P9-DVV-399

The Americanization of Benjamin Franklin

ALSO BY GORDON S. WOOD

The Creation of the American Republic, 1776–1787

The Radicalism of the American Revolution

The American Revolution: A History

THE AMERICANIZATION OF BENJAMIN FRANKLIN

GORDON S. WOOD

THE PENGUIN PRESS
NEW YORK
2004

THE PENGUIN PRESS
a member of
Penguin Group (USA) Inc.
375 Hudson Street
New York, New York 10014

Copyright © Gordon Wood, 2004
All rights reserved

Illustration credits appear on pp. 285–86.

Library of Congress Cataloging-in-Publication Data

Wood, Gordon S.
The Americanization of Benjamin Franklin / Gordon S. Wood.
p. cm.
Includes bibliographical references (p.) and index.
ISBN 1-59420-019-X
1. Franklin, Benjamin, 1706–1790. 2. Franklin, Benjamin, 1706–1790—Influence. 3. Franklin, Benjamin, 1706–1790—Public opinion. 4. Statesmen—United States—Biography. 5. Scientists—United States—Biography. 6. Inventors—United States—Biography. 7. Printers—United States—Biography. 8. Public opinion—United States. I. Title
E302.6.F8W84 2004 2003063254
973.3'092—dc22
[B]

This book is printed on acid-free paper. ♾

Printed in the United States of America
1 3 5 7 9 10 8 6 4 2

DESIGNED BY MARYSARAH QUINN

Without limiting the rights under copyright reserved above, no part of this publication may be reproduced, stored in or introduced into a retrieval system, or transmitted, in any form or by any means (electronic, mechanical, photocopying, recording, or otherwise), without the prior written permission of both the copyright owner and the above publisher of this book.

The scanning, uploading, and distribution of this book via the Internet or via any other means without the permission of the publisher is illegal and punishable by law. Please purchase only authorized electronic editions and do not participate in or encourage electronic piracy of copyrighted materials. Your support of the author's rights is appreciated.

TO CHRISTOPHER, ELIZABETH, AND AMY

Preface

"Of making many books there is no end," and with the upcoming tricentennial celebration of Benjamin Franklin's birth in 2006, this seems to be especially true of Franklin biographies. But this book is not meant to be a traditional biography of Franklin. It does not contain every event in his long life, nor does it deal with all of his multitudinous relationships and writings. Instead, it is a relatively selective study, focusing on specific aspects of this extraordinary man's life that reveal a Benjamin Franklin who is different in important ways from the Franklin of our inherited common understanding.

First of all, the book attempts to penetrate beneath the many images and representations of Franklin that have accumulated over the past two hundred years and recover the historic Franklin who did not know the kind of massively symbolic folk hero he would become. At the same time it hopes to make clear how and why Franklin acquired these various images and symbols. It tries to place Franklin's incredible life in its eighteenth-century context and explain why he retired from business and became a gentleman, why he came to admire the British Empire and sought to become its architect, why he began writing his *Autobiography* when he did, and why he belatedly joined the American Revolution, and joined it with a vengeance. It seeks to clarify the personal meaning the Revolution had for him and to describe his extraordinary achievements as America's envoy to France—achievements that were never fully appreciated by many of his countrymen at the time. It attempts also to account for the way in which the French came to see Franklin as the symbol of America even before his fellow Americans did. Indeed, without understanding Franklin's intimate connection with France we will never make sense of the remarkable degree of hostility Franklin faced in the last years of his life from members of Congress and other influential Americans. Even after his death in 1790 the hostility continued, especially as Franklin emerged as the representative American, as the hardworking self-made businessman, for hundreds of thousands of middling Americans in the early decades of the nineteenth century.

This early-nineteenth-century image of Franklin was not the image of Franklin known to people in his own lifetime; it was a product of the turbulent capitalism of the age of Jackson, the age so brilliantly depicted by Alexis de Tocqueville in his *Democracy in America.* And it is that popular image that seems to have the most resonance even today. Despite the continuing power of Franklin's symbolic significance as the entrepreneurial American, however, the historic Franklin of the eighteenth century was never destined to be that symbol. Franklin was not even destined to be an American. How he became one is the theme of this book.

Acknowledgments

THIS BOOK HAS BEEN in my mind for many years. I first became interested in writing about Franklin when I reviewed several volumes of his papers in the early 1970s. I let my thoughts about this extraordinary character stew for a decade. Then in 1983 the late William B. Cohen, chair of the Department of History of Indiana University, invited me to present a lecture on Franklin as part of Indiana University's bicentennial celebration of the signing of the Treaty of Paris, which ended the Revolutionary War against Britain. This invitation forced me to put some of my thoughts about Franklin on paper. So I am grateful to Professor Cohen and Indiana University for the invitation that got me started on this book. Franklin next became an important figure in my book *The Radicalism of the American Revolution,* and the several paragraphs devoted to him there anticipate some of what is in this study. Indeed, what happened to Franklin and Franklin's image between the middle of the eighteenth century and the early decades of the nineteenth century seems to me to demonstrate vividly the radical social and cultural changes that the American Revolution brought about.

Much of the book was written when I was a fellow at the Institute for United States Studies in London in the winter and spring of 2002, and I want to thank the institute and its staff for their hospitality. For their editorial expertise I am grateful to my wife, Louise, and my daughter

Elizabeth, and my friends Lesley Herrmann and Barbara Oberg. I am especially indebted to Ellen Cohn, who is currently the editor in chief of the Franklin Papers, not only for her careful reading of the manuscript, which saved me from many errors, but also for her making available to me a CD-ROM of the Franklin Papers, which includes those papers not yet published in the magnificent letterpress edition of Yale University Press. I am grateful too to my agent, Andrew Wylie, for all his support. My thanks also to Sophie Fels at The Penguin Press for her considerable and always cheerful aid in preparing the manuscript. My final thanks go to my editor at The Penguin Press, Scott Moyers, who is every author's dream of what an editor ought to be. He could not have been more helpful, and I am very grateful to him.

GORDON S. WOOD
Providence, Rhode Island

Contents

ILLUSTRATIONS

The Americanization of Benjamin Franklin

INTRODUCTION

THE FOLKSY FOUNDER

Benjamin Franklin has a special place in the hearts and minds of Americans. He is, of course, one of the most preeminent of the Founders, those heroic men from the era of wigs and knee breeches. Men as diverse as Henry Cabot Lodge and Garry Wills have ranked him along with Washington as the greatest of the Founders.[1] Of these heroic men of the eighteenth century, Franklin seems to have a unique appeal. He seems the most accessible, the most democratic, and the most folksy of the Founders. His many portraits suggest an affable genial old man with spectacles and a twinkle in his eye ready to tell us a humorous story. He seems to be the one we would most like to spend an evening with. Ordinary people can identify with him in ways they cannot with the other Founders. Stern and thin-lipped George Washington, especially as portrayed by Gilbert Stuart, is too august and awesome to be approachable. Although Thomas Jefferson has democratic credentials, he is much too aristocratic and reserved for most people to relate to; besides, he was a slaveholder who failed to free most of his slaves. John Adams seems human enough, but he is too cranky and idiosyncratic to be in any way the kind of American hero ordinary folk can get close to. James Madison is much too shy and intellectual, and Alexander Hamilton is much too arrogant and hot tempered: neither of them makes a congenial popular idol. No, of all these great men of the eighteenth century, it is Franklin who seems to have the most common touch and who seems to symbolize better than any other Founder the plain democracy of ordinary folk.

Indeed, perhaps no person in American history has taken on such emblematic and imaginative significance for Americans as has Franklin. We may not agree with his enemy John Adams that Franklin combined "practical cunning" with "theoretick Ignorance," but we may well share Adams's belief that he is "one of the most curious Characters in History."[2] Franklin has become, in the view of literary historian Perry Miller, one of the most "massively symbolic" figures in American history.[3]

Scholars today tend not to believe anymore in the notion of an American character, but if there is such a thing, then Franklin exemplifies it. In 1888 William Dean Howells called Franklin "the most modern, the most American, of his contemporaries," and many other commentators have agreed.[4] He seems to have embodied much of what most Americans have valued throughout their history. His "homely aphorisms and observations," one historian has written, "have influenced more Americans than the learned wisdom of all the formal philosophers put together."[5] Although Franklin was naturally talented, declared one nineteenth-century admirer, he achieved his success by character and conduct that were "within the reach of every human being." All of his teachings entered into the "everyday manners and affairs" of people; they "pointed out the causes which may promote good and ill fortune in ordinary life." That was what made him such a democratic hero.[6]

Unlike the other great Founders, Franklin began as an artisan, a lowly printer who became the architect of his own fortune. He is the prototype of the self-made man, and his life is the classic American success story—the story of a man rising from the most obscure of origins to wealth and international preeminence. Franklin, the author of *The Way to Wealth,* has stood for American social mobility—the capacity of ordinary people to make it to the top through frugality and industry and to flourish. The unforgettable images of Franklin that he himself helped to create—the youth of seventeen with loaves of bread under his arms, the scientist flying a kite to capture lightning in a storm, the fervent moralist outlining his resolves that once followed will lead to success—have passed into American mythology and folklore. If any single figure could symbolize all of America, it was Franklin. Not surprisingly, he became for historian Frederick Jackson Turner and many subsequent biographers and panegyrists "the first great American."[7]

He was the nation itself, declared the *Atlantic Monthly* in 1889, "the personification of an optimistic shrewdness, a large, healthy nature, as of a young people gathering its strength and feeling its broadening power." He has represented everything Americans like about themselves—their levelheadedness, common sense, pragmatism, ingenuity, and get-up-and-go. Because of his inventions of the lightning rod, bifocals, the Franklin stove, and other useful instruments, he has been identified with the happiness and prosperity of common people in the here and now. He was the one, as an 1833 history of the United States put it, "who has made our dwellings comfortable within, and protected them from the lightning of heaven." He spoke to common people, to "that rank of people who have no opportunity for study," as the Columbian Class Book declared in 1827. He was, as one admirer wrote in 1864, "a genuine product of American soil."[8] Millions of people have quoted and tried to live their lives by his Poor Richard sayings and proverbs, such as "Early to bed and early to rise, makes a man healthy wealthy and wise."[9] Those who wanted to know the way to wealth read Franklin. He has stood for industry, frugality, thrift, and every materialistic virtue that Americans have valued.

During the nineteenth century Franklin became not only an icon that ordinary people could emulate but also the most important mythical figure used to assimilate foreigners to American values. Franklin came to represent the America of innovation and enterprise, of moneymaking and getting ahead. He was everything that immigrants thought America was about. America, even into our own time, as one twenty-first-century immigrant put it, has remained "a land of opportunity, and one [where] if you worked hard you could get ahead."[10] No one has stood for that promise of getting ahead better than Franklin. Schools in the nineteenth century began using his *Autobiography* to teach moral lessons to students. Many people seemed to know his writings as well as they knew the Bible. It is not surprising that the book Davy Crockett had with him when he died at the Alamo was not the Bible but Franklin's *Autobiography*.[11]

DEBUNKING FRANKLIN

So overwhelming did Franklin's image of the boy who worked hard and made it become in the nineteenth century that humorists like Mark Twain could scarcely avoid mocking it. Franklin's example, said Twain in 1870, had become a burden for every American youngster. The great man, said Twain, had "early prostituted his talents to the invention of maxims and aphorisms calculated to inflict suffering upon the rising generation of all subsequent ages. His simplest acts, also, were contrived with a view to their being held up for the emulation of boys forever—boys who might otherwise have been happy. . . . With a malevolence which is without parallel in history," wrote Twain, "he would work all day and then sit up nights and let on to be studying algebra by the light of the smouldering fire, so that all other boys might have to do that also or else have Benjamin Franklin thrown up to them."[12]

As Twain's sardonic humor suggests, Franklin has had many detractors. And most of them have been much more genuinely critical than Twain. Indeed, the criticism that Franklin has aroused over the past two centuries has been as extraordinary as the praise. Franklin may be the most folksy and popular figure among the Founding Fathers, yet at the same time he is also the one who has provoked the most derision.

Of course, from the beginning of professional history-writing at the end of the nineteenth century, historians have been busy trying to strip away the many myths and legends that have grown up around all the Founding Fathers in order to get at the human beings presumably hidden from view. Indeed, during modern times this sort of historical debunking of the Founders has become something of a cottage industry. But the criticism leveled at Franklin has been different. Historians did not have to rip away a mantle of godlike dignity and loftiness from Franklin, as they had to do with the other Founders, in order to recover the hidden human being; Franklin already seemed human enough. Indeed, it was his Poor Richard ordinariness that made him vulnerable to criticism. As William Dean Howells noted, Franklin came down to the end of the nineteenth century "with more reality than any of his contemporaries." Although this "by no means hurt him in the popular regard," it certainly did not help his reputation with many intellectuals.[13] Precisely because of his massive identification with middling and materialistic America, he became the Founder whom many critics most liked to mock. As John Keats pointed out as early as 1818, there was nothing sublime about Franklin, or about Americans in general, for that matter.[14]

Like Franklin, Thomas Jefferson has often been identified with America, and thus he too has come in for some hard knocks, especially over the past generation, mostly for his hypocrisy, his ideological rigidity, and his unwillingness to free his slaves. But as intense as this criticism of Jefferson has been, it is not quite comparable to the ridicule and condemnation that Franklin has suffered over the past two centuries. Jefferson has never been accused of lacking elegance or of being a lackey of capitalism.

Almost from the beginning of America's national history, many imaginative writers, defenders of elegance, and spiritual seekers of various sorts found that by attacking Franklin they could attack many of America's middle-class values. Aristocratic-minded Federalists scorned the emerging penny-getting world of 1800 and saw Franklin as its symbol. He was the one "who has the *pence table* by heart and knows all the squares of multiplication."[15] All of the things that turned Franklin into a middling folk hero became sources of genteel contempt and ridicule. Those who believed that Franklin's *Autobiography* was supposed "to promote good morals, especially among the uneducated class of the community," declared the *North American Review* in 1818, could not be more wrong. "The groundwork of his character, during this period, was bad; and the moral qualities, which contributed to his rise, were of a worldly and very profitable kind."[16] In the minds of these imaginative intellectuals Franklin came to stand for all of America's bourgeois complacency, its get-ahead materialism, its utilitarian obsession with success—the unimaginative superficiality and vulgarity of American culture that kills the soul. He eventually became Main Street and Babbittry rolled into one—a caricature of America's moneymaking middle class.

When Edgar Allan Poe wrote a satirical piece on the dry and systematic ways of "The Businessman" (1845), he never mentioned Franklin by name, but any reader would have known who his model was. A businessman, said Poe, loved order and regularity and hated geniuses—all those imaginative sorts who violated the "fitness of things." Unlike fanciful geniuses who were apt to write poetry, a businessman was the product of "those habits of methodical accuracy" that had been "thumped" into him; thus with his "old habits of *system*," wrote Poe, using one of Franklin's favorite phrases, the successful businessman was carried "swimmingly along."[17]

Everyone who had a quarrel with superficial bourgeois America necessarily had a quarrel with Franklin, for he was, as Herman Melville said, "the type and genius of his land. Franklin was everything but a poet." In his novel *Israel Potter* (1855), Melville created a vivid and wonderfully satiric picture of Franklin. His Franklin was "the homely sage and household Plato," who possessed "deep worldly wisdom and polished Italian tact, gleaming under an air of Arcadian unaffectedness." He was at one and the same time "the diplomatist and the shepherd . . . ; a union not without warrant; the apostolic servant and dove. A tanned Machiavelli in tents." Melville's Franklin, as his character Israel Potter describes him, was "sly, sly, sly." "Having carefully weighed the world, Franklin," wrote Melville, "could act any part in it . . . printer, postmaster, almanac maker, essayist, chemist, orator, tinker, statesman, humorist, philosopher, parlorman, political economist, professor of housewifery, ambassador, projector, maxim-monger, herb-doctor, wit," anything and everything but a poet.[18]

Nineteenth-century Americans, like the characters in Nathaniel Hawthorne's "Biographical Stories," were not sure why Franklin had become so famous. It was doubtful, said Hawthorne's storyteller, "whether Franklin's philosophical discoveries, important as they were, or even his vast political services, would have given him all the fame which he acquired." Instead, it was as the author of *Poor Richard's Almanack* that Franklin had become "the counselor and household friend to almost every family in America." No matter that Franklin's proverbs "were all about getting money and saving it," they were "suited to the condition of the country."[19]

The condition of the country was capitalistic, and that was what made Franklin both a hero and a villain to so many people. He was the patron saint of business, and since the business of America, as President Calvin Coolidge liked to say, was business, Franklin became America itself. Gilded Age defenders of business like T. L. Haines simply borrowed Franklin's maxims and turned them into manuals for making money and getting ahead.[20]

Since Franklin had become so identified with the art of getting, saving, and using money, it was inevitable that scholars seeking to understand the sources of capitalism would sooner or later fasten upon Franklin. In his famous work *The Protestant Ethic and the Spirit of Capitalism* (1905), the great German sociologist Max Weber found Franklin to be a perfect exemplar of the modern capitalistic spirit. No one, wrote Weber, expressed the moral maxims underlying the ethic of capitalism better than Franklin. For Franklin, "honesty is useful, because it assures credit; so are punctuality, industry, frugality, and that is the reason they are virtues." But Franklin was not a hypocrite, wrote Weber; as revealed by his character "in the really unusual candidness of his autobiography," his virtues were not designed to aggrandize the individual. "In fact," said Weber, "the *summum bonum* of this ethic, the earning of more and more money, combined with the strict avoidance of all spontaneous enjoyment of life," had nothing to do with individual happiness. "It is thought of so purely as an end in itself, that from the point of view of the happiness of, or utility to, the single individual, it appears entirely transcendental and absolutely irrational." In Weber's opinion Franklin believed that "man is dominated by the making of money, by acquisition as the ultimate purpose in life," regardless of his actual material needs. This was "a leading principle of capitalism," akin to certain religious feelings in its intensity and asceticism. "Benjamin Franklin himself, although he was a colourless deist, answers in his autobiography with a quotation from the Bible, which his strict Calvinist father drummed into him again and again in his youth: 'Seest thou a man diligent in his business? He shall stand before kings.'" Franklin's ethic, Weber concluded, was the ethic of capitalism, expressed "in all his works without exception."[21]

Since apparently no imaginative writer, artist, or intellectual could like capitalism, it went without saying that nearly all these sensitive souls would dislike Franklin, the proto-capitalist. Someone who thought that the end of life was merely the making of money obviously lacked depth and spirituality. And if Franklin was superficial and soulless, so too was America. With his apparently shriveled spirit, Franklin was everything that imaginative artists found wrong with America.

No artist found more wrong with Franklin and America than did the English writer D. H. Lawrence. Lawrence's hilarious attack in his *Studies in Classic American Literature* in 1923 is the most famous criticism of Franklin ever written. To Lawrence, Franklin embodied all those shallow bourgeois moneymaking values that intellectuals are accustomed to dislike. Franklin was "this dry, moral, utilitarian little democrat," the "sharp little man," the "middle-sized, sturdy, snuff-coloured Doctor Franklin," "sound, satisfied Ben," who was a "virtuous little automaton" and "the first downright American."[22]

Lawrence was not the only creative writer to find Franklin a convenient means for saying something about America. F. Scott Fitzgerald's Jay Gatsby, one of the most American characters in all of literature, was an earnest believer in Franklin's message of self-improvement as a young boy.[23] Franklin's resolutions in fact became a model for the young Gatsby's self-imposed schedule: "Rise from bed, 6.00 A.M.," "Dumbbell exercise and wall-scaling, 6.15–6.30," "Study electricity, etc., 7.15–8.15," "Work, 8.30–4.30 P.M.," "Baseball and sports, 4.30–5.00," "Practice elocution, poise and how to attain it, 5.00–6.00," "Study needed inventions, 7.00–9.00." If these weren't enough, Gatsby added some "General Resolves" that the abstemious Franklin might have approved of: "No wasting time at Shafters," "No more smokeing or chewing," "Read one improving book or magazine per week," "Save . . . $3.00 per week." With such resolutions, as Gatsby's father said, the young boy "was bound to get ahead." Franklin's resolves became part of what Fitzgerald wanted to say about Gatsby's desire to realize the so-called American dream.

No matter that this dream eluded Gatsby, as Fitzgerald thought it eluded all Americans. As long as Americans keep trying to grasp that "green light, the orgiastic future that year by year recedes before us," Franklin will remain a central figure in American mythology. His remarkable life seems to reaffirm for all Americans the possibility of anyone's, however humble his birth and background, making it.[24]

THE HISTORIC EIGHTEENTH-CENTURY FRANKLIN

Gatsby may be a powerful representative American character, but he is a fictional figure. Franklin, on the other hand, was a real person, not invented. Or was he? Does Franklin's *Autobiography*, perhaps the most widely read autobiography in the world, give us an accurate picture of the man? Much of twentieth-century literary criticism of the *Autobiography* has emphasized Franklin's sophistication, humor, and sense of irony as a writer. How seriously must we take Franklin? Is young Franklin, the character of the first two sections of the *Autobiography*, really the same person as the older Franklin, the author? Do we really know Franklin, know him as well as we know, say, Fitzgerald's Jay Gatsby?

In fact, the historic Franklin, the Franklin of the eighteenth century, seems to elude us as much as Gatsby's ever receding green light eluded him. When we actually recover the Franklin of the eighteenth century, he does not seem to fit the image we have created of him. First of all, his life was not really about the making and saving of money. He was in fact the most benevolent and philanthropic of the Founders and in some respects the least concerned with the getting of money. Despite achieving fame as a scientist, he never believed that science was as important as public service. Indeed, at the age of forty-two, he retired from business and devoted the remainder of his life to serving his city, his colony, his empire, and then, after independence in 1776, his state and the United States.

Far from being the spokesman for moneymaking and bourgeois values, Franklin repeatedly mocked those who were caught up "in the Pursuit of Wealth to no End." In 1750, he wrote that at the end of his life "I would rather have it said, *He lived usefully*, than, *He died rich*."[25] He continually warned against the abuse of money in politics and in fact urged that governmental officials should serve without pay. After his retirement from business in 1748 he often thought like a genteel aristocrat, not a tradesman.

Although he may have eventually become the supreme symbol of America, he was certainly not the most American of the Founders during his lifetime. Indeed, one might more easily describe him as the least American and the most European of the nation's early leaders. He was undoubtedly the most cosmopolitan and the most urbane of that group of leaders who brought about the Revolution. He hobnobbed with lords and aristocrats in Britain and the rest of Europe. He conversed with kings and even dined with one. No other American, even Jefferson, knew more Europeans or was more celebrated abroad in more countries than Franklin.

As historian Carl Becker once pointed out, Franklin "was acquainted personally or through correspondence with more men of eminence in letters, science, and politics than any other man of his time."[26]

Certainly no other American leader lived more years abroad than Franklin. In fact, Franklin spent the bulk of the last thirty-three years of his life living outside of America, in Britain and France. At several points it was doubtful whether he would ever return to America, or wanted to—or even cared much about America. Far from being a natural and thoroughgoing American, Franklin at several points in his life experienced what we today might call the anxiety of national identity. He was not sure where he rightly belonged. Was he English? Or British? Or did he really belong in France? We should not take his Americanness for granted. Nor should we take his participation in the Revolution for granted.

At the beginning of the imperial crisis in the early 1760s—the crisis that would end with the breakup of the British Empire and the independence of the United States—no one could have identified Franklin with a radical cause. Certainly, no one could have predicted that he would become one of the leaders of the American Revolution. In 1760 there were few Englishmen who were as dedicated to the greatness of the British Empire as he.

It was then hard to see any difference at all between Franklin and the man who would eventually come to symbolize for Americans the arch-Tory and the foremost enemy of American liberty and American independence: Thomas Hutchinson. Both Franklin and Hutchinson were good Enlightenment figures—literate, reasonable men, with a deep dislike of religious enthusiasm. Both were imperial officials, dedicated to the British Empire. They had in fact cooperated in forming the Albany Plan of Union in 1754, which presented a farsighted proposal for intercolonial cooperation and imperial defense. Both Franklin and Hutchinson were getting-along men—believers in prudence, calculation, affability—and they made their way in that monarchical society by playing their parts. Both were believers in the power of a few reasonable men, men like themselves, to run affairs. Both regarded the common people with a certain patronizing amusement, unless, of course, they rioted—then the two officials were filled with disgust.

It is hard from the vantage point of the early 1760s to predict that the paths of Franklin and Hutchinson would eventually diverge so radically. In many respects Franklin seems the least likely of revolutionaries. Certainly his participation in the Revolution was not natural or inevitable; indeed, Franklin came very close to remaining, as his son did, a loyal member of the British Empire. On the face of it, it is not easy to understand why Franklin took up the Revolutionary cause at all.

First of all, Franklin, unlike the other Founders, was not a young man. He was seventy in 1776—not the age that one associates with passionate revolutionaries. He was by far the oldest of the Revolutionary leaders—twenty-six years older than Washington, twenty-nine years older than John Adams, thirty-seven years older than Jefferson, and nearly a half century older than Madison and Hamilton. Because he came from an entirely different generation from the rest of the Founders, he was in some sense more deeply committed to the British Empire than they were.

More important, unlike these other Revolutionary leaders, Franklin already had an established reputation; indeed, prior to the Revolution he was already world-famous. He had everything to lose and seemingly little to gain by participating in a revolution. The other American Revolutionary leaders were young men, virtually unknown outside of their remote provinces. We can generally understand why they might have become revolutionaries. They were men of modest origins with high ambitions who saw in the Revolution opportunities to achieve that fame that Hamilton called "the ruling passion of the noblest minds."[27] But Franklin was different. He alone already had the position and the fame that the others only yearned for. He was already known all over Britain and the rest of Europe. Because of his discoveries concerning electricity, which were real contributions to basic science, he had become a celebrity throughout the Atlantic world. He had become a member of the Royal Society and had received honorary degrees from universities in America and Britain, including St. Andrews and Oxford. Philosophers and scientists from all over Europe consulted him on everything from how to build a fireplace to why the oceans were salty. Well before the Revolution he was one of the most renowned men in the world and certainly the most famous American.

Since he scarcely could have foreseen how much the Revolution would enhance his reputation and turn him into one of America's greatest folk heroes, why at his age would he have risked so much?

We do not usually ask the question of why Franklin became a revolutionary. Somehow we take his participation in the Revolution for granted. Because he is so identified with the Revolution and with America, we can scarcely think of him as anything but a thoroughgoing American. But this is a problem of what historians generally call whiggism—the anachronistic foreshortening that tends to see the past and persons in the past as anticipations of the future. Franklin has become such a symbol of America that we have a hard time thinking of him as anything but an American folk hero or the spokesman for American capitalism. We have more than two hundred years of images imposed on Franklin that have to be peeled away before we can recover the man who existed before the Revolution. Franklin in the late 1760s and early 1770s was not fated to abandon the British Empire and join the American cause. How he became estranged from that empire and became, almost overnight, a fiery revolutionary is an important part of the story of his Americanization.

In many respects Franklin in 1776 emerged as the quintessential republican, dedicated to a world in which only talent counted, not who your father was or whom you married. Once Franklin joined the Revolutionary cause, he inevitably became a fervent believer in a republican world where leaders were disinterested gentlemen, free from any occupation and the cares of making money. Franklin, long since retired from his printing business, was in 1776 more than willing to devote himself to the service of the new United States without any expectation of monetary reward. No one except Washington gave more of himself to the new nation.

The eight years Franklin spent abroad as the chief envoy from the United States to France furthered the process of his Americanization. Amid the luxury of the French court, the most sophisticated in all of Europe, Franklin became much more self-conscious of his image as the representative American, as the symbol of the simplicity of the New World and its difference from the corruptions of the Old World. Because the French needed this symbol before the Americans themselves did, they first created the image of Franklin as the rustic democrat, as the simple untutored genius from the wilds of America who had become one of the world's great scientists and writers. Franklin was well aware of this image and developed and used it on behalf of the American cause.

As important as Franklin's French experience was in his Americanization, however, it was in the several decades immediately following his death in 1790 that the modern image of Franklin as the self-made bourgeois moralist and spokesman for capitalism was really created. As the new American republic developed into much more of a democratic, moneymaking society than anyone had anticipated, the need for a Founder who could represent the age's new egalitarian and commercial forces became ever more pressing. Only with the publication of his *Autobiography* in 1794 did the idea of Franklin as the folksy embodiment of the self-made businessman and the creator of the American dream begin to gather power, until today, more than two centuries later, the historic Franklin of the eighteenth century remains buried beneath an accumulation of images. Consequently, despite hundreds of biographies and studies of Franklin and over three dozen volumes of his papers magnificently published in a modern letterpress edition, we still do not fully know the man.

THE MAN OF MANY MASKS

Franklin is not an easy man to get to know. Although he wrote more pieces about more things than any of the other Founders, Franklin is never very revealing of himself. He always seems to be holding something back—he is reticent, detached, not wholly committed. We sense in Franklin the presence of calculated restraint—a restraint perhaps bred by his spectacular rise and the kind of hierarchical and patronage-ridden world he had to operate in.[28] Certainly there were people in Philadelphia who never let him forget "his original obscurity," and that he had sprung from "the meanest Circumstances."[29] Despite his complaining that he was never able to order things in his life, we sense that he was always in control and was showing us only what he wanted us to see. Only at moments in the early 1770s and at the end of his life do we sense that the world was spinning out of his grasp.

Beyond the restrained and reserved character of his personal writings is the remarkable character of his public writings, especially his

Autobiography—"this most famous of American texts," as one scholar calls it.[30] Literary scholars have continually interpreted and reinterpreted the *Autobiography* but still cannot agree on what Franklin was trying to do in writing it. Among the Founders, Jefferson and Adams also wrote autobiographies, but theirs are nothing like Franklin's. His resembles a work of fiction in that we cannot be sure that the narrative voice is the same as the author's. Indeed, much of the reader's enjoyment of the *Autobiography* comes from the contrast between Franklin's descriptions of the "awkward ridiculous Appearance" the teenaged printer made upon his arrival in Philadelphia and "the Figure I have since made there."[31] It is hard to interpret the *Autobiography,* since, as scholars have pointed out, Franklin moves between several personas, especially between the innocence of youth and the irony of a mature man.[32]

In all of Franklin's writings, his wit and humor, his constant self-awareness, his assuming different personas and roles, make it difficult to know how to read him. He was a man of many voices and masks who continually mocks himself.[33] Sometimes in his newspaper essays he was a woman, like "Silence Dogood," "Alice Addertongue," "Cecilia Shortface," and "Polly Baker," saucy and racy and hilarious. At other times he was the "Busy Body," or "Obadiah Plainman," or "Anthony Afterwit," or "Richard Saunders," also known as "Poor Richard," the almanac maker. Sometimes he wrote in the London newspapers as "An American" or "A New England-Man." But other times he wrote as "A Briton" or "A London Manufacturer," and shaped what he wrote accordingly. During his London years he wrote some ninety pseudonymous items for the press using forty-two different signatures.[34] For each of the many pieces he wrote both in Philadelphia and in London he had a remarkable ability to create the appropriate persona. Indeed, all of his many personas contribute nicely to the particular purpose of his various works, whether they are essays, skits, poems, or satires. "Just as no other eighteenth-century writer has so many moods and tones or so wide a range of correspondents," declares the dean of present-day Franklin scholars, "so no other eighteenth-century writer has so many different personae or so many different voices as Franklin." No wonder we have difficulty figuring out who this remarkable man was.[35]

Of all the Founders, Franklin had the fullest and deepest understanding of human nature. He had a remarkable capacity to see all sides of human behavior and to appreciate other points of view. He loved turning conventional wisdom on its head, as, for example, when he argued for the virtue and usefulness of censure and backbiting.[36] But then again are we sure that he is not putting us on? He certainly enjoyed hoaxes and was the master of every rhetorical ploy. No American writer of the eighteenth century could burlesque, deride, parody, or berate more skillfully than he. He could praise and mock at the same time and could write on both sides of an issue with ease.

It is easy to miss the complexity and subtlety of Franklin's writing. He praises reason so often that we forget his ironic story about man's being a reasonable creature. In his *Autobiography* he tells us about how he abandoned his youthful effort to maintain a vegetarian diet. Although formerly a great lover of fish, he had come to believe that eating fish was "a kind of unprovok'd Murder." But one day when he smelled some fish sizzling in a frying pan, he was caught hanging "between Principle and Inclination." When he saw that the cut-open fish had eaten smaller fish, however, he decided that "if you eat one another, I don't see why we mayn't eat you." And so he had heartily dined on cod ever since. "So convenient a thing it is to be a *reasonable Creature*," he concluded, "since it enables one to find or make a Reason for every thing one has a mind to do."[37]

None of the Founders was more conscious of the difference between appearance and reality than Franklin. Not only did he continually comment on that difference, but he was never averse to maintaining it. If one could not actually be industrious and humble, he said, at least one could appear to be so.

Although he wrote against disguise and dissimulation and asked, "Who was ever cunning enough to conceal his being so?" we nevertheless know that he was the master of camouflage and concealment. "We shall resolve to be what we would seem," he declared, yet at the same time he seems to have delighted in hiding his innermost thoughts and motives. "Let all Men know thee," Poor Richard said, "but no man know thee thoroughly: Men freely ford that see the shallows."[38]

While sometimes bowing to the emerging romantic cult of sincerity, he remained firmly rooted in the traditional eighteenth-century world of restraining one's inner desires and feelings in order to be civil and get along. He never thought that his characteristic behavior—his artful posing, his role playing, his many masks, his refusal to reveal his inner self—was anything other than what the cultivated and sociable eighteenth century admired. He was a thoroughly social being, enmeshed in society and civic-minded by necessity. Not for him the disastrous assertions of antisocial autonomy and the outspoken sincerity of Molière's character Alceste in *Le Misanthrope.* Like many others of his day, Franklin preferred the sensible and prudent behavior of Alceste's friend Philinte, who knew that the path of good sense was to adapt to the pressures and contradictions of society.[39] Unlike, say, John Adams, Franklin never wore his heart on his sleeve; he kept most of his intentions and feelings to himself. He was a master at keeping his own counsel. As Poor Richard said, "Three may keep a Secret, if two of them are dead."[40]

Franklin is so many-sided, he seems everything to everyone, but no image has been more powerful than that of the self-improving businessman. This modern image of Franklin began to predominate with the emergence of America's democratic capitalism in the early republic; and, like Alexis de Tocqueville's description of that rambunctious democratic America, Franklin's personification of its values has had a remarkable staying power. Just as we continue to read Tocqueville's *Democracy in America* for its insights into the democratic character of our society in our own time nearly two centuries later, so too do we continue to honor Franklin as the Founder who best exemplifies our present-day democratic capitalist society. As the symbol of an American land of opportunity where one works hard to get ahead, Franklin continues to have great meaning, especially among recent immigrants.

But to recover the historic Franklin we must shed these modern images and symbols of Franklin and return to that very different, distant world of the eighteenth century. Only then can we go on to understand how the symbolic Franklin was created.

ONE

BECOMING A GENTLEMAN

BOSTON BEGINNINGS

Franklin was born in Boston on January 17, 1706 (January 6, 1705, in the old-style calendar), of very humble origins, origins that always struck Franklin himself as unusually poor. Franklin's father, Josiah, was a nonconformist from Northamptonshire who as a young man had immigrated to the New World and had become a candle and soap maker, one of the lowliest of the artisan crafts. Josiah fathered a total of seventeen children, ten, including Benjamin, by his second wife, Abiah Folger, from Nantucket. Franklin was number fifteen of these seventeen and the youngest son.

In a hierarchical age that favored the firstborn son, Franklin was, as he ruefully recounted in his *Autobiography*, "the youngest Son of the youngest Son for 5 Generations back."[1] In the last year of his life the bitterness was still there, undisguised by Franklin's usual irony. In a codicil to his will written in 1789 he observed that most people, having received an estate from their ancestors, felt obliged to pass on something to their posterity. "This obligation," he wrote with some emotion, "does not lie on me, who never inherited a shilling from any ancestor or relation."[2]

Because the young Franklin was unusually precocious ("I do not remember when I could not read," he recalled), his father initially sent

Franklin's birthplace on Milk Street, Boston, across from the Old South Church

the eight-year-old boy to grammar school in preparation for the ministry.[3] But his father soon had second thoughts about the expenses involved in a college education, and after a year he pulled the boy out of grammar school and sent him for another year to an ordinary school that simply taught reading, writing, and arithmetic. These two years of formal education were all that Franklin was ever to receive. Not that this was unusual: most boys had little more than this, and almost all girls had no formal schooling at all. Although most of the Revolutionary leaders were college graduates—usually being the first in their families to attend college—some, including Washington, Robert Morris, Patrick Henry, Nathanael Greene, and Thomas Paine, had not much more formal schooling than Franklin. Apprenticeship in a trade or skill was still the principal means by which most young men prepared for the world.

Franklin's father chose that route of apprenticeship for his son and began training Franklin to be a candle and soap maker. But since cutting wicks and smelling tallow made Franklin very unhappy, his father finally agreed that the printing trade might better suit the boy's "Bookish Inclination."[4] Printing, after all, was the most cerebral of the crafts, requiring the ability to read, spell, and write. Nevertheless, it still involved heavy manual labor and was a grubby, messy, and physically demanding job, without much prestige.

In fact, printing had little more respectability than soap and candle making. It was in such "wretched Disrepute" that, as one eighteenth-century New York printer remarked, no family "of Substance would ever put their Sons to such an Art," and, as a consequence, masters were "obliged to take of the lowest People" for apprentices.[5] But Franklin fit the trade. Not only was young Franklin bookish, but he was also nearly six feet tall and strong with broad shoulders—ideally suited for the difficult tasks of printing. His father thus placed him under the care of an older son, James, who in 1717 had returned from England to set himself up as a printer in Boston. When James saw what his erudite youngest brother could do with words and type, he signed up the twelve-year-old boy to an unusually long apprenticeship of nine years.

That boy, as Franklin later recalled in his *Autobiography,* was "extremely ambitious" to become a "tolerable English Writer."[6] Although literacy was relatively high in New England at this time—perhaps 75 percent of males in Boston could read and write and the percentage was rapidly growing—books were scarce and valuable, and few people read books the way Franklin did.[7] He read everything he could get his hands on, including John Bunyan's *Pilgrim's Progress,* Plutarch's *Lives,* Daniel Defoe's *Essay on Projects,* the "do good" essays of the prominent Boston Puritan divine Cotton Mather, and more books of "polemic Divinity" than Franklin wanted to remember.[8] He even befriended the apprentices of booksellers in order to gain access to more books. One of these apprentices allowed him secretly to borrow his master's books to read after work. "Often," Franklin recalled, "I sat up in my Room reading the greatest Part of the Night, when the Book was borrow'd in the Evening & to be return'd early in the Morning lest it should be miss'd or wanted."[9] He tried his hand at writing poetry and other things but was discouraged with the poor quality of his attempts. He discovered a volume of Joseph Addison and Richard Steele's *Spectator* papers and saw in it a tool for self-improvement. He read the papers over and over again and copied and recopied them and tried to recapitulate them from memory. He turned them into poetry and then back again into prose. He took notes on the *Spectator* essays, jumbled the notes, and then attempted to reconstruct the essays in order to understand the way Addison and Steele had organized them. All this painstaking effort was designed to improve and polish his writing, and it succeeded; "prose Writing" became, as Franklin recalled in his *Autobiography*, "of great Use to me in the Course of my Life, and was a principal Means of my Advancement." In fact, writing competently was such a rare skill that anyone who could do it well immediately acquired importance. All the Founders, including Washington, first gained their reputations by something they wrote.[10]

In 1721 Franklin's brother, after being the printer for another person's newspaper, decided to establish his own paper, the *New England Courant*. It was only the fourth newspaper in Boston; the first, published in 1690, had been closed down by the Massachusetts government after only one issue. The second, the Boston *News-Letter*, was founded in 1704; it became the first continuously published newspaper not only in Boston but in all of the North American colonies. The next Boston paper, begun in 1719 and printed by James Franklin for the owner, was the Boston *Gazette*.[11] These early newspapers were small, simple, and bland affairs, two to four pages published weekly and containing mostly reprints of old European news, ship sailings, and various advertisements, together with notices of deaths, political appointments, court actions, fires, piracies, and such matters. Although the papers were expensive and numbered only in the hundreds of copies, they often passed from hand to hand and could reach beneath the topmost ranks of the city's population of twelve thousand, including even into the ranks of artisans and other "middling sorts."

These early papers were labeled "published by authority." Remaining on the good side of government was not only wise politically, it was wise economically. Most colonial printers in the eighteenth century could not have survived without government printing contracts of one sort or another. Hence most sought to avoid controversy and to remain neutral in politics. They tried to exclude from their papers anything that smacked of libel or personal abuse. Such material was risky. Much safer were the columns of dull but innocuous foreign news that they used to fill their papers, much to Franklin's later annoyance. It is hard to know what colonial readers made of the first news item printed in the newly created *South Carolina Gazette* of 1732: "We learn from Caminica, that the Cossacks continue to make inroads onto polish Ukrania."[12]

James Franklin did not behave as most colonial printers did. When he decided to start his own paper, he was definitely not publishing it by authority. In fact, the *New England Courant* began by attacking the Boston establishment, in particular the program of inoculating people for smallpox that was being promoted by the Puritan ministers Cotton Mather and his father. When this inoculation debate died down, the paper turned to satirizing other subjects of Boston interest, including pretended learning and religious hypocrisy, some of which provoked the Mathers into replies. Eager to try his own hand at satire, young Benjamin in 1722 submitted some essays to his brother's newspaper under the name of Silence Dogood, a play on Cotton Mather's *Essays to Do Good,* the name usually given to the minister's *Bonifacius,* published in 1710. For a sixteen-year-old boy to assume the persona of a middle-aged woman was a daunting challenge, and young Franklin took "exquisite Pleasure" in fooling his brother and others into thinking that only "Men of some Character among us for Learning and Ingenuity" could have written the newspaper pieces.[13]

These Silence Dogood essays lampooned everything from funeral eulogies to "that famous Seminary of Learning," Harvard College. Although Franklin's satire was generally and shrewdly genial, there was often a bite to it and a good deal of social resentment behind it, especially when it came to his making fun of Harvard. Most of the students who attended "this famous Place," he wrote, "were little better than Dunces and Blockheads." This was not surprising, since the main qualification for entry, he said, was having money. Once admitted, the students "learn little more than how to carry themselves handsomely, and enter a Room genteely, (which might as well be acquire'd at a Dancing-School,) and from whence they return, after Abundance of Trouble and Charge, as great Blockheads as ever, only more proud and self-conceited."[14] One can already sense an underlying anger in this precocious and rebellious teenager, an anger with those who claimed an undeserved social superiority that would become an important spur to his ambition.

When Franklin's brother found out who the author of the Silence

Dogood pieces was, he was not happy, "as he thought, probably with reason," that all the praise the essays were receiving tended to make the young teenager "too vain." Franklin, as he admitted, was probably "too saucy and provoking" to his brother, and the two brothers began squabbling. James was only nine years older than his youngest brother, but he nonetheless "considered himself as my Master & me as his Apprentice." Consequently, as master he "expected the same Services from me as he would from another; while I thought he demean'd me too much in some he requir'd of me, who from a Brother expected more Indulgence."[15]

Since the fraternal relationship did not fit the extreme hierarchical relationship of master and apprentice, the situation became impossible, especially when James began exercising his master's prerogative of beating his apprentice.

Indentured apprentices were under severe contractual obligations in the eighteenth century and were part of the large unfree population that existed in all the colonies. In essence they belonged to their masters: their contracts were inheritable, and they could not marry, play cards or gamble, attend taverns, or leave their masters' premises day or night without permission. With such restraints it is understandable that Franklin was "continually wishing for some Opportunity" to shorten or break his apprenticeship.[16]

In 1723 that opportunity came when the Massachusetts government—like all governments in that pre-modern age, acutely sensitive to libels and any suggestion of disrespect—finally found sufficient grounds to forbid James to publish his paper. James sought to evade the restriction by publishing the paper under Benjamin's name. But it would not do to have a mere apprentice as editor of the paper, and James had to return the old indenture of apprenticeship to his brother. Although James drew up a new and secret contract for the remainder of the term of apprenticeship, Franklin realized his brother would not dare to reveal what he had done, and he thus took "Advantage" of the situation "to assert my Freedom."

His situation with his brother had become intolerable, and his own standing in the Puritan-dominated community of Boston was little better. Since Franklin had become "a little obnoxious to the governing Party" and "my indiscreet Disputations about Religion began to make me pointed at with Horror by good People, as an Infidel or Atheist," he determined to leave Boston. But because he still had some years left of his apprenticeship and his father opposed his leaving, he had to leave secretly. With a bit of money and a few belongings, the headstrong and defiant seventeen-year-old boarded a ship and fled the city, a move that was much more common in the mobile eighteenth-century Atlantic world than we might imagine. Thus Franklin began the career that would lead him "from the Poverty & Obscurity in which I was born & bred, to a State of Affluence & some Degree of Reputation in the World."[17]

PHILADELPHIA

Franklin arrived in the Quaker city renowned for its religious freedom in 1723, hungry, tired, dirty, and bedraggled in his "Working Dress," his "Pockets stuffed out with Shirts and Stockings," with only a Dutch dollar and copper shilling to his name. He bought three rolls, and "with a Roll under each Arm, and eating the other," he wandered around Market, Chestnut, and Walnut Streets, and in his own eyes, and the eyes of his future wife, Deborah Read, who watched him from her doorway, made "a most awkward ridiculous Appearance." He finally stumbled into a Quaker meetinghouse on Second Street, and "hearing nothing said," promptly "fell fast asleep, and continu'd so till the Meeting broke up, when one was kind enough to wake me."

Franklin tells us in his *Autobiography* that he offers us such a "particular"—and unforgettable—description of his "first Entry" into the city of Philadelphia so "that you may in your Mind compare such unlikely Beginnings with the Figure I have since made there." Although he tried in his *Autobiography* to play down and mock his achievements, Franklin was nothing if not proud of his extraordinary rise. He always knew that it was the enormous gap between his very obscure beginnings and his later worldwide eminence that gave his story its heroic appeal.[18]

Philadelphia in the 1720s numbered about six thousand people, but it was growing rapidly and would soon surpass the much older city of Boston.[19] The city, and the colony of Pennsylvania, had begun in the late seventeenth century as William Penn's "Holy Experiment" for poor persecuted members of the Society of Friends. But by the time Franklin arrived, many of the Quaker families, such as the Norrises, Shippens, Dickinsons, and Pembertons, had prospered, and this emerging Quaker aristocracy had come to dominate the mercantile affairs and politics of the colony. At the same time, however, many non-English immigrants—Germans at first and later Scotch-Irish—had begun to pour into the colony in increasing numbers. Most of these new immigrants came as servants; indeed, at least half the population of Philadelphia during the early and middle decades of the eighteenth century was composed of indentured servants.

Since the Philadelphia that Franklin moved to was still a very small town, knit together by face-to-face relationships, Franklin was able to become acquainted with people fairly quickly. He first looked for work with the dominant printer of the colony, Andrew Bradford, who was the government printer and since 1719 had been publishing Pennsylvania's only newspaper, the *American Weekly Mercury*. When Franklin discovered that Bradford had no place for him, he ended up working in the shop of a rival printer, Samuel Keimer.[20] He eventually found lodging in the home of a plain carpenter, John Read, the father of the woman who had watched his awkward and ridiculous entry into the city.

He soon made friends in the town with clerks and other middling sorts who had intellectual and literary ambitions similar to his. He was unusually amiable, told a good story, and worked at getting along with people. He tells us that very early on he developed "the Habit of expressing my self in Terms of modest Diffidence, never using when I advance any thing that may possibly be disputed, the Words, *Certainly, undoubtedly*, or any others that give the Air of Positiveness to an Opinion." Looking back, he realized that this habit had been "of great Advantage" to him in persuading people to come round to his point of view.[21]

With his amiability and talent he soon became an artisan to be reckoned with. He knew more about printing than his employer, Samuel Keimer; indeed, as Governor William Keith of Pennsylvania quickly surmised, this talented teenager knew more about printing than anyone in Philadelphia. He was extremely bright and naturally affable, and his future as an artisan looked very promising.

PATRONAGE

Although Franklin certainly wanted to make something of himself in Philadelphia, he could not have anticipated becoming what he eventually became—the archetype of the self-made man. Indeed, it would be a mistake to overemphasize this aspect of his life, as if his career was unique and he was somehow prefiguring the Horatio Alger success stories of the next century. Rising from obscure origins to success and eminence was not unheard of in the eighteenth century or earlier, and Franklin's rise, however spectacular, was not unique in English history. Wasn't it said that Cardinal Wolsey's father had been a butcher?

In the eighteenth century many young men moved up the social ladder in both America and Britain. William Strahan, Franklin's lifelong British friend and associate, began as a journeyman printer like Franklin and eventually became very rich, richer perhaps than Franklin, and even acquired a seat in Parliament. And then there was Edmund Burke, the Irishman of undistinguished origins who rose to become one of the great writers and orators of his age. But most of this mobility in the eighteenth century was sponsored mobility. On both sides of the Atlantic bright Englishmen of obscure origins could have spectacular rises, but they needed patrons and sponsors to do so. Burke would never have acquired the eminence he did without the patronage of William Hamilton and the Marquess of Rockingham. In that very different monarchical world, patrons were often on the lookout for bright young lads, and when they found them, they were eager to bring them along. Patronizing inferiors and creating obligations, after all, was an important mark of an aristocrat in that rank-conscious age.

The examples of such patronage in the colonial world are many. One evening in 1720 a swollen Virginia river forced John Carter, the provincial secretary and "a man of immense wealth," to seek shelter in the home of a "plain planter" named John Waller. During the course of the evening Carter, impressed with the "quickness" and the "uncommon parts" of Waller's ten-year-old son, Benjamin, proposed to the father that he take the boy and educate him. Perhaps money changed hands. At any rate, the bright young Benjamin Waller was brought into the Carter household, educated, sent to the College of William and Mary, and trained in the law. Eventually Waller became a member of the House of Burgesses, the holder of several crown offices, and a great man in his own right.[22]

Other examples of patrons' sponsoring young men may not be as remarkable as this one, but the practice was common. Edmund Pendleton in Virginia succeeded in just this manner, as did many young New England farm boys discovered by their local ministers and sent on to Harvard and Yale. And then there was a brilliant seventeen-year-old merchant's clerk, named Alexander Hamilton, who was rescued from his "groveling" obscurity in St. Croix by perceptive patrons and sent to the mainland for an education.[23]

Patronage was the basic means of social mobility in the eighteenth century, and Franklin's rise was due to it—as a careful reading of his *Autobiography* shows. He could never have made it in the way he did in that hierarchical society if he had not been helped by men of influence and supported at crucial points. When Franklin's brother-in-law, a ship captain who sailed a commercial sloop between Massachusetts and the Delaware region, learned that Franklin was in Philadelphia, working in a print shop, he wrote to persuade the young runaway to return to Boston. The brother-in-law happened to show Franklin's reply to Governor Keith, who could not believe that a seventeen-year-old could have written such a letter. "He said," Franklin recalled, "I appear'd a young Man of promising Parts, and therefore should be encouraged."[24] Unhappy with the two existing printers in Philadelphia, Bradford and Keimer, the governor called on Franklin, who was working for Keimer. The governor invited Franklin out for a drink in a local tavern and offered to help establish him as an independent printer if his father would supply the capital. When his father refused to put up the money, Governor Keith promised to do so himself.

Keith was not the only colonial governor to notice Franklin. When the young man was returning from Boston, having failed to get the money from his father, he stopped off in New York with a trunk of his books that he had retrieved from home. A youth with a trunk of books was rare enough in colonial New York that Governor William Burnet asked to meet with the young man to converse about authors and books.

During Franklin's trip to Boston, even Cotton Mather, whom Franklin had satirized so successfully in the Silence Dogood essays, had asked to meet the learned young man.

Once prominent Pennsylvanians grasped what Franklin was like, they were quick to patronize him. Thomas Denham, a Quaker merchant, befriended him, gave him money at a crucial moment, and brought him into his business. Even Franklin's later enemy William Allen, who was Philadelphia's richest man, helped Franklin at various times, especially in securing for him the position of deputy postmaster. Prominent Philadelphia lawyer Andrew Hamilton would continue to patronize Franklin throughout his life.[25] Franklin's patrons supported him in a variety of ways, lending money, inviting him to their homes, introducing him to others, becoming his "friends," which was the common euphemism of the day for patron-client relations. All of "these Friends were . . . of great Use to me," Franklin recalled, "as I occasionally was to some of them."[26] No doubt his own conspicuous talent was the main source of his rise, but once he had caught people's attention, "the leading Men . . . thought it convenient to oblige and encourage me."[27] So it went. In the end Franklin was never quite as self-made as he sometimes implied or as the nineteenth century made him out to be.

In the end, of course, he did succeed in rising higher than any of his patrons could have imagined. But at the outset Franklin did not think much beyond becoming his own independent printer in the city of Philadelphia—a remarkable enough feat in itself, given the lowliness of his origins. We know the teenage printer's social horizons were still limited; otherwise he would not have begun seeking the hand in marriage of Deborah Read, whose family was anything but rich or distinguished. When Deborah's father suddenly died, her widowed mother suggested that marriage wait until Franklin was established. Trusting in Governor Keith's promise to finance him in setting up his own printing firm, Franklin planned a trip to London to purchase the necessary equipment. There was time enough to get married after he returned from England. In November 1724, a year after he had arrived in Philadelphia, Franklin, with a friend, James Ralph, was on his way to the metropolitan center of the British Empire.

LONDON, 1724–1726

London, with a population of over a half million people in the 1720s, was a far cry from any city in North America. London was growing rapidly, but since its death rate was so horrendous—two persons died for every child born—this growth was entirely from people moving into the city. The city teemed with movement. One third of its population were, like Franklin, recent arrivals; the city was absorbing about one half of the entire natural increase of England's population. All these people made for congestion and confusion in the city's labyrinth of narrow streets and dark alleys, which contrasted sharply with the neatly rectangular layout of colonial Philadelphia.[28]

London's society was as different from that of Philadelphia in its hierarchical complexity and its luxurious splendor as in its number of people. It was dominated by a monarchical court and wealthy hereditary aristocrats who were busy buying property and erecting opulent town houses everywhere. Some of these nobles had annual incomes in the tens of thousands of pounds, exorbitant sums that no colonial aristocrat could match. Some of them spent on a single supper and ball what many Englishmen could not earn in a lifetime. These nobles lived in the country but maintained homes in London that they visited annually at fabulous cost. Lord Ashburnham, for example, spent over £4000 a year for his annual visit to London. But the British aristocracy was larger than the two hundred or so hereditary peers who sat in the House of Lords. It included not only several titled ranks of knights and esquires but also the large body of gentry, the lowest social rank entitled to bear a coat of arms. Below these were rich merchants and the growing numbers of middling shopkeepers, traders, artisans, and craftsmen, all resting on a huge population of beggars, sailors, prostitutes, street sellers, porters, servants, and laborers of every conceivable description.[29]

When Franklin arrived in this maelstrom of humanity, he discovered that Governor Keith had reneged on his promise to supply credit for him. Franklin the innocent youth was stunned. "Unsolicited as he was by me, how could I think his generous Offers insincere? I believ'd him one of the best Men in the World." Since Keith had been, after all, the knighted governor of the colony, Franklin in his *Autobiography* milked the deception for all it was worth: "What shall we think of a Governor's playing such pitiful Tricks, and imposing so grossly on a poor ignorant Boy!"[30]

Although Franklin learned from Governor Keith's behavior something about the arbitrary nature of power in that severely hierarchical world, he had no recourse but to seek work as a printer in the great metropolis. Despite the complexity of London he seems to have made his way about with remarkable ease. He naturally impressed his London employers and indeed everyone else he met. In London he soon forgot about his engagement to Deborah Read and spent most of his money "going to Plays & other Places of Amusement."[31] In addition to these "Expenses" that kept him from earning enough to pay for his return passage, he seems to have indulged what he later called "that hard-to-be-govern'd Passion of Youth" that hurried him "frequently into Intrigues with low Women."[32] He did, however, avoid the vices of smoking, drinking, and gambling. Unlike his fellow printers and most workers in those days, who were "great Guzzlers of Beer," he drank only water while working.[33] His extraordinary lifelong temperance, as he later pointed out, contributed not only to his health but also to his remarkable success in business. Unlike most other workers, Franklin had no "St. Mondays," no absences from Monday work because of excessive weekend drinking.[34]

These initial experiences in London made a lasting impression on the nineteen-year-old Franklin, and he devoted a considerable number of pages in his *Autobiography* to them. Although he mentions several "errata" that he committed while in London, he clearly was proud of the way he had survived in the big city. At a time when most people, even many sailors, did not know how to swim, he tells us that the English much admired his prowess as a swimmer; he even imagined that he might have made a living teaching swimming and water sports to the sons of the English gentry.

While in London he wrote and printed on his employer's press a rather sophomoric *Dissertation on Liberty and Necessity, Pleasure and Pain* that argued that since God determined everything, it was useless to debate the right and wrong of anything. This would seem to have been a nice justification for his self-indulgent behavior in London—except that he also argued that all pleasure was accompanied by equal sensations of pain or uneasiness, which suggests that his conscience may have been bothered by his apparent freedom from religious restraints. The essay attracted some attention from deists and gave him entrée to some intellectual circles, where he met Bernard Mandeville, the author of *The Fable of the Bees, or Private Vices, Public Benefits.* Since Mandeville believed that private vice could have beneficial public consequences, he seemed to be a writer after the young Franklin's own hard-to-be-governed heart.

Franklin later repudiated his *Dissertation on Liberty and Necessity,* burning all but one of the copies still in his possession. He came to conclude that all such "Metaphysical Reasonings" were useless, and he gave them up. Although he never accepted the Bible as divine revelation or believed in the divinity of Christ, he always affirmed "the Existence of the Deity, that he made the World, and govern'd it by his Providence." He came to believe that the only important thing about religion was morality, and the only basis for that morality was utility. "Sin is not hurtful because it is forbidden," he later wrote in his *Poor Richard's Almanack,* "but it is forbidden because it's hurtful.... Nor is a Duty beneficial because it is commanded, but it is commanded, because it's beneficial."[35]

Although Franklin had been "religiously educated as a Presbyterian," he never accepted the Calvinist conviction that faith alone was the source of salvation; indeed, he became convinced that "the most acceptable Service of God was the doing Good to Man." His respect for the various religions in eighteenth-century America came to depend solely on their contributions to virtue or morality. After concluding in a 1735 newspaper polemic that "a virtuous Heretick shall be saved before a wicked Christian," Franklin thereafter decided that religion was not a subject worth disputing in public. Although he continued to make contributions to many churches, he never belonged to any of them—a problem for his reputation in the early nineteenth century.[36]

BACK TO PHILADELPHIA

After eighteen months in London, Franklin got tired of the big city and wanted to get back to Philadelphia. Surely it was not because of his pining for Deborah Read—he wrote her only once during the nearly two years he was gone, and then simply to tell her that he was not likely soon to return. In London, he tells us, he had proceeded "by degrees" to forget his engagement to Deborah.[37] Perhaps he wished to return because London in the 1720s was experiencing food shortages and more outbreaks of diseases than usual. Or perhaps he had come to realize that he would be a much bigger fish in the relatively small pond of Philadelphia than he was in the huge ocean of London with its hundreds of thousands of people. Or perhaps he sensed that printers in England were losing control of the publishing business, and he would have many more opportunities for advancement back in the colonies.[38] At any rate, in 1726, when Philadelphia merchant Thomas Denham offered to pay Franklin's passage back home and bring him into his business, he jumped at the opportunity.

Denham's untimely death soon drove Franklin back into the printing trade, managing the shop of his former boss Samuel Keimer. In addition to training the five workers in the shop, Franklin cast type, engraved, made ink, and acted as warehouseman: "in short," he recalled, he was "quite a Factotum."[39] The patrons of Keimer's printing firm soon came to realize that young Franklin the employee was far more competent and presentable than his employer. Not only was Keimer an "odd Fish," grouchy and "ignorant of common Life," said Franklin, but he was "slovenly to extream dirtiness." Consequently, the firm's patrons, who included Judge William Allen, Samuel Bustill, the secretary of the province, Isaac Pearson, Joseph Cooper, several members of the important Smith family, and members of the assembly, found Franklin a much better companion than they did the owner of the business. "They had me to their Houses, introduc'd me to their Friends, and show'd me much Civility, while he, tho' the Master, was a little neglected." One of these patrons, Isaac Decow, the surveyor general, helped to fill Franklin with dreams of what he might become. Decow told the young artisan that he himself had begun humbly, wheeling clay for bricklayers and carrying chains for surveyors, but had "by his Industry acquir'd a good Estate." Decow predicted that Franklin would soon work his employer out of his business and "make a fortune in it in Philadelphia."[40]

In 1728 Franklin and one of his fellow workers, Hugh Meredith (whose father put up the capital), left Keimer and opened up their own printing business. There were now three printing firms in Philadelphia, which was more than most people thought the town could support.

Franklin was determined that it would not be his business that would fail. He worked incredibly hard, "and this Industry visible to our Neighbours began to give us Character and Credit."[41] When in 1729 Meredith lost interest in printing and began drinking heavily, Franklin, with the aid of friends, bought him out. At last at age twenty-three, he was sole owner of his own printing firm. But he also had debts.

MARRIAGE

At the same time Franklin was thinking about getting married and settling down. Ever since he had returned from London, he recalled, he had come to realize that his frequent "Intrigues with low Women that fell in my Way . . . were attended with some Expence & great Inconvenience, besides a continual Risque to my Health." Marriage would allow free rein to "that hard-to-be-govern'd Passion of Youth" while removing the expense and the risk. He might have added that bachelors were regarded with a certain amount of suspicion in many of the colonies.

Since Deborah Read, to whom he had been engaged, had given up on him during his absence in London and married a potter named John Rogers, Franklin never gave her a thought and began courting the daughter of a relative of one of his friends. However, when he asked the young woman's parents for a dowry of about £100 to pay off his debts, he was turned down. He asked acquaintances about other marital prospects and discovered that "the Business of a Printer being generally thought a poor one, I was not to expect Money with a Wife unless with such a one, as I should not other wise think agreeable."[42]

Only then did Franklin realize that he might have to settle for Deborah Read. Although Deborah was already married, her husband had turned out to be a wastrel and perhaps a bigamist. Consequently, Deborah had left John Rogers and returned to her mother's house. Rogers in turn ran off to the West Indies, where rumor had it he died, but no one could be sure. Since Pennsylvania law did not allow divorce for desertion, Franklin and Deborah in 1730 decided to avoid legal difficulties by simply setting up housekeeping as husband and wife.

Franklin's entering at the age of twenty-four upon a common-law marriage (a much more prevalent practice in the eighteenth century than today) to the loud and lowly and scarcely literate Deborah Read suggests that his social ambitions were still quite limited. The other Founders generally made something of themselves by their marriages. Indeed, most of them tended to think of marriage in dynastic terms, as a means of building alliances and establishing or consolidating their position in society. Washington acquired a considerable estate by marrying the rich young widow Martha Custis. Upon his marriage to the widow Martha Wayles Skelton, Jefferson received 135 slaves, including the Hemings family, and 11,000 acres of land. Hamilton married Elizabeth Schuyler, a member of one of the most distinguished families of New York. Only John Adams seems not to have worried much about his wife's dowry, though Abigail Smith's father was the minister in Weymouth and her mother was a Quincy, a member of a wealthy and important Massachusetts family.

Franklin's marriage was very different from that of the other Founders. It was sudden and seemingly without great advantage. Only two months after telling his sister that he was definitely not planning to get married, Franklin unexpectedly changed his mind.[43] We are not sure why. Franklin tells us in his *Autobiography* that marrying Deborah Read eased his conscience over his earlier treatment of her, but we have no evidence of his guilt except his later recollection of it. If he felt guilty over his earlier treatment of her, how much more guilty he must have felt over his later treatment of her; but we have no evidence of that either. No doubt, as he recalled, the couple "throve together," but the marriage scarcely helped Franklin socially.[44] She may in fact have become something of an embarrassment to him. Certainly the Philadelphia gentry, when they began mingling with Franklin, never included his wife in invitations to their homes. Deborah did, however, help him economically; she was as shrewd and as frugal as he was, and she never ceased working to bring money into the household.[45]

In newspaper essays written shortly after his marriage Franklin expressed his dislike of tradesmen's wives who aspired to become gentlewomen. Such wives shunned work, refused to knit their husbands' stockings, bought extravagant goods, and lived beyond their means.[46] Franklin knew that Deborah would never behave in this way. Indeed, in his "Rules and Maxims for Promoting Matrimonial Happiness," written at the time of his marriage, he advised a prospective wife to "have a due Regard to [her husband's] Income and Circumstances in all your Expenses and Desires." But, most important, the wife was to "Read frequently with due Attention the Matrimonial Service; and take care in doing so, not to overlook the Word obey." His experience with Deborah eventually proved that such wives did not have to bring dowries to their artisan husbands. As he later pointed out to a prospective tradesman contemplating marriage, "If you get a prudent healthy Wife, your Industry in your Profession, with her good Economy, will be a Fortune sufficient."[47]

There may have been other reasons for Franklin to marry Deborah. Franklin almost immediately took into his home an illegitimate son born to him and another woman, a son whom his new wife had to raise. Under the circumstances Deborah may have been the only woman in Philadelphia who would have put up with this added responsibility, and she did so only reluctantly. (After three centuries the identity of the mother of the illegitimate son, whom Franklin named William, remains a mystery. Franklin apparently made some small provision for the mother who, as the son of one of Franklin's close friends later said, "being none of the most agreeable of Women," was neither noticed nor acknowledged by Franklin or William.)[48]

Franklin indeed ought to have been grateful to Deborah for taking on the burden of bringing up some other woman's child. Deborah never liked the boy and, according to a visiting Virginian who lived in the Franklin household for a short time in 1755, often treated the then twenty-four-year-old William with unusual coldness. To the visitor's consternation, she called William "the greatest Villain upon Earth," denounced him in foul and vulgar language, and kept trying to put him down in front of their guest. She apparently never said any such thing in front of her husband, however, for Franklin adored his son.[49]

Franklin's marriage to Deborah seemed to confirm his status as a commoner. As a printer who had to work for a living and with a wife like Deborah, he was a long way from being regarded as a gentleman.

GENTLEMEN AND COMMONERS

Many people in the eighteenth-century English-speaking world, especially those in the topmost ranks, still tended to divide the society into only two parts, a tiny elite of gentlemen on the top dominating the bulk of commoners on the bottom. A gentleman was someone quite different from ordinary folk—even in the colonies, which lacked the extremes of English society, with its great opulent aristocrats set against the most appalling poverty. "The title of a gentleman," wrote one early-eighteenth-century observer, "is commonly given in England to all that distinguish themselves from the common sort of people, by a good garb, genteel air, or good education, wealth or learning." Although the numbers trying to enter the rank of gentleman were increasing, becoming a gentleman was still not easy, especially as the bar of politeness and refinement kept being raised. "A finished Gentleman," wrote the English essayist Richard Steele, someone whose writings Franklin knew well, "is perhaps the most uncommon of all the great Characters in Life."[50]

This separation between gentlemen and commoners, which John Adams called "the most ancient and universal of all Divisions of People," overwhelmed all other divisions in colonial culture, even that between free and enslaved that we today find so horribly conspicuous. Although the eighteenth century was becoming increasingly confused over precisely who ought to constitute the categories of gentlemen and ordinary people, many were still sure that in all societies some were patricians and most were plebeians, some were officers and most were common soldiers, some were "the better sort" and most were not. The awareness of the "difference between gentle and simple," recalled the Anglican minister Devereux Jarratt of his humble youth in colonial Virginia, was "universal among all of my rank and age."[51]

Since this distinction has lost almost all of its older meaning (Jarratt himself lived to see "a vast alteration, in this respect"), it takes an act of imagination to recapture the immense importance of the difference between gentleman and commoner in the eighteenth century.[52] Common soldiers captured in war were imprisoned; captured officers, however, could be released "on parole," after giving their word to their fellow gentleman officers that they would not flee the area or return to their troops. Southern squires entered their churches as a body and took their pews only after their families and the ordinary people had been seated. The courts of Massachusetts debated endlessly over whether or not particular plaintiffs and defendants were properly identified as gentlemen, for, as John Adams noted, it was important in law that writs "not call Esquires Labourers, and Labourers Esquires."[53] Inevitably, the law treated gentlemen and commoners differently. Although English colonial law was presumably equal for all, the criminal punishments were not: gentlemen, unlike commoners, did not have their ears cropped or their bodies flogged.

In the southern parts of colonial America the distinction between gentleman and commoner was there practically from birth: "Before a boy knows his right hand from his left, can discern black from white, good from evil, or knows who made him, or how he exists," wrote one Virginian, "he is a Gentleman." And as a gentleman, "it would derogate greatly from his character, to learn a trade; or to put his hand to any servile employment."[54] Although the precise nature of a gentleman might have been in more doubt in the northern colonies, even there the distinction was very real. As late as 1761 the young attorney John Adams at least thought he knew when someone was not a gentleman, "neither by Birth, Education, Office, Reputation, or Employment," nor by "Thought, Word, or Deed." A person who springs "from ordinary Parents," who "can scarcely write his Name," whose "Business is Boating," who "never had any Commissions"—to call such a person a gentleman was "an arrant Prostitution of the Title."[55]

For most people the principal means of distinction between the gentry and commoners was still "Birth and Parentage." Many colonists continued to believe that all men were created unequal. God, it was said, had been "pleas'd to constitute a Difference in Families." Although most children were of "low Degree or of Common Derivation, Some are Sons and Daughters of the Mighty: they are more honorably descended, and have greater Relations than others."[56] The word "gentry" was after all associated with birth, derived from the Latin *gens,* or stock. English and colonial writers such as Henry Fielding and Robert Munford, even when poking fun at the false pretensions of the aristocracy, had to have—for the harmony of their stories and the comfort of their genteel audiences—their apparently plebeian heroes or heroines turn out to be secretly the offspring of gentlemen.

In addition to genealogy, wealth was important in distinguishing a gentleman, for "in vulgar reckoning a mean condition bespeaks a mean man." But more and more in the eighteenth century these traditional sources of gentry status—birth and wealth—were surrounded and squeezed by other measures of distinction—artificial, man-made criteria having to do with manners, taste, and character. "No man," it was increasingly said, "deserves the appellation *a Gentleman* until he has done something to merit it."[57]

Gentlemen walked and talked in certain ways and held in contempt those who did not. They ate with silver knives and forks while many common people still ate with their hands. Gentlemen prided themselves on their classical learning, and in their privately circulated verse and in their public polemics they took great pains to display their knowledge. They took up dancing and fencing, for both "contribute greatly to a graceful Carriage." "A Gentleman," they were told, "should know how to appear in an Assembly [in] Public to Advantage, and to defend himself if attacked." Young aspiring gentlemen were urged by their parents to study poetry and to learn to play musical instruments. Unlike common people, gentlemen wore wigs or powdered their hair, believing that "nothing [was] a finer ornament to a young gentleman than a good head of hair well order'd and set forth," especially when appearing "before persons of rank and distinction." They dressed distinctively and fashionably. In contrast to the plain shirts, leather aprons, and buckskin breeches of ordinary men, they wore lace ruffles, silk stockings, and other finery. They sought to build elaborate houses and to have their portraits painted. Little gratified the gentry's hearts more than to have a "coach and six," or at least a "chariot and four," to have servants decked out in "fine liveries," to have a reputation for entertaining liberally, to be noticed.[58]

But central to these cultural attributes of gentility was "politeness," which had a far broader and richer significance for the eighteenth century than it does for us. It meant not simply good manners and refinement but being genial and sociable, possessing the capacity to relate to other human beings easily and naturally. It was what most obviously separated the genteel few from the vulgar and barbaric mass of the population.

"Politeness," said the Reverend William Smith in 1752, "is the Bond of social life,—the ornament of human nature." By "softening . . . our natural roughness," politeness developed in men "a certain Easiness of Behavior," which, said Smith, was the main "Characteristic of the Gentleman." Gentlemen were admired for their "real humility, condescension, courteousness, affability, and great good manners to all the world."[59]

Only a hierarchical society that knew its distinctions well could have placed so much value on a gentleman's capacity for condescension—that voluntary humiliation, that willing descent from superiority to equal terms with inferiors. For us today condescension is a pejorative term, suggesting snobbery or haughtiness. But for the eighteenth century it was a positive and complimentary term, something that gentlemen aspired to possess and commoners valued in those above them. Rufus Putnam, a young Massachusetts enlisted man serving with the provincial forces attached to the British army in northern New York during the Seven Years War, was especially taken with the ability of one British officer to condescend. The officer frequently came among his men, said Putnam, "and his manner was so easy and fermiller, that you loost all that constraint or diffidence we feele when addressed by our Superiours, whose manners are forbidding."[60]

Ultimately, beneath all these strenuous efforts to define gentility was the fundamental classical quality of being free and independent. The liberality for which gentlemen were known connoted freedom—freedom from material want, freedom from the caprice of others, freedom from ignorance, and freedom from having to work with one's hands. The gentry's distinctiveness came from being independent in a world of dependencies, learned in a world only partially literate, and leisured in a world of laborers.

We today have so many diverse forms of work and recreation and so much of our society shares in them that we can scarcely appreciate the significance of the earlier stark separation between a leisured few and a laboring many. In the eighteenth century, labor, as it had been for ages, was still associated with toil and trouble, with pain, and manual productivity did not yet have the superior moral value that it would soon acquire. To be sure, industriousness and hard work were everywhere extolled, and the puritan ethic was widely preached—but only for ordinary people, not for gentlemen. Hard steady work was good for the character of common people: it kept them out of trouble; it lifted them out of idleness and barbarism; and it instilled in them the proper moral values.

Most people, it was widely assumed, would not work if they did not have to. Franklin certainly thought so: it was conventional wisdom. "It seems certain," he wrote in 1753, "that the hope of becoming at some time of Life free from the necessity of care and Labour, together with fear of penury, are the mainsprings of most people's industry."[61] People labored out of necessity, out of poverty, and that necessity and poverty bred the contempt in which laboring people had been held for centuries. Since servants, slaves, and bonded laborers did much of the work of the society, it seemed natural to associate leisure with liberty and toil with bondage.[62] A gentleman's freedom was valued because it was freedom from the necessity to labor, which came from being poor.

Indeed, only the need of ordinary people to feed themselves, it was thought, kept them busy working. "Everyone but an idiot knows that the lower class must be kept poor or they will never be industrious," declared the English agricultural writer Arthur Young. Only "poverty," wrote Thomas Hutchinson in 1761, by then the lieutenant governor of Massachusetts, "will produce industry and frugality" among the common people. Franklin agreed. Since people were naturally indolent, "giving mankind a dependence on anything for support in age and sickness, besides industry and frugality during youth and health, tends . . . to encourage idleness and prodigality, and thereby to promote and increase poverty, the very evil it was intended to cure."[63]

Thus even in the eighteenth century the age-old contempt for those who had to work for a living, those who had occupations, lingered on. In the ideal polity, Aristotle had written thousands of years earlier, "the citizens must not live a mechanical or commercial life. Such a life is not noble, and it militates against virtue." Not even agricultural workers could be citizens, for men "must have leisure to develop their virtue and for the activities of a citizen."[64] This leisure, or what was best described as not exerting oneself for profit, was supposed to be a prerogative of gentlemen only. Gentlemen, James Harrington had written in the seventeenth century, were those who "live upon their own revenue in plenty, without engagement either to the tilling of their lands or other work for their livelihood." In the early eighteenth century Daniel Defoe defined "the gentry" as "such who live on estates, and without the mechanism of employment, including the men of letters, such as clergy, lawyers and physicians." A half century later Franklin's colleague, Richard Jackson, similarly characterized the gentry as those who "live on their fortunes."[65]

Ideally gentlemen did not work for a living. A gentleman, it was said, was someone "who has no visible means of support." His income was supposed to come to him indirectly from his wealth—from rents and from interest on bonds or money out on loan—and much of it often did. Although some northern colonists might suggest that gentlemen-farmers ought to set "a laborious example to their Domesticks," perhaps by taking an occasional turn in the fields, a gentleman's activity was supposed to be with the mind. Managing one's landed estate in the way that Cicero and other Roman patricians had managed theirs meant exercising authority—the only activity befitting a truly free man. Therefore, when a planter like George Washington totaled up his accounts or rode through his fields to check on his slaves or even when he occasionally took a hand at some task, he was not considered to be engaged in work.[66]

Immense cultural pressure often made gentlemen pretend that their economic affairs were for pleasure or for the good of the community, and not for their subsistence. They saw themselves and, more important, were seen by others as gentlemen who happened to engage in some commercial enterprises. Unlike ordinary people, gentlemen, or the better sort, traditionally were not defined or identified by what they did, but by who they were. They had avocations, not vocations. The great eighteenth-century French naturalist the Comte de Buffon did not like to think of himself as anyone other than "a gentleman amusing myself with natural history." He did not want to be called a "naturalist," or even a "great naturalist." "Naturalists, linkboys, dentists, etc."—these, said Buffon, were "people who live by their work; a thing ill suited to a gentleman." The fifth Duke of Devonshire knew exactly his cousin's status: "He is not a gentleman; he works."[67] Clergymen, doctors, and lawyers were not yet modern professionals, working long hours for a living like common artisans. Their gentry status depended less on their professional skills than on other sources—

on family, wealth, or a college education in the liberal arts—and those doctors, lawyers, and clergymen who had none of these were therefore something less than gentlemen: pettifoggers, charlatans, or quacks.

Without understanding the age-old belief, as John Locke had expressed it, that "trade is wholly inconsistent with a gentleman's calling," we will never be able to fully comprehend Franklin's career or his reputation following his death. Dr. Johnson defined the word "mechanic" as "mean, servile; of mean occupation." Such mechanics or artisans were supposed to know their place. So in 1753 when printer Hugh Gaines attempted to defend himself in writing against opponents of his *New-York Mercury*, he was forced to apologize for his boldness. He was wrong, he said, "to appear in print in any other Manner, than what merely pertains to the Station in Life in which I am placed."[68] In the eighteenth century artisans and mechanics—shoemakers, coopers, silversmiths, printers—all those who worked for a living, especially with their hands, no matter how wealthy, no matter how many employees they managed, could never legitimately claim the status of gentleman. Even a great painter with noble aspirations like John Singleton Copley was socially stigmatized because he worked with his hands. Copley painted the portraits of dozens of distinguished colonial gentlemen, and he knew what his patrons thought of his art. For them, Copley said bitterly in 1767, painting was "no more than any other useful trade, as they sometimes term it, like that of a Carpenter tailor or shoemaker."[69]

THE MIDDLING SORTS

By the first third of the eighteenth century this dichotomous social structure was changing, and changing rapidly. The astonishing growth of commerce, trade, and manufacturing in the English-speaking world was creating hosts of new people who could not easily be fitted into either of the two basic social categories. Commercial farmers, master artisans, traders, shopkeepers, petty merchants—ambitious "middling" men, as they were increasingly called—were acquiring not only wealth but some learning and some awareness of the world and were eager to distance themselves from the "vulgar herd" of ordinary people. Already there were thinkers like Daniel Defoe who were trying to explain and justify these emerging middling people, including the "working trades, who labour hard but feel no want."[70] These were people who more and more prided themselves on their industriousness and frugality and their separation from the common idleness and dissipation of the gentry above them and the poor beneath them. These were the beginnings of what would become the shopkeepers, traders, clerks, and businessmen of the new middle class of the nineteenth century.[71]

This was the incipient middling world that Franklin entered in the early decades of the eighteenth century, and no one epitomized it in all of its aspirations and ambitions better than he did. Almost immediately after returning to Philadelphia in 1726, he revealed his interest in intellectual and literary activities in the city. In effect, he began acquiring some of the attributes of a gentleman while still remaining one of the common working people. In 1727 he organized a group of artisans who met weekly for learned conversation—a printer, several clerks, a glazier, two surveyors, a shoemaker, a cabinetmaker, and subsequently "a young Gentleman of some Fortune," named Robert Grace, who did not have to work for a living.[72] Calling themselves first the Leather Apron, then the Junto (perhaps because they had admitted a gentleman, and the mechanics' title was no longer applicable), they aimed at self-improvement and doing good for the society.

Not that they ignored their businesses and the making of money. At their meetings they asked themselves such questions as "Have you lately heard of any citizen's thriving well, and by what means?" or "Have you lately heard how any present rich man, here or elsewhere, got his estate?"[73] It was this kind of aspiring and prosperous middling man that was beginning to challenge the hierarchical network of privilege and patronage that dominated eighteenth-century society, and in the process blurring the traditionally sharp social division between gentlemen and commoners.

Already Franklin's field of vision extended far beyond the boundaries of Philadelphia, and even of Pennsylvania. In 1731 he toyed with the idea of forming a United Party for Virtue that would organize "the Virtuous and good Men of all Nations into a regular Body, to be govern'd by suitable good and wise Rules, which good and wise Men may probably be more unanimous in their Obedience to, than common People are to common Laws."[74] In that same year he discovered just the organization he was looking for: Freemasonry.

FREEMASONRY

Although the origins of Masonry supposedly went back centuries, it was only in 1717 in England that it had become the modern secret fraternity that expressed Enlightenment values. The institution, which worked to blur the distinction between gentlemen and commoners, was made for someone like Franklin. Although fewer than one in ten of its members in Philadelphia were artisans, Masonry became a means by which those men—usually the most ambitious and wealthy artisans—could mingle with members of the upper social ranks without themselves formally becoming gentlemen. (Maybe for that reason many of the gentry elite did not take their own membership as seriously as they might otherwise have.) Most of the Masonic artisans tended to belong to those crafts, like printing, that involved close association with gentlemen or large amounts of capital, and because of the high fees involved in membership they tended to be fairly well off. Since Masonry emphasized benevolence and sociability, all those members of the brotherhood who were still working artisans and tradesmen could believe that they were nevertheless participating in the world of genteel politeness and thus were separated from the vulgar and barbaric lower orders beneath them. For such men Masonry became a kind of halfway house to gentility. Although the brothers wore aprons, a reminder of the organization's artisanal roots, their aprons were not the leather ones of common craftsmen but instead were made of soft white lambskin, befitting their quasi-genteel status.[75]

With Franklin's affable nature and his obsession with benevolence, not to mention his rapidly growing wealth, he was naturally attracted to the organization. He joined the St. John's Lodge of Free Masons, the earliest known lodge in America. It satisfied his growing desire to dominate affairs. Knowing that only a "few in Public Affairs act from a meer View of the Good of their Country, whatever they may pretend," he wanted to be one of those few. He still thought that his projected United Party for Virtue, which the Masonic society resembled, could contain artisans and tradesmen like him. He thought one of the functions of his proposed party was to have its members give "their Advice Assistance and Support to each other in promoting one another's Interest, Business and Advancement in Life."[76]

Freemasonry more than fulfilled Franklin's Enlightenment dreams of establishing a party for virtue, and he became an enthusiastic and hard-working member of the fraternity. Two years after he joined St. John's Lodge in Philadelphia, he drafted its bylaws and became its warden. A year later, in 1734, he printed the *Constitutions of the Free-Masons,* the first Masonic book in America. A month later he became master of St. John's Lodge. Eventually he became the grand master of all the lodges in the colony of Pennsylvania. No organization could have been more congenial to Franklin, and although he seldom mentioned the organization in his correspondence, he remained a Mason throughout his life. Not only was Masonry dedicated to the promotion of virtue throughout the world, but this Enlightenment fraternity gave Franklin contacts and connections that helped him in his business.

CIVIC AFFAIRS

Franklin, as he said in his *Autobiography,* "always thought that one Man of tolerable Abilities may work great Changes, and Accomplish great Affairs among Mankind, if he first forms a good Plan and . . . makes the Execution of that same Plan his sole Study and Business."[77] To the young Franklin it made no difference whether this man of tolerable abilities was an artisan or not. He had set out from the beginning to demonstrate that middling sorts of craftsmen, tradesmen, and shopkeepers like himself could fulfill this Enlightenment hope in Philadelphia.

In 1731 Franklin and the other members of the Junto organized a subscription lending library, the Library Company, which would enable subscribers to have access to many more books than they otherwise would. Although he was the originator of the library, he soon came to realize that people were suspicious of a mere printer soliciting money and objected to his raising his reputation above that of his neighbors. Consequently, he decided to remain in the background and pass off his library as "a Scheme of a *Number of Friends.*" By his willingness to deny himself credit, his "Affair went on more smoothly," a lesson he applied when he came to promote subsequent ventures. As he later said, with some excusable exaggeration, the Library Company became "the Mother of all the North American Subscription Libraries now so numerous.... These Libraries had improv'd the general Conversation of the Americans, [and] made the common Tradesmen & Farmers as intelligent as most Gentlemen from other Countries."[78]

This was just one part of his civic activity. In 1729 he wrote a pamphlet promoting the printing of paper money, which was a boon for "every industrious Tradesman" and all those who bought and sold goods. (It was also a boon to those printers like Franklin who received government contracts to print the paper money.) With a sufficient supply of paper currency, wrote Franklin, "Business will be carried on more freely, and Trade be universally enlivened by it." Although he tried to assure gentlemen-creditors and others who lived on fixed incomes that they should not fear such paper currency, he knew that these leisured gentlemen were not the real source of prosperity in the society. It was the *"Labouring and Handicrafts Men"* who were *"the chief Strength and Support of a People."*[79]

But Franklin was not just interested in creating wealth in the community. No civic project was too large or too small for his interest. Because of the ever present danger of fire, he advised people on how to carry hot coals from one room to another, how to keep chimneys safe, how to organize fire companies for the city, and how to insure themselves against the damages of fire. He worked hard to promote inoculation against smallpox in the face of strong opposition, taking the position of the Mathers, which his brother James's paper had opposed in 1721.[80] To make the city streets safe he proposed organized night watchmen to be supported by taxes. To earn support for a hospital to be open free of charge to the poor of the city he concocted the idea of matching grants and persuaded the Pennsylvania General Assembly to put up £2000 if the same amount could be raised privately. To deal with smoky chimneys and poor indoor heating he invented his Pennsylvania stove. Almost single-handedly he made life notably more comfortable for his fellow citizens and helped to create a civic society for the middling inhabitants of Philadelphia. Individually, these were small matters perhaps, but they were all designed to add to the sum of human happiness—which after all was what the eighteenth-century Enlightenment was all about. "Human Felicity," Franklin noted, "is produc'd not so much by great Pieces of good fortune that seldom happen, as by little Advantages that occur every Day."[81]

FRANKLIN'S AWKWARD MIDDLING STATUS

With all his success Franklin found himself caught between two worlds, between that of aspiring artisans and tradesmen and that of wealthy gentlemen, with whom he mingled constantly. Because he came to believe that "common Tradesmen and Farmers" in America were "as intelligent as most Gentlemen from other Countries," he thought commoners in America often expected to pass as gentlemen more easily than elsewhere. He had discovered earlier in his life that an ordinary person with the right sponsorship could be admitted to the society of gentlemen. When he and James Ralph had boarded their ship to sail to England in 1724, they "were forc'd to take up with a Berth in the Steerage," since "none on board knowing us, [we] were considered as ordinary Persons." But when Colonel John French, justice of the Delaware Supreme Court, later came on board, recognized the eighteen-year-old Franklin, and paid him "great Respect," he was "more taken Notice of," and he and Ralph were immediately invited "by the other Gentlemen to come into the Cabin."[82]

Yet he knew that such socializing was often the consequence of gentry condescension. He knew too that no matter how successful and wealthy he had become, he still remained a laborer in the eyes of most of the gentry, and thus one of the common people or "meaner Sort" who had to work for a living as a printer. The gentry knew how to put a mere mechanic, no matter how wealthy or talented, in his place.

In 1740 Franklin came up with the idea of starting a magazine in Philadelphia and offered the job of editing it to John Webbe, a lawyer he knew. But Webbe took the idea to Franklin's competitor Andrew Bradford, who quickly brought out *The American Magazine.* (The next year in his *Almanack,* Poor Richard proclaimed: "If you would keep your Secret from an enemy, tell it not to a friend.") A week later Franklin announced that he would publish his own periodical, *The General Magazine.* At the same time he told the world that he had originated the idea of a magazine and that Webbe had betrayed him. Webbe, the lawyer, using the usual gentry put-down of a mechanic, replied that Franklin had never been expected to participate in the magazine "in any other capacity than that of a *meer* Printer."[83]

This was just the sort of sneer that would have made Franklin both angry and uncomfortable. He naturally preferred to call himself a member of the new emerging middling sort. But when confronted with the dichotomous social division favored by the gentry—"the BETTER SORT of People" set against "the meaner Sort"—he was willing to be lumped with those he considered to constitute the populace, which, he pointed out, "your Demosthenes' and Ciceroes, your Sidneys and Trenchards never approached . . . but with Reverence." Writing in his newspaper in 1740 as Obadiah Plainman, Franklin let loose some of his resentment at those who used the expression "the BETTER SORT of People." Such gentlemen, he said with a good deal of scorn, looked upon "the Rest of their Fellow Subjects in the same Government with Contempt, and consequently regard them as Mob and Rabble," who constituted nothing more than "a stupid Herd, in whom the Light of Reason is extinguished." In contrast to this arrogant "better Sort," he said, he was but "a poor ordinary Mechanick of this City, obliged to work hard for the Maintenance of myself, my Wife, and several small Children."[84]

Yet, of course, he knew that in reality he was anything but "a poor ordinary Mechanick." His genteel newspaper opponent Richard Peters, a former clergyman and secretary of the colony's land office, knew that too. When pressed to defend his use of the "better Sort," Peters declared that he could think of no better example of such persons than those who were members of the Library Company—to which Franklin, as Obadiah Plainman, had already admitted in the newspaper exchanges to belonging. If "poor ordinary Mechanicks" could be classed as members of "the better Sort," the gentry's dichotomous social categories were not working well at all. More so perhaps than anyone in colonial America, Franklin was living in two social worlds simultaneously.[85]

Franklin's proposals for education vividly reveal the ambivalence he felt as someone caught between the better and meaner sorts. As early as 1743 he had drawn up plans for an academy in Philadelphia, but it was not until 1749 that he laid them out in a pamphlet, *Proposals Relating to the Education of Youth in Pensilvania.* He originally wanted a school dedicated to teaching the English language and not Latin. The school, in other words, was mainly designed for young men with origins similar to his own—tradesmen and mechanics who wished to better themselves. But, as he recalled with some resentment in an unpublished tract written at the end of his life, this plan was foiled by a number of "Persons of Wealth and Learning, whose Subscriptions and Countenance we should need," and who believed that the school "ought to include the learned Languages."[86]

With his original plan for an English academy transformed into a traditional Latin school favoring the sons of the gentry, Franklin had to create a separate English school that he hoped would fulfill his original intentions. "Youth would come out of this School," he wrote in a piece published in 1751, "fitted for learning any Business, Calling or Profession, except wherein Languages are required; and tho' unacquainted with any antient or foreign Tongue, they will be Masters of their own, which is of more immediate and general Use."[87] Unfortunately, however, the gentry trustees who were in charge of both schools so discriminated against the English school in favor of the Latin school—paying the Latin head twice as much as the English head, for example, even though he taught fewer students—that the English school eventually dwindled into insignificance. At the end of his life, however, Franklin had some consolation to discover that things had changed. The executor of his estate told him that *"public opinion"* had now "undergone a revolution," and was now "undoubtedly in favor of an English Education, in spite of the prejudices of the learned on this subject."[88]

Franklin's attempt to form a philosophical society revealed a similar tension between the different worlds of tradesmen and gentry. In 1743 he published *A Proposal for Promoting Useful Knowledge Among the British Plantations in America,* in which he suggested the formation of a society composed of "Virtuosi or ingenious Men residing in the several Colonies," a kind of intercolonial version of his old Junto. This organization, to be called *"The American Philosophical Society,"* would promote "all philosophical Experiments that let Light into the Nature of Things, tend to increase the Power of Man over Matter, and multiply the Conveniences or Pleasures of life." He got the society on its feet, but at the outset it was not as active as Franklin had hoped. "The Members of our Society are very idle Gentlemen," he complained to the New York official and scientist Cadwallader Colden in 1745. "They will take no Pains."[89] Apparently the ambitious middling sorts that had made up his Junto had had more energy and more intellectual curiosity than the gentry.

Despite all his gentlemanly activities—his philanthropic ventures and his practical projects for self-education in the art of virtue—Franklin still saw himself as a printer and businessman and not a gentleman in these early Philadelphia years. But if he was not a gentleman, he was obviously not a commoner either. Instead, he had become the principal spokesman for the growing numbers of artisans, shopkeepers, and other middling sorts in Philadelphia who were his main supporters in all of his civic endeavors. He identified completely with these middling people: "Our Families and little Fortunes," he said, were "as dear to us as any Great Man's can be to him." And he was not at all embarrassed to call himself publicly "an honest Tradesman."[90]

"THE MOLATTO GENTLEMAN"

Although he was constantly mingling with gentlemen, he did not yet think of turning himself into one; that is, he had not yet imagined himself having all the qualities that would allow him to retire from his business and shed his leather apron entirely. However wealthy an artisan he might become, and Franklin's income was growing rapidly, this young printer well knew that entering into the status of a gentleman was not a simple matter, and he was not at all sure that he even wanted to try.

There were many people, he wrote in an anonymous newspaper piece in 1733, who, "by their Industry or good Fortune, from mean Beginnings find themselves in Circumstances a little more easy." Many of these people were immediately seized by "an Ambition . . . to become *Gentlefolks*." But it was "no easy Thing for a Clown or a Labourer, on a sudden to hit in all respects, the natural and easy Manner of those who have been genteely educated: And 'tis the Curse of *Imitation,* that it almost always either under-does or over-does."

Franklin's newspaper persona—"an ordinary Mechanick" who prays that "I may always have the Grace to know my self and my Station"—went on to describe the problems faced by the newly wealthy artisan trying to pass as a gentleman. "The *true Gentleman,* who is well known to be such, can take a Walk, or drink a Glass, and converse freely, if there be occasion, with honest Men of any Degree below him, without degrading or fearing to degrade himself in the least." In other words, a true gentleman, confident of his status, could condescend with ease. The parvenu was not able to act in this easy manner. Whenever Franklin's persona witnessed such a person acting "mighty cautious" in company with those who appear to be his inferiors, he knew that that person was "some *new Gentleman,* or rather *half Gentleman,* or *Mungrel,* an unnatural Compound of Earth and *Brass* like the Feet of *Nebuchadnezzar's* Image."

The same was true of women who did not know how to act with their supposed inferiors. If Franklin's artisan persona found "some young Woman Mistress of a new fine furnished House, treating me with a kind of Superiority, a distant sort of Freedom, and high Manner of Condescension that might become a Governor's Lady, I cannot help imagining her to be some poor Girl that is but lately married." Or if she acted in a "very haughty and imperious" manner, "I conclude that 'tis not long since she was somebody's Servant Maid."

These kinds of upstarts had the respect of neither the gentry nor the commoners. "They are the Ridicule and Contempt of both sides." A "lumpish stupid" artisan who "kept to his natural Sphere" may not have been envied by his fellow artisans, but "none of us despis'd him." Yet when he got "a little Money, the Case is exceedingly alter'd."

> Without Experience of Men or Knowledge of Books, or even common Wit, the vain Fool thrusts himself into Conversation with People of the best Sense and the most polite. All his Absurdities, which were scarcely taken Notice of among us, stand evident among them, and afford them continual Matter of Diversion. At the same time, we below cannot help considering him as a Monkey that climbs a Tree, the higher he goes, the more he shows his Arse.

There were many kinds of *"Molattoes"* in the world, Franklin concluded—in race, in religion, in politics, in love. "But of all sorts of *Molattoes,* none appear to me so monstrously ridiculous as the *Molatto Gentleman.*"[91]

Since Franklin did not want to appear ridiculous, he was not about to act the gentleman unless he was fully prepared to assume the rank and the rank was fully prepared to accept him. Like Daniel Defoe, who was wrestling with some of the same problems of tradesmen trying to become gentlemen, Franklin knew only too well the nature of the society he lived in. Since Defoe had written that a gentleman was someone "whose Ancestors have at least for some time been rais'd above the Class of Mechanicks," Franklin knew it would not be easy for him to hoist himself up in one generation.[92]

Besides, he had the example of the failure of David Harry, who had taken over Samuel Keimer's print shop, to make him cautious. Earlier Franklin had actually proposed a partnership with Harry, which Harry, said Franklin, "fortunately for me, rejected with Scorn." Harry, observed Franklin, messed up his life by trying to become a gentleman without having the wherewithal to bring it off. "He was very proud, dress'd like a Gentleman, liv'd expensively, took much diversion and Pleasure abroad, ran in debt, and neglected his Business, upon which all Business left him."[93]

Franklin knew better.

FRANKLIN'S WEALTH

If he was not yet one of "the better sort," as a printer and tradesman Franklin had prospered beyond what anyone could have expected and become wealthier than most of the so-called gentlefolk. Contemporaries never described Franklin in any great detail, and we have no portraits of Franklin during this period of his late twenties and thirties. But we can imagine that he was a fairly tall man, a shade under six feet and well built, perhaps already tending toward that corpulence that was for the eighteenth century a mark of prosperity. He had brown hair, a head that was large in proportion to his body, and a mild and pleasant countenance. He still worked in his printing firm, no doubt more as an editor, writer, and manager of his journeymen and apprentices and his other businesses than as someone who wore a leather apron and set type.

Despite his growing wealth, the several houses on lower Market Street that he rented at various times were modest and unpretentious. Home was still the place where he worked. Attached to his home was a shop where his wife and mother-in-law sold books and stationery and a wide variety of other goods, including soap, cheese from Rhode Island, and bohea tea. Franklin seems to have also acted as agent for the sale of the unexpired indentures of servants and a few slaves. Although apprentices, journeymen, servants, and some relatives, including his mother-in-law, often lodged in the house, Franklin's immediate family was small. In 1732 Deborah had given birth to a baby boy, Francis, called Franky, who died of smallpox at the age of four, a loss that Franklin never got over. In 1743 the Franklins had a second child, a baby girl, Sarah, called Sally. With them lived Franklin's illegitimate teenage son, William, whom his father increasingly indulged.[94]

Despite all of his unpretentiousness he could not help making money, a great deal of it. He had a natural genius for business. Not only did he run his printing business successfully, but he never stopped looking out for new opportunities. In 1736 he was appointed clerk to the Pennsylvania Assembly, which, he said, gave him "a better Opportunity of keeping up an Interest among the Members." This interest paid off when he became the official printer for the assembly, securing for him the "Business of Printing the Votes, Laws, Paper Money, and other occasional Jobbs for the Public that on the whole were very profitable."[95] Eventually he became the public printer for Delaware, New Jersey, and Maryland as well.

Unlike printers in London, who had enough business to specialize exclusively in printing, printers in the colonies always lacked sufficient work to support themselves, and they were generally driven to expand into related fields.[96] Franklin was especially adept at adding on new businesses to his printing firm. In 1729 he started a newspaper, the *Pennsylvania Gazette,* which became the leading paper in the colony. With all of his government contracts, mostly from the patronage of the colony's legislature, it was important for Franklin's newspaper not to offend people in authority. Therefore he continually voiced the conventional wisdom that he was a mere mechanic, impartially delivering the various views of other people to his readers.

He wrote in his famous "Apology for Printers" (1731) that, as a printer, he was just like any other artisan—a blacksmith, a shoemaker, or a carpenter—an ordinary tradesman, just trying to make a living. Printers "chearfully serve all contending Writers that pay them well, without regarding on which side they are of the Question in Dispute. . . . Being thus continually employ'd in serving all Parties," he wrote, "Printers naturally acquire a vast Unconcernedness as to the right or wrong Opinions contain'd in what they print; regarding it only as the Matter of their daily labour."[97] This neutral and impartial conception of his role as a printer may have significantly affected his political behavior later on when he was in London as an agent of the Pennsylvania Assembly.[98]

Most important for Franklin's income was his launching of an almanac. He considered an almanac "a proper Vehicle for conveying Instruction among the common People, who bought scarce any other Books." By featuring both Poor Richard's essays and proverbs in the almanac, he "endeavour'd to make it both entertaining and useful." His almanac soon "came to be in such Demand," recalled Franklin, "that I reape'd considerable Profit from it, vending annually near ten Thousand."[99] In fact, it became the most successful almanac in all of colonial America. Franklin's persona Poor Richard noted that his almanac's printer—who, of course, was also Franklin—was making most of the profit, but "I do not grudge it him; he is a Man I have a great Regard for, and I wish his Profit ten times greater than it is." (Poor Richard even blamed his printer for the errata in the almanacs.)[100]

In 1737 Franklin became postmaster of Philadelphia. "Tho' the salary was small," he said, "it facilitated the Correspondence that improv'd my Newspaper, encreas'd the Number demanded, as well as the Advertisements to be inserted, so that it came to afford me a very considerable Income."[101] In addition to his store, which brought in a good income, Franklin began as early as 1731 to set up or sponsor printing shops in other colonies, usually by entering into partnerships with younger men who were often his own journeymen—such as Thomas Whitmarsh in South

Carolina and James Parker in New York. He supplied presses and type and other materials, and in return took one third of the profits of his partner's printing shop for the duration of the contract, which was usually for six years. By 1743 he owned three printing firms in three different colonies and was thinking of opening more.[102] Before he was done he had partnerships and other working arrangements with over two dozen individuals all over the colonies, from New England to Antigua.[103] He was more than a craftsman; he was an entrepreneur, and an extremely successful one.

We do not know a great deal about his business activities or his income. But we do know that he became a very wealthy man, perhaps one of the richest colonists in the northern parts of the North American continent. His print-shop partnership with David Hall, established in 1748, in itself brought in well over £600 a year on average for him alone, a considerable sum when we realize that Washington's Mount Vernon was earning only £300 a year in the early 1770s.[104] Between 1756 and 1765 more than £250 annually came to the partnership from work for the government, and this doesn't include the money Franklin and Hall made from printing the colony's paper currency.[105] Some have estimated that Franklin's total income eventually reached nearly £2000 a year, twice the salary of Pennsylvania's governor and ten times the salary of the rector of Franklin's proposed academy.[106] When we realize that manufacturers in England made about £40 a year and lawyers about £200 a year, we know that Franklin was very well off indeed. Not only did he have his partnerships and his shares in a number of printing businesses in other colonies, but he also established at least eighteen paper mills at one time or another; in fact, he may have been the largest paper dealer in the English-speaking world.[107] He also owned a good deal of rental property in Philadelphia and in many coastal towns.[108] He was a substantial creditor, practically a banker, with a great amount of money out on loan, some loans as small as two shillings and others as large as £200.[109] And throughout much of his life he was deeply involved in land speculation. The fact that in the mid-1740s he refused to acquire exclusive patent rights to his immensely popular and profitable stove on the grounds that his invention offered him *"an Opportunity to serve others"* suggests that he was already rich enough to begin thinking like a public-spirited gentleman.[110]

A GENTLEMAN AT LAST

In 1748, at the age of forty-two, Franklin believed he had acquired sufficient wealth and gentility to retire from active business. This retirement had far more significance in the mid-eighteenth century than it would today. It meant that Franklin could at last become a gentleman, a man of leisure who no longer would have to work for a living.

Up to this point Franklin had made a name for himself in Philadelphia essentially as an ingenious tradesman. In organizing and promoting all of his benevolent and philanthropic projects for the city he had generally relied on his fellow middling sorts. As late as 1747 he still chose to identify himself as "A Tradesman of Philadelphia," which was the pseudonym he used for his pamphlet *Plain Truth: Or, Serious Considerations on the Present State of the City of Philadelphia and Province of Pennsylvania.* Franklin directed his pamphlet at "the middling People, the Farmers, Shopkeepers and Tradesmen of this city and country," who, being ignored by "those Great and rich Men"—that is, wealthy merchants and government officials—had to unite and protect themselves from the war with the French that raged all around the colony.[111] Franklin followed up his pamphlet by drafting a charter for a "Militia Association" composed of volunteers drawn from the people at large. In essence he proposed that the people of Pennsylvania form a private army.

But that year Franklin realized that middling sorts could not do everything by themselves. When he met with a group of mostly artisans, as Richard Peters reported to the Penn family, he assumed "the Character of a Tradesman" and praised his "middling" audience for being "the first Movers in every useful undertaking that had been projected for the good of the City—Library Company, Fire Company &c.... By this Artifice," said Peters, he sought "to animate all the middling Persons to undertake their own Defense in Opposition to the Quakers and the Gentlemen." But after Franklin had pulled out a draft of his association and read it, and all the middling people present approved it and immediately offered to sign on, Franklin told them that that was not enough. "No," he said, "let us not sign yet, let us offer it at least to the Gentlemen and if they come into it, well and good, we shall be the better able to carry it into Execution." It worked, because a few days later, according to Peters, "all the better sort of the People" agreed to the plan.[112]

By 1747 Franklin was changing his mind about his notion of a United Party for Virtue. In 1731 he had thought that virtuous and ingenious men from all ranks could constitute its membership. But now he thought he might be mistaken. Perhaps only gentlemen were the "few in Public Affairs" who were capable of acting "from a meer View of the Good of their Country." Perhaps those middling people who had occupations—craftsmen and tradesmen, merchants and mechanics—were as yet too occupied with their particular interests to look after the common good. They were, as one genteel poet put it, the "vulgar" caught up "in trade, / Whose minds by miser avarice were sway'd."[113] In other words, Aristotle's principle that people who worked for a living could never possess virtue was still alive in the mid-eighteenth century. Only gentlemen, as Adam Smith later pointed out, only "those few, who being attached to no particular occupation themselves, have leisure and inclination to examine the occupations of other people."[114] Franklin had come to believe that only those who were free of the need for money should be involved in public affairs—a principle that eventually became a fixation with him. He had decided that to be a mover and shaker in the province, he would have to become a gentleman, one of "the better Sort of People" he had earlier scorned.

He had no intention, however, of becoming one of those "molatto gentlemen," one of those stupid rich artisans who was way over his head in genteel circles. He had read enough, knew enough, was worldly enough to mingle and converse with the most polite and cultivated gentry in America, indeed, as he later demonstrated, in the courts of Europe as well. He taught himself languages, and learned enough Latin, French, Italian, Spanish, and German to read what he needed. And he was rich enough not to have to work as a printer ever again. Few parvenus in history have ever been as well prepared to assume a genteel station in life as Franklin.

His retirement was a major event for him, and he took it very seriously. He now acquired several slaves and moved to a new and more spacious house in "a more quiet Part of the Town," renting a house on the northwest corner of Sassafras (Race) and Second Streets. He left his printing office and shop in the old quarters on Market Street, where his new partner David Hall moved in to run the firm. Since most artisans worked where they lived, separating his home from his business in this way was a graphic reminder that Franklin had left his occupation as a tradesman behind.

As he had long been interested in his family genealogy, sometime before 1751 he adopted a Franklin coat of arms and began sealing his letters with it. He continued to write his *Poor Richard's Almanack* without violating his new gentry status, writing being acceptable as a genteel activity, especially if it was done anonymously. For its final decade, until 1757, Franklin called the almanac *Poor Richard Improved* and made it much more didactic and condescending—perhaps befitting his recently heightened rank.[115]

With the same patronizing tone that he brought to the revised version of the almanac, he also wrote in 1748 "Advice to a Young Tradesman, Written by an Old One." He more or less designed this piece to counsel all those young men who would emulate his achievement in becoming rich. The secret to "the Way to Wealth," he said, was plain: "It depends chiefly on two Words, INDUSTRY and FRUGALITY; i.e., Waste neither Time nor Money, but make the best Use of both." Without industry and frugality nothing will do, and with them, everything is possible, unless "that Being who governs the World" determines otherwise. Only someone who had been as successful as he had could write with such confidence. Of course, Franklin left out of his advice the most important ingredient involved in his success—his genius.[116]

Most important in distinguishing his move into gentility, he had a remarkable coming-out portrait painted to mark the occasion (see page 58). Portraits, after all, had long been attributes of nobility and family rank and were expensive, which is why aspiring gentlemen would be eager to have one. This first portrait of Franklin is attributed to the American-born painter Robert Feke and is like no other of the Franklin portraits we are familiar with. The painting announces the arrival of a gentleman: there is none of the famous Franklin simplicity of dress found in his later portraits. Although his dress is not as elegant as that of many colonial aristocrats, Franklin nevertheless stands in an aristocratic

Franklin, portrait of a new gentleman, by Robert Feke, 1748

pose, stiff and mannered and wearing a dark green velvet coat and tightly curled brown wig, with his right arm extended to reveal the frilled ruffle of his silk sleeve.[117]

Franklin had waited until he was fully ready for this important step; he did not want to rush it. In that rank-conscious age Franklin had always been sensitive not to act too much beyond his station. "In order to secure my Credit and Character as a Tradesman," he wrote in his *Autobiography,* "I took care not only to be in Reality Industrious & frugal, but to avoid all *Appearances* of the Contrary." As a tradesman he dressed plainly, shunned places of idle diversion, and put on no airs. Indeed, "to show that I was not above my Business, I sometimes brought home the Paper I purchas'd at the Stores, thro' the Streets on a Wheelbarrow." He won his superiors over by allowing them to patronize him. When one member of the legislature, a gentleman of fortune and education, opposed his election as clerk of the assembly, Franklin made him his friend by borrowing a book from him, thus, he would say, demonstrating the truth of an old maxim, *"He that has once done you a Kindness will be more ready to do you another, than he whom you yourself have obliged."*[118]

Franklin was not the only wealthy colonial artisan or merchant who moved into the gentry in eighteenth-century America, but he was certainly one of the most prominent of those who did. In fact, he had been so long mingling with the gentry and engaged in civic affairs that most gentlemen in Philadelphia scarcely noticed the significance of his retirement. No doubt there were some gentlemen who wondered what this prosperous upstart printer was doing organizing clubs, starting libraries, promoting schools, leading the Masons, and becoming involved in dozens of activities that were well beyond the reach and consciousness of nearly all tradesmen and artisans. Franklin knew he had to take their views and prejudices very much into account and not move upward too rapidly or too conspicuously. Since bright rich colors and elaborate patterns in clothing were associated with nobility and especially high rank, even the dark green, almost black, color of Franklin's coat in his coming-out portrait suggests that he did not want to overstep his exact position in the social order. He was at last a gentleman, but, sure as he was that he was smarter and more talented than any of them, he was not as yet ready to presume full equality with the leading aristocrats of colonial Philadelphia.[119]

Franklin was always sensitive about his proper place in the world. When he had organized the extra-legal Militia Association in Philadelphia in 1747, the year before his retirement, the officers of the Philadelphia regiment had chosen him its colonel. "Conceiving myself unfit," he had declined the honor. Instead, he recommended Thomas Lawrence, a "Man of Influence," and instead took his turn as a common soldier in the regiment.[120] He conceived himself unfit not because he was ignorant of military matters—this never stopped other eighteenth-century gentlemen from becoming militia colonels—but because he realized that he was not yet quite a gentleman and it might be thought presumptuous of him to act above his social rank.

By 1756, a decade later, he had become a full-fledged gentleman and was more than ready to become an officer. He then accepted another election to the colonelcy of the militia regiment. His military rank now seemed commensurate with his social status as a well-established gentleman. But by that time he was more than a gentleman. He had become a major player in the politics of the British Empire.[121]

TWO

BECOMING A BRITISH IMPERIALIST

FRANKLIN'S ELECTRICAL EXPERIMENTS

Becoming a gentleman changed Franklin's life. He was no longer merely the "honest Tradesman." He was a different person with different goals. Although he did not hide the fact that he had had only a tradesman's education (which made his achievements all the more impressive), he certainly did not go about Philadelphia bragging of his humble and obscure origins.[1] As his portrait, new home, and new style of living suggested, he was eager to be accepted as a complete gentleman. Of course, there were some in Philadelphia who never forgot where he came from, and no doubt he had to overcome a thousand slights and snubs by sheer genius and persistence and by his remarkable ability to act the part not only of a gentleman of means but, more important for the enlightened eighteenth century, of a gentleman of learning.

Having "disengag'd . . . from private Business," Franklin was now free to devote himself openly to gentlemanly activities. Once he became a gentleman and a "master of my own time," Franklin says that he thought he would do what other gentlemen did—write and engage in "Philosophical Studies and Amusements." As he told the New York official and scientist Cadwallader Colden, he now had "leisure to read, study, make experiments, and converse at large with such ingenious and worthy Men as are pleas'd to honour me with their Friendship or Acquaintance on such Points as may produce something for the common benefit of Mankind, uninterrupted by the little Cares and Fatigues of Business."[2]

For Franklin the most significant of those "Philosophical Studies and Amusements," and an important inducement for his retiring, was his involvement with electricity. From his earliest years Franklin had been fascinated by all aspects of nature and human behavior. Indeed, throughout his life he retained a childlike sense of curiosity that led him to wonder about the workings of nearly everything. So he wondered about some pelagic crabs he found in seaweed; he wondered about the effects of differing amounts of oil on water; he wondered why an ocean voyage took two weeks longer going west than it did going east. Indeed, he could not drink a cup of tea without wondering why the tea leaves at the bottom gathered in one way rather than in another.[3] Things that struck him as new and odd were always worth thinking about, for explaining them might advance the boundaries of knowledge. "For a new appearance," he later wrote, "if it cannot be explain'd by our old principles, may afford us new ones, of use perhaps in explaining some other obscure parts of natural knowledge." With such an enlightened need to know and to understand, it was inevitable that he would investigate the wonders of electricity.[4]

Electricity was one of those hidden forces, like gravity and magnetism, that came to fascinate every knowledgeable person in the eighteenth century. Initially, however, like so much that we today label "science," electricity was simply a curious amusement, just a matter of showmen-savants or "electricians" playing parlor tricks with electrostatics, trying to get people to laugh at the way things attracted and repelled one another. The court electrician to Louis XV of France once sent an electric shock through 180 soldiers of the guard who were touching one another, in order to get them to jump simultaneously and amuse the court. To top himself, he did the same with 700 monks, and the king and court were greatly amused.[5] On a visit to Boston in 1746 Franklin witnessed a performance by one of these electricians, Dr. Archibald Spencer from Scotland, who had begun his career as a male midwife and would end it as a clergyman.[6] One of Spencer's most spectacular tricks was to suspend a little boy from the ceiling by silken threads while drawing "electric fire"—

that is, sparks—from his hands and feet. Although Spencer's electrical experiments were "imperfectly performed," they were new to Franklin, and "they equally surpriz'd and pleas'd" him.[7] It was just the kind of thing that would excite Franklin's insatiable curiosity, and soon after he jumped at the opportunity to purchase all Spencer's apparatus.

At about the same time Peter Collinson, a wealthy English Quaker merchant interested in science, sent to the Library Company a glass tube and instructions for conducting various electrical experiments. Thomas Penn, the son of William Penn, also presented some electrical apparatus to the Library Company. Franklin borrowed more stuff from his household: thimbles, a vinegar cruet, a cake of wax, a pump handle, the gold leaf of a book binding—anything and everything that could help him experiment with this mysterious force.[8] Finally he acquired a Leyden jar, or capacitor ("this miraculous Bottle," Franklin called it), which allowed for the accumulation of far greater electrical charges.[9] With all this equipment Franklin's enthusiasm ran wild. He threw himself into studying and playing with electricity. "I never was before engaged in any study that so totally engrossed my attention and my time as this has lately done," he told Collinson in 1747. He practiced his experiments alone and then invited crowds of friends and acquaintances to witness them. For months he had "little leisure for anything else."[10]

Franklin sent Collinson piecemeal reports of his ideas and his experiments. Because he could not know what European philosophers had already discovered and was never really sure of the significance of his findings, he presented them diffidently. He apologized for the crudity and hastiness of his thoughts and generously urged Collinson to share them with whomever he pleased.

But despite the fact that he was out of touch with the centers of European thought, his ideas were truly original. He concocted for the first time in history what he called an electrical battery for the storing of electrical charges; he created new English words for the new science—conductor, charge, discharge, condense, armature, electrify, and others; he replaced the traditional idea that electricity was of two kinds—vitreous and resinous—with the fact that it was a single "fluid" with positive and negative or plus and minus charges; and he came to understand that the plus and minus charges or states of electrification of bodies must occur in exactly equal amounts—a quantitative principle that is known today as the law of conservation of charge, a principle fundamental to all science.[11]

Although he was excited by his findings, he was chagrined that he could not at first discover any practical use for them, and for Franklin, science or philosophy—indeed, every area of thought—had to be useful. Initially the best he could do was to suggest using an electric shock to kill hens and turkeys for eating: it made them unusually tender. The French eventually picked up this technique and, predictably, spent many years trying to use electricity to improve the cooking of food. They even wondered if electricity might not make large animals more tender for eating, but Franklin thought the electrical charge necessary to kill large animals might end up killing the cook instead.[12]

Many people had guessed that lightning was an electrical phenomenon, but no one had ever set out a method for proving it until Franklin did in 1749.[13] Not only did Franklin explain how lightning was generated, he also suggested that points grounded with conducting wires might be attached to houses, ships, and churches in order to draw off the lightning. The Royal Society in London showed little interest in publishing Franklin's letters in full; in fact, according to Franklin, some members even laughed at some of his findings, probably convinced that no colonist living on the outer edges of Christendom could produce anything worthwhile. Collinson turned them over to a publisher, who in 1751 brought them out in an eighty-six-page book entitled *Experiments and Observations on Electricity, Made at Philadelphia in America.*[14]

During the eighteenth century Franklin's book went through five English editions, three in French, one in Italian, and one in German. Although Franklin became known everywhere, it was the French who were most excited by his theories and who first successfully tested them. (Franklin's own secret test of his ideas—his famous flying of a kite in a thunderstorm—came in the summer of 1752, after the successful French experiments but before news of them reached America.) Suddenly Franklin was an international celebrity. "All Europe is in Agitation on Verifying Electrical Experiments on points," Collinson told Franklin in September 1752. "All commends the Thought of the Inventor. More I dare not Saye least I offend Chast Ears."[15]

Collinson need not have worried about offending Franklin's modesty, for Franklin, as he himself admitted, had his share of vanity. He had, of course, so much more ability than others to be vain about, but, knowing the effect on people, he wisely worked hard at restraining his vanity as much as possible. Although he was genuinely surprised by the acclaim he received for his experiments, he certainly welcomed it. He knew that people love to be praised, "tho'," as he told a friend in 1751, "we are generally Hypocrites in that respect, and pretend to disregard Praise."[16]

The praise was extraordinary, to say the least. Franklin began to emerge as a symbol of the primitive New World's capacity to produce an untutored genius, a standing that he would use to great effectiveness when he later became the United States minister to France. Joseph Priestley declared that Franklin's discoveries were "the greatest, perhaps, since the time of Sir Isaac Newton."[17] Immanuel Kant went so far as to call Franklin the modern Prometheus who had stolen fire from the heavens.[18] Many honors soon followed. In May 1753 Harvard College awarded him an honorary master of arts degree, the first M.A. granted to someone not a member of its faculty. In September 1753 Yale followed with another M.A. degree, and three years later the College of William and Mary did the same. "Thus without studying in any College I came to partake of their Honours."[19] In 1753 the Royal Society awarded him the Sir Godfrey Copley Medal for "his curious experiments and observations on electricity," and three years later, much to Franklin's delight, made him a member.[20] Ezra Stiles, later president of Yale, wanted Franklin to be honored with a knighthood or some "hereditary Dignity." Franklin, said Stiles, in one of his typical unctuous outbursts, "the Electrical Philosopher, the American Inventor of the pointed Rods will live for Ages to come." Even the king of France sent his congratulations.[21]

He became the premier electrician in a world fascinated by electricians and electricity. He transformed what had been a curious wonder into a science, although he continued to think about science, as almost everyone in the eighteenth century did, in terms of its inventiveness and usefulness. For Franklin, all his discoveries would have meant little without the resultant lightning rod. And others agreed. Even those who did not read his writings or delve into his experiments could understand the significance of the lightning rod for the safety of their homes, churches, or ships.

His name spread widely throughout Europe and not just among the learned few. He became in fact the most famous American in the world.

Yet through all the applause and acclaim Franklin remained skeptical of the fickle world of science and invention. People, he told the South Carolinian physician and scientist John Lining in 1755, did not really admire inventors. Not having any inventive faculty themselves, they could not easily conceive that others may possess it. "A man of *their own acquaintance;* one who has no more sense than themselves, could not possibly, in their opinion, have been the inventor of anything." Perhaps he was thinking of the reaction of some of his genteel Philadelphia neighbors to his sudden fame—Franklin the printer (a printer!), married to Deborah Read, had become a world-renowned philosopher! Who would have guessed?

Franklin went on to describe the vanity, envy, and jealousy that afflicted the world of science and invention—passions that made it impossible for any inventor to claim much reputation for long. We can scarcely remember who invented spectacles or the compass, he said; even paper and printing, which record everything else, have not been able to preserve with certainty their inventors. Do not wish therefore, he told Lining, for a friend or child to possess any special faculty of invention. "For his attempts to benefit mankind in that way, however well imagined, if they do not succeed, expose him, though very unjustly, to general ridicule and contempt; and if they do succeed, to envy, robbery, and abuse." There was no humor or irony here to deflect the bitterness: Franklin had felt all the envy and ridicule that he spoke of.[22]

THE IMPORTANCE OF PUBLIC SERVICE

As much as Franklin appreciated the importance of his scientific achievements, science was not what he came to value most. Given the skeptical reactions of some of his Philadelphia neighbors to his scientific experiments, it could never be what he would most prize. At first, he had exulted in the leisure that his retirement from business had given him, even discouraging his friends from promoting his election to the assembly. But he soon had second thoughts. He came to realize that science and philosophy could never take the place of service in government.

Being a public official—that was what counted, that was how the community was best served, that was where true greatness and lasting fame could be best achieved. In 1750 he warned his fellow scientist Cadwallader Colden not to "let your Love of Philosophical Amusements have more than its due Weight with you. Had Newton been Pilot but of a single common Ship, the finest of his discoveries would scarce have excus'd, or atton'd for his abandoning the Helm one Hour in Time of Danger; how much less if she had carried the Fate of the Commonwealth."[23] In other words, the greatest scientist of the age would have had no excuse for not serving the government if the state had needed him.

Franklin thought that the province of Pennsylvania needed him. Pennsylvania, founded in 1681 by William Penn as a refuge for his fellow Quakers, was a fast-growing colony continually beset by factionalism and conflict between its legislature and its Penn family–controlled executive. Its population in 1750 numbered over 120,000, making it the fourth-largest colony after Virginia, Massachusetts, and Maryland; by 1770 it would be the second largest. The lack of any established church and the Quaker reputation for religious toleration had attracted the most varied mixture of religious groups in all of North America. By midcentury the Quakers had become a minority in their own colony, dipping to just a quarter of the population. The Scotch-Irish Presbyterians made up another quarter and the Germans, composed of a wide assortment of religious sects, totaled nearly 40 percent. Favoring the Quaker policies of pacifism, no militia, and low taxes, the Germans tacitly agreed to let a Quaker oligarchy run the assembly. But Indian problems on the frontier, where most of the Scotch-Irish were settled, and the fact that the Penn family, which had converted to Anglicanism, refused to pay what many thought was its fair share of taxes, meant that politics in the colony remained contentious and turbulent.

This was the faction-ridden political mixture that Franklin entered. Following his retirement from business, as he recalled in his *Autobiography,* "the Publick, now considering me as a Man of Leisure, laid hold of me for their Purposes." Indeed, he said, "Every Part of our Civil Government, and almost at the same time, impos[ed] some Duty on me."[24] As a gentleman, that is, as a man of leisure, he was brought into government. He became a member of the Philadelphia City Council in 1748; he was appointed a justice of the peace in 1749; and in 1751 he became a city alderman and was elected from Philadelphia to be one of the twenty-six members of the very clubby eastern- and Quaker-dominated Pennsylvania Assembly.

His "Ambition," he admitted, was "flatter'd by all these Promotions... for considering my low Beginnings they were great Things to me. And they were still more pleasing, as being so many spontaneous Testimonies of the public's good Opinion, and by me entirely unsolicited." Indeed, Franklin was very proud of his aristocratic sense of obligation to serve the public and of his genteel disdain for electioneering. Like any good eighteenth-century gentleman, he stood, not ran, for office. Campaigning for public office was regarded as vulgar and contemptible. No self-respecting gentleman would engage in it, and certainly not Franklin, whose status as a gentleman was still suspect in the eyes of some. His election to the assembly, he recalled with pride, "was repeated every Year of Ten Years, without my ever asking any Elector for his Vote, or signifying either directly or indirectly any Desire of being chosen."[25]

In the legislature he immediately became influential and was at once able to get his son William appointed to succeed him as its clerk. During all those years he had been clerk he had become bored stiff listening to tedious legislative debates in which he could take no part, and he had amused himself by inventing arithmetical games. Now it was different. He was at the center of assembly affairs, and very much in demand. No responsibility was too great or too small for his involvement, and he served on every kind of committee, dealing with both the most prestigious and the most minor matters. His committees drafted messages and responses to the governor, reviewed the history of and need for paper money, investigated the share of expenses borne by the province and the proprietors for Indian expenses, studied official fees, regulated the number of dogs in the city of Philadelphia, and recommended where a bridge across the Schuylkill should be built. Franklin seldom spoke in the assembly, for public speaking was never his strong point. Instead, he worked quietly behind the scenes, bringing people together, shaping opinions, and writing reports. By 1753 he had become the leader of the dominant Quaker party in the assembly, much opposed to the Penn family and the proprietary government.[26]

Pennsylvania was an unusual colony. Because Charles II had granted William Penn a proprietary charter, the Penn family more or less owned the colony in a quasi-feudal manner. Maryland was also a proprietary colony held by the Baltimore family. These two provinces, together with Connecticut and Rhode Island, which were corporate colonies with separate charters, were the only colonies in British North America not controlled directly by the Crown and whose governors were not royally appointed. The fact that Pennsylvania was not a royal colony eventually became something of an obsession with Franklin.

Well before he became a member of the assembly, Franklin had been concerned with the way the Pennsylvania government had neglected the defense of the colony against America's French and Indian enemies, largely because of the Quakers' pacifist principles and their sympathy for the Indians. When the legislature didn't act to defend the colony in 1747, Franklin almost single-handedly had privately raised 10,000 armed men in the Militia Association and had organized lotteries to raise funds to purchase cannons and to build batteries on the Delaware River.

Obviously these private efforts at raising an army posed a threat to the legitimate government; as soon as the most prominent of the proprietors, Thomas Penn, now living in England, learned of them, he became alarmed. Penn saw Franklin's formation of the Association as "acting a part little less than Treason." If the people of Pennsylvania could act "independent of this Government, why should they not Act against it." The man behind these actions, said Penn, was "a dangerous Man and I should be very Glad he inhabited any other country, as I believe him of a very uneasy Spirit." But Penn realized that Franklin was "a sort of Tribune of the People," and as such, at least for the time being, "he must be treated with regard."[27] Thus, even before Franklin had become a member of the assembly, the lifelong enmity between him and Thomas Penn had taken root.

Although William Penn, the father of Thomas Penn, had founded Pennsylvania as a "holy experiment" for the Society of Friends, the present generation of Penns had abandoned their ancestor's Quakerism for the Church of England, and they had come to regard their proprietary colony as more a source of income than a religious experiment. With such attitudes on the part of the proprietors, it was inevitable that the bulk of the population of Pennsylvania would come to believe that the Penns ought to do more to pay for the costs of supporting the colony. Above all, they ought to allow the assembly to tax the hundreds of thousands of acres of proprietary lands they had not yet granted or sold to settlers; after all, everyone else in Pennsylvania was paying taxes on their land. Franklin and the Quaker party were very much in the forefront of this opposition to the Penn family.

FRANKLIN'S VISION OF THE NEW WORLD

Before long Franklin began to see that there was more to America than the province of Pennsylvania. He had no sooner become a member of the assembly than he became eager to apply his immense intelligence and imagination to the issues and problems of the entire British Empire in North America.

In 1751, in his *Observations Concerning the Increase of Mankind, Peopling of Countries, Etc.*, Franklin set forth basic principles that explained the difference between life in Europe and life in America. In Europe land was scarce in relation to people and therefore was expensive. Hence, unable to afford their own land to farm, Europeans were compelled to work for others, either by becoming laborers for landowners in the countryside or, more often, by migrating to the cities to engage in manufacturing goods in factories. In both cases since labor, because of its plentifulness, was cheap, the workers' wages were low. Because their wages were so low, the European workers tended to postpone marriage and thus to have fewer children than if they had owned their own land.

In America, he wrote, the situation was reversed. Land was cheap and labor, which was relatively scarce, was expensive. Since land was so plentiful, a laborer in America who understood farming could in a short time save enough money to buy land for a family farm. Such people were not afraid to marry early and raise many children, for these American married couples could look ahead and "see that more Land is to be had at rates equally easy." In America twice as many people per hundred married every year than in Europe and had twice as many children. Consequently, said Franklin, the population of America "must at least be doubled every

20 years." He went on, "But notwithstanding this Increase, so vast is the Territory of North-America that it will require many Ages to settle it fully, and till it is fully settled, Labour will never be cheap, where no Man continues long a Labourer for others, but gets a Plantation of his own, no Man continues long a Journeyman to a Trade, but among those new Settlers, and sets up for himself, Etc."

Franklin could scarcely restrain his excitement as he contemplated the future of this prolific New World that would eventually outnumber the Old. At the rate the colonies were increasing, he said, the population of North America "will in another Century be more than the People of England, and the greatest Number of *Englishmen* will be on this Side the Water. What an Accession of Power to the *British* Empire by Sea as well as Land! What Increase of Trade and Navigation! What Numbers of Ships and Seamen!"[28]

With this vision of the people in North America eventually outnumbering those in Britain itself, Franklin was not anticipating the separation of the colonies from Great Britain. Quite the contrary: he was a true-blue Englishman; he had no thought that America should not be a part of England, at least as connected to England as Scotland was.[29] He thought the colonists were as much British subjects as those in Britain itself. They spoke the same language, possessed the same manners, read the same books, and shared the same religion. The growth of British subjects in America could only benefit the entire empire.

The glorious English empire he envisioned was supposed to be a single community made up only of Englishmen, which is why he interrupted his pamphlet on population growth with an angry outcry against the massive immigration of Germans into Pennsylvania, a development he was not alone in protesting. "Why should the *Palatine Boors* be suffered to swarm into our Settlements, and by herding together establish their Language and Manners to the Exclusion of ours?" Indeed, if he had his way he would exclude all the Germans and black people from the New World. The country, he said, ought to belong to only the English and the Indians, "the lovely White and Red." But then again, he said, "perhaps I am partial to the Complexion of my Country, for such Kind of Partiality is natural to Mankind."[30]

To Franklin the rise of the British Empire was the greatest phenomenon of the eighteenth century, and with his ever growing ambition he wanted very much to be part of it. In the same year, 1751, that he wrote his *Observations Concerning the Increase of Mankind,* he solicited the aid of Peter Collinson and Chief Justice William Allen to lobby on his behalf for the position of postmaster general for North America. His provincial offices were fine, but he had his sights on something bigger than postmaster of a single city.

Finally, in 1753, the Crown did appoint Franklin and William Hunter, postmaster at Williamsburg, joint deputy postmasters general for all the colonies of North America. Franklin was supposedly responsible for the northern colonies and Hunter for the southern colonies, but since Hunter's health was not good, most of the responsibility of the post office fell on Franklin. He applied all he had learned running the Philadelphia post office to the colonial post office. He introduced strict accounting and increased the speed and reliability of mail delivery, and he made the post office profitable. By 1757 he had completely reorganized postal delivery in North America, exercised the patronage expected of someone in his position to secure postal jobs up and down the continent for nearly all of his many relatives, and helped to make the scattered colonies more aware of one another.

THE ALBANY PLAN OF UNION

Franklin had been thinking about the union of the North American colonies for a long while. The American Philosophical Society, which he had proposed in 1743, had been designed to bring intellectuals from the various colonies together. In 1751 his partner James Parker sent him a pamphlet by a New York official, Archibald Kennedy, entitled *The Importance of Gaining and Preserving the Friendship of the Indians to the British Interest Considered,* and asked Franklin's advice on reprinting it in Philadelphia. Franklin very much agreed with the argument of the pamphlet and offered some additional suggestions. If the British Empire were to become as great as Franklin imagined, then the French had to be driven back and the Indians had to become allies of the English. If nothing were done, the French could occupy the entire Ohio Valley, take over the Indian trade, and cut Britain off from access to the continent's interior. In order to prevent these dire developments, said Franklin, the colonists had to create some sort of intercolonial union for Indian affairs and defense, some kind of structure that would transcend the governments of the several colonies. If the Iroquois could unite, why couldn't the colonists? "It would be a very strange Thing," he wrote, "if six Nations of ignorant Savages should be capable of forming a Scheme for such an Union, and be able to execute it in such a Manner as that it has subsisted for Ages, and appears indissoluble; and yet a like Union should be impracticable for ten or a Dozen English Colonies, to whom it is more necessary, and must be more advantageous; and who cannot be supposed to want an equal Understanding of their Interests."[31]

For such an imperial union the colonists could not rely on the governors and members of the assemblies of each of the colonies to act; they were much too caught up in their local squabbles to think about the empire as a whole. Instead, Franklin presented a solution that he was to return to time and again in his career—a reliance on a few good men, or even a single man, to set matters straight. That was the way he had operated with such success in Philadelphia, but whether he could operate the same way in larger arenas was the challenge of his career.

> Now, if you were to pick out half a Dozen Men of good Understanding and Address, and furnish them with a reasonable Scheme and proper Instructions, and send them in the Nature of Ambassadors to the other Colonies, where they might apply particularly to all the leading Men, and by proper Management get them to engage in promoting the Scheme; where, by being present, they would have the Opportunity of pressing the Affair both in publick and private, obviating Difficulties as they arise, answering Objections as soon as they are made, before they spread and gather Strength in the Minds of the People, &c., &c. I imagine such a Union might thereby be made and established: For reasonable sensible Men, can always make a reasonable Scheme appear such to other reasonable Men, if they take Pains, and have Time and Opportunity for it.

At this point he thought a voluntary union entered into by the colonies themselves was preferable to one imposed by Parliament. After all, the colonists in the seventeenth century had formed confederations without the approval of Parliament. Why couldn't they do the same now? Besides, it would be easier to make future changes in the union if people believed they had consented to it from the beginning.[32]

In detailing his plan for Indian affairs and colonial defense, Franklin proposed an intercolonial council made up of representatives from all the colonies, with a governor appointed by the Crown. Money for the union might be raised by an excise tax on liquor. To avoid jealousy among the colonies, the council might rotate its meeting place from colony to colony. If the colonists were to defend themselves during the war with the French and the Indians that seemed destined to come, Franklin was convinced, they had to put together some kind of union.

Other Englishmen were also worried about the French and Indians in North America. Even before fighting broke out on the Ohio frontier between English and French forces, the British Board of Trade in London had called for an unprecedented meeting of commissioners from the several colonies to negotiate a treaty with the Six Nations of the Iroquois. In June 1754 commissioners from each of the colonies were to meet in Albany with the Indians and consider issues of intercolonial defense and security. Franklin was one of the four commissioners selected to represent Pennsylvania, along with Richard Peters, secretary of the province, Isaac Norris, the speaker of the assembly, and John Penn, a grandson of the colony's founder—a high-powered group that gives us some indication of Franklin's remarkable political rise. Although Pennsylvania instructed its delegates merely to hold an interview with the Iroquois and renew friendship with them, Franklin had grander ideas. He went to Albany well prepared with a plan for union.[33]

Although Franklin had been moving in the highest circles of Pennsylvania's political society for several years, he now saw new political worlds opening up. On his way to Albany, he stopped in New York and showed his proposal to James Alexander and Archibald Kennedy, "two Gentlemen of great Knowledge in public Affairs," whose approval fortified his confidence to present his proposal to the upcoming congress.[34] In Albany he met and impressed some of the most influential officials of the other colonies, including William Smith Sr., Yale graduate and member of the New York council, and Thomas Hutchinson, Harvard graduate and member of the Massachusetts council. In the few years since the public had "laid hold" of him, he had come a long way.

A squabble among the colonies over precedence at the conference did not bode well for their cooperation. Virginia, perhaps the most important colony of all, did not even send a delegation. But finally the representatives who attended agreed that some sort of colonial union was needed, and they appointed a committee made up of a commissioner from each colony to draw one up. Franklin was the Pennsylvania representative. Although a few other commissioners came with proposals for union, none had thought out or detailed his plan as fully as Franklin. His 1754 proposal was essentially the same as his earlier one, with one big difference. Whereas in 1751 he had believed that the union ought to be organized by the colonies themselves, he now thought the plan ought to be sent to England and unilaterally established by Parliament. His experience with the Pennsylvania Assembly's reluctance to resist French encroachments in the Ohio Valley and his frustration with the parochialism of some other colonies had convinced him that only imposition by act of Parliament could bring about the kind of union he wanted.[35]

On the committee, Thomas Hutchinson of Massachusetts, in collaboration with Franklin, took the lead in presenting a case for some sort of colonial union—no easy task, since most of the delegates, like those from Pennsylvania, had been instructed simply to negotiate with the Indians, not construct a union. But the Albany Congress unanimously accepted the committee's report and delegated Franklin, as the strongest proponent of the idea, to draw up a detailed plan of union. In doing so Franklin had to make some concessions to the views of his fellow commissioners. "When one has so many different People with different Opinions to deal with in a new Affair," he explained to Cadwallader Colden, "one is oblig'd sometimes to give up some smaller Points in order to obtain greater."[36] But the plan that the Albany Congress adopted in July 1754 came pretty close to his original proposal.

The union was to be headed by a president general appointed and paid by the Crown. This president general was to be aided by a grand council composed of representatives from each of the colonies and selected by the respective colonial legislatures in proportion to their monetary contributions to the general treasury. Until that could be determined, the grand council would comprise seven delegates each from Massachusetts and Virginia, six from Pennsylvania, and so on, down to two each from New Hampshire and Rhode Island. The president general with the advice of the grand council would be responsible for making war and peace with the Indians, raising soldiers and building forts, regulating the Indian trade, purchasing land from the Indians, granting that land to colonists, making laws, and levying taxes "as to them shall appear most equal and just."[37] It was an extraordinary proposal—totally out of touch with the political realities of the day, which was often the case when one relied on a few reasonable men for solutions to complicated political problems.

The plan was sent to the colonies for their approval, to be followed by confirmation by the king and Parliament. Franklin confessed that he had no idea how the assemblies or the home government would view the plan. Within a few months he realized that the prospects were not good. The colonial assemblies were not willing to adopt any plan of union at all. Even the Pennsylvania Assembly refused to go along with the Albany proposal. He had come to realize that the colonies would never unite without pressure from the mother country. Although everyone cried that a union was "absolutely necessary," the "weak Noodles" who dominated the colonial assemblies were too distracted to act. "So if ever there be a Union," he told Peter Collinson in December 1754, "it must be form'd by the Ministry and Parliament. I doubt not that they will make a good one."[38]

But the ministry (or what later would be called the cabinet) and Parliament were no more eager to adopt the Albany Plan than the colonial assemblies, and officials in Britain rejected it as well. Although most Americans in 1754 could scarcely conceive of the colonies' becoming independent from Great Britain, many British officials continued to worry, as they had for decades, that the colonies were becoming too rich and strong to be governed any longer from London.[39] Bringing the colonies together in any way seemed to make such a possibility more likely. The Speaker of the House of Commons warned the Duke of Newcastle, the official responsible for American affairs, of the "ill consequences to be apprehended from uniting too closely the northern colonies with each other, an Independency upon this country to be feared from such an union."[40] With such opinions flying about it is not surprising that the British government dismissed the Albany Plan out of hand. As Franklin later recalled, "Its Fate was singular. The Assemblies did not adopt it as they all thought there was too much [crown] *Prerogative* in it; and in England it was judg'd to have too much of the *Democratic*."[41]

Despite the failure of his Albany Plan, the whole experience of making plans for the empire was exhilarating. Being deputy postmaster for North America could not compare with this kind of top-level participation in imperial affairs. When word spread of Franklin's major involvement in drawing up the plan of union, prominent imperial officials were eager to talk with him. One of these was William Shirley, royal governor of Massachusetts, who became commander in chief of the British forces in North America in 1755. Franklin had not previously met Shirley but knew him to be "a wise, good and worthy Man," who, as governor, had been "made the Subject of some public virulent and senseless Libels."[42] Acquiring these kinds of imperial connections was a heady experience for Franklin, and he could not help feeling some pride. He was eager to tell his son that during his meeting with Governor Shirley in 1754 the governor had been "particularly civil to me."[43]

He presumably began exchanging views with Shirley over the nature of the British Empire and the kind of union that might be possible in North America. Apparently, Shirley proposed that the colonial assemblies be bypassed not only in establishing a general government but also in the administering of such a government. Franklin admitted that a "general Government might be as well and faithfully administer'd without the people, as with them," but he reminded Shirley that "where heavy burthens are to be laid on them, it has been found useful to make it, as much as possible, their own act."[44] The colonists themselves, he argued, knew better the needs of the colonies for defense than did the distant Parliament. Franklin said all this at the very moment he was telling his friend Collinson that the colonial assemblies were so fuzzy-headed that the ministry and Parliament not only had to impose a plan of union on the colonies but would do it right. This raises the question of just how sincere he was with Shirley, or whether he in fact then wrote this to Shirley at all. (His three letters to Shirley in December 1754 were printed in a London newspaper in 1766, but the originals in Franklin's hand do not survive.)[45]

If he did write this to Shirley that winter, he was sufficiently confident of himself to tell a crown-appointed governor to his face that such royal governors were not to be trusted to look after the colonists' interests. Royal governors, he informed Governor Shirley, were "not always Men of the best Abilities and Integrity, have no Estates here, nor any natural Connections with us," and "often come to the Colonies merely to make Fortunes, with which they intend to return to Britain." He went on to remind Shirley "that it is suppos'd an undoubted Right of Englishmen not to be taxed but by their own Consent given thro' their Representatives." Since the colonists had no representatives in Parliament, for Parliament to tax the colonists "would be treating them as a conquer'd People, and not as true British Subjects."[46]

In reply, Shirley suggested that the colonists might be granted representation in Parliament. Franklin liked this idea, as long as the colonists "had a reasonable number of Representatives allowed them; and that all the old Acts of Parliament restraining the trade or cramping the manufacturing of the Colonies, be at the same time repealed, and the British Subjects on this side the water put, in those respects, on the same footing with those in Great Britain." What he wanted above all in 1754 was for the people of Great Britain and the people of the colonies to "learn to consider themselves, not as belonging to different Communities with different Interests, but to one Community with one Interest." This plea for treating the colonists as equals of those living in England itself was a measure of Franklin's heightened sense of his own personal equality with nearly anyone in the British Empire. Once he actually began meeting some of the so-called great men of the empire, such as Lord Loudoun, he came to realize that they had no more ability than he had.[47]

PENNSYLVANIA POLITICS

When the French and Indian War (or the Seven Years War, as it was called in Europe) began in 1754 with the expedition into the Ohio Valley by a young Virginia militia colonel named George Washington, Franklin inevitably became involved. By the next year, when the British government sent General Edward Braddock with two regiments of regulars to engage the French in the interior, Franklin had already persuaded the Pennsylvania Assembly to create a land bank to finance the war effort. The assembly deputed Franklin to meet with Braddock, disabuse him of his prejudices against Pennsylvania, and explain to him just how much the colony was contributing to the war effort. When Braddock discovered that he was short of horses and wagons to haul his expedition westward, Franklin offered to gather the horses and wagons and to stand bond for them personally. That Braddock's expedition ended in a shocking disaster in July 1755 was not Franklin's fault; he had warned the arrogant general that frontier warfare would not be easy.

By the fall of 1755 the situation had become desperate. Frontier defenses had collapsed, westerners were fleeing eastward in droves, and with virtually no military force to stop them French-inspired hostile Indians were closing within a day's ride of Philadelphia. Thoroughly alarmed, the Pennsylvania Assembly finally authorized expenditures for defense, and to raise the money passed a bill taxing all the property in the colony, including the proprietary estates. Under instructions from the proprietors in England, the governor vetoed the bill.

Thus were renewed the increasingly angry exchanges between the governor and the legislature over the issue of taxing the proprietors' lands, with Franklin writing most of the assembly's messages. Franklin later recalled that "our Answers as well as his Messages were often tart, and sometimes indecently abusive."[48] But as much as Franklin abused the governor, it was the proprietors, especially Thomas Penn, who really aroused his ire. That the proprietors, who were subjects of the king as well as he, refused to pay taxes on their lands in Pennsylvania along with everyone else galled Franklin to no end.

But something had to be done, and Franklin worked out a compromise that allowed the governor and legislature to agree to the organization of a militia. Unlike Franklin's Militia Association of 1747, this army was public and legal, though military men regarded its democratic organization with soldiers electing their own officers as absurd. Franklin not only wrote a public defense of the militia but also took charge of raising the troops. With no military title this corpulent forty-nine-year-old civilian led a commission escorted by fifty mounted militiamen to the northwest frontier of the province in order to organize its defense. Governor Robert Morris of Pennsylvania finally recognized Franklin's military role, and in January 1756 formally appointed him sole military commander of that area of the frontier. After overseeing the building of several forts, Franklin got word that the assembly was convening and he was needed back in Philadelphia. Franklin later recalled that the governor even proposed making him a general in charge of provincial troops to do what Braddock had failed to do and take Fort Duquesne.[49] He could hardly help thinking that he had become a kind of indispensable one-man government for the colony.

All this, together with the accolades he was receiving at the same time for his scientific accomplishments, was enough to turn any man's head, and Franklin began to become pretty full of himself. When later that year he was elected once again to the colonelcy of the militia regiment, he accepted gladly and was even escorted by his regiment with drawn swords, an honor never paid to the proprietor of Pennsylvania or to any of the colony's governors, as Franklin delighted in pointing out.[50]

Rumors reached Thomas Penn in London of the incident, and it alarmed him. He had earlier thought Franklin a dangerous man, and Franklin's presuming to be escorted with drawn swords, "as if he had been a member of the Royal Family or Majesty itself," made Penn even more suspicious of this parvenu printer.[51] Penn's confidants in Pennsylvania told him that Franklin was trying to dupe everyone in order to take over all power in the province.[52]

Even Franklin's friends were distressed that he seemed to be overreaching himself. Colden found Franklin's conduct "most surprising," and alerted Collinson. When a worried Collinson wrote Franklin about his display of arrogance, Franklin dismissed the matter. "The People happen to love me. Perhaps that's my Fault." Besides, he had nothing but contempt for the proprietors and had "not the least Inclination to be in their good Graces." They were petty and mean men, and he had a "natural Dislike to Persons" like them. His opposition to the proprietors was based not on personal pique or resentment but on his "Regard to the Publick Good." He may be mistaken about what that public good may be, he told Collinson, "but at least I mean well." That's more than could be said for the proprietors. He was ashamed for them. They should have become "Demi Gods" in the eyes of the people; instead they have "become the Objects of universal Hatred and Contempt." Despite all the power their charter, laws, and wealth gave them, "a private Person (forgive your Friend a little Vanity)," he said to Collinson, was able to "do more Good in their Country than they." And this "private Person" was able to do so much more than the proprietors "because he has the Affections and Confidence of their People, and of course some Command of the Peoples Purses."[53]

By 1756 Franklin must have thought he was on top of the world. No one had seen more of America, and no one knew more important people in the colonies, than he. He was in a position, he thought, to accomplish extraordinary things. "Life," he wrote that year, was "like a dramatic Piece" and thus "should not only be conducted with Regularity, but methinks it should finish handsomely. Being now in the last Act, I begin to cast about for something fit to end with."[54] Of course, he could scarcely have foreseen how handsomely it would end. At this point in the drama of his life he wanted only to help shape the future of the entity he most admired—the British Empire.

In 1754, while formulating the Albany Plan, he had envisioned two new colonies being created in the West "between the present frontiers of our colonies on one side, and the lakes and Mississippi on the other." These colonies, he said, would lead "to the great increase of Englishmen, English trade, and English power." The Crown should grant to the contributors and settlers of these colonies "as many and as great privileges and powers of government . . . as his Majesty in his wisdom shall think for their benefit and encouragement, consistent with the general good of the British empire."[55]

This dream of landed empires in the West was one he long clung to and one he shared with his son William. Two years later he fantasized with his friend the evangelical preacher George Whitefield about their being "jointly employ'd by the Crown to settle a Colony on the Ohio. . . . What a glorious Thing it would be, to settle in that fine country a large Strong Body of Religious and Industrious People! What a Security to the Other Colonies: and Advantageous to Britain, by Increasing her People, Territory, Strength, and Commerce." He and Whitefield could spend the remainder of their lives in such an endeavor, and "God would bless us with Success, if we undertook it with a sincere Regard to his Honour, the Service of our gracious King, and (which is the same thing) the Publick Good."[56]

MISSION TO GREAT BRITAIN

Franklin was very much the loyal Englishman. Although few Americans in the 1750s expressed anything other than deep loyalty to the mother country, Franklin did seem to have an unusual degree of confidence in his gracious king. He was in fact coming to believe that royal authority might even supplant the proprietary government of Pennsylvania.

With the legislature and the governor continuing to wrangle over the issue of taxing the proprietary lands, the assembly early in 1757 decided to send a mission to England to argue its case with the proprietors and, if that should fail, with the British government. The assembly's ostensible aim was to get the proprietors to change their attitude toward taxing their lands and to cease issuing oppressive instructions to their gubernatorial appointees; but behind the negotiations with the proprietors lay the threat of seeking to have Parliament remove the Penns from control of Pennsylvania.

Naturally, the fifty-one-year-old Franklin was selected as emissary. He could not have been more excited by the prospect of going "home to England," to the metropolitan center of the empire.[57] At last he would have an arena fit for what he assumed would be the final act of his remarkable life.[58]

He knew he was leaving "some Enemies in Pensilvania, who will take every Opportunity of injuring me in my Absence." To "watch" these enemies and "guard my Reputation and Interest as much as may be from the Effects of their Malevolence," he turned to the young lawyer Joseph Galloway, a friend who had helped to train his son William in the law. Indeed, this wealthy and well-connected future loyalist, in whose care Franklin "chearfully" left his "dearest Concerns," became his principal political ally and Pennsylvania confidant during his many years in London.[59]

Not surprisingly, Franklin decided to take the twenty-seven-year-old

William with him to London. The father and son had grown increasingly close in recent years. William had accompanied his father to the Albany conference, had aided him in rounding up supplies for General Braddock's ill-fated expedition, and had enjoyed his father's company during the military buildup on the frontier. In fact, from the beginning Franklin had sought to give William every advantage that he had lacked as a boy. Instead of being taken out of school after only two years, William was sent to the best schools in Philadelphia. William did not have to borrow books or learn a trade. It was clear at the outset that William would be a gentleman who would never have to work for a living with his hands.

If it was inevitable that Franklin would take his son with him to London, it was equally inevitable that he would leave Deborah and his fourteen-year-old daughter, Sally, at home. To be sure, Deborah said she feared crossing the ocean, but no doubt she also knew that the London world that Franklin was entering would not be for her. If she was not invited to the homes of the Philadelphia gentry, how much more out of place would she be amid the sophistication and elegance of London? Besides, Franklin was becoming used to being with William away from the women of the family. In the summer of 1755, a visitor to the Franklin household reported that Deborah had accused her husband of "having too great an esteem for his son in prejudice of herself and daughter." She certainly had misgivings about her husband and William's leaving for what was likely to be an extended stay in London, but she promised her husband that she would never complain.[60]

THE WAY TO WEALTH

Knowing he was off to England for some time, Franklin decided to bring the writing of his *Poor Richard's Almanack* to an end. While at sea in the summer of 1757, he completed a preface for the final, 1758 edition. Unlike his earlier prefaces, which were usually a page long, this preface, entitled "Father Abraham's Speech," and later known as *The Way to Wealth,* ran about a dozen pages. It eventually became the most widely reprinted of all Franklin's works, including the *Autobiography.*

In this preface Franklin introduced a new persona, Father Abraham, who presumably carries biblical authority and wisdom and yet in fact seems to be a comic figure. When a crowd of shoppers waiting for an auction to begin asks Father Abraham to comment on the economic condition of the country, the old man rises and begins spouting a series of aphorisms taken from previous editions of *Poor Richard's Almanack,* repeating over and over again "as Poor Richard Says." But instead of drawing indiscriminately from the wide variety of proverbs in the earlier almanacs that dealt with all sorts of social and domestic issues, Father Abraham cites only those proverbs that concern hard work, thrift, and financial prudence, such as *"Early to bed, early to rise, makes a Man healthy, wealthy and wise."* At the end of Father Abraham's harangue, says Franklin's Richard Saunders persona, the audience heard his counsel, "approved the Doctrine, and immediately practised the contrary, just as if it had been a common sermon." When the auction finally opened, "they began to buy extravagantly, notwithstanding his Cautions and their own Fear of Taxes."[61]

It has been suggested that Franklin was taking the opportunity in this, his last almanac and last series of proverbs, to question the whole project of using maxims to reform behavior. In other words, he was warning his readers not to take all his proverbial advice too literally. Remember, he has Father Abraham finally caution, people cannot get rich on their own; God has something to do with a person's prosperity.[62]

Franklin could only believe that God was now firmly on his side. He had all the wealth he needed, and this time, unlike thirty years earlier, he was off to London as a full-fledged gentleman.

LONDON

This time he was emotionally prepared for London; indeed, he so fell in love with Britain that he eventually found it difficult to contemplate going back to America. Along with Dr. Johnson, he came to believe that to love London was to love life and to love life was to love London. London, with its three quarters of a million people, was much larger than it had been thirty years earlier and even more a world unto itself. One in ten Englishmen lived there. Despite its own exceedingly rapid growth, Philadelphia, with fewer than twenty thousand people, could not compare at all to this teeming metropolis. London's appalling poverty and gin-soaked slums were still present, but the city was improving itself, erecting impressive new Palladian buildings and laying out large elegant squares and crescents. The expensive Westminster Bridge across the Thames had just recently been completed, and the West End, "the polite end of the town," was being rapidly developed. London was drawing talented people from all over the greater British world—men such as David Hume, Oliver Goldsmith, Edmund Burke, Dr. Johnson, David Garrick, James Boswell, and now, of course, Benjamin Franklin. Not only was London the largest city in Europe, but, some thought, it might become the most grand as well. But this was not to be: it was too noisy, too busy, too turbulent, and too free. In London, James Boswell discovered, "we may be in some degree whatever character we choose."[63]

Amid the cosmopolitan excitement of this world-class cultural center—with its numerous clubs, coffeehouses, and theaters—Franklin began to realize just how limited and parochial life was in the distant colonies. Instead of the brief mission that he originally expected, he stayed for more than five years, and then, after a two-year trip back to Philadelphia, he returned to London for another ten years. He came close to staying forever.

He and William and two slaves were soon comfortably ensconced in the apartments of Margaret Stevenson, a widow living with her daughter Mary, called Polly, at No. 7 (later No. 36) Craven Street, near Charing Cross and the fabulous shopping mall of the Strand, and only a short walk from the government offices of Whitehall (see page 86).[64] As long as he stayed in London, he lived with the Stevensons, where everything, he said, was "pretty genteel." Mrs. Stevenson and Polly seemed to make up for the absence of Deborah Franklin and Sally. Indeed, he soon came to lavish much more emotion on this surrogate family than he did on his real one back in Philadelphia. The best he could do for his wife and daughter back home, it seemed, was to send them portraits of himself that he commissioned.[65]

At last he met friends with whom he had corresponded for years but had never set eyes upon, men like Peter Collinson, the Quaker merchant,

Franklin's house on Craven Street, London

naturalist, and member of the Royal Society, and William Strahan, the Scottish-born printer of Dr. Johnson's dictionary and the first volumes of David Hume's history of England and later a member of Parliament. They in turn introduced him to ever widening circles of important people. With his affable nature Franklin was as "clubbable" as Dr. Johnson said James Boswell was, and he joined several clubs, where he met all sorts of scientists, philanthropists, and explorers, including Captain James Cook and Joseph Priestley.[66] His favorite club was the Club of Honest Whigs, whose members included his close friends the Quaker physician Dr. John Fothergill and the Scottish scientist John Pringle, who was physician to the Earl of Bute, George III's confidant and favored minister in the early 1760s. Dr. Pringle, soon to be president of the Royal Society and physician to the king himself, eventually became one of Franklin's most intimate friends.

Franklin's scientific reputation preceded him and opened dozens of doors. He was invited to Cambridge University, where in May 1758 he performed some of his electrical experiments. He enjoyed his visit so much that he and his son went back in July for the university's commencement ceremonies. He and William, he told Deborah, "were present at all the ceremonies, dined every day in their halls, and my vanity was not a little gratified by the particular regard showed by the chancellor and vice-chancellor of the university, and the heads of colleges."[67] A year later the University of St. Andrews in Scotland conferred on him the honorary degree of Doctor of Laws, which resulted in his thereafter being called "Dr. Franklin." Another honorary doctoral degree from Oxford followed in 1762.

His fame was extraordinary; it was not simply that he was a world-celebrated scientist but that he was a colonial from the far wilderness across the Atlantic. So celebrated was he that enterprising individuals could make money from his image: one of his portraitists, Benjamin Wilson, had engraver James McArdell make mezzotints for sale to the general public. The 1761 print features Franklin in a great white wig with a static electric machine and writing materials on a table with a lightning storm raging in the background. A year or so later a portrait by another artist, Mason Chamberlain, was likewise reproduced, by engraver Edward Fisher, and widely distributed in England and the colonies (see page 88). This portrait also emphasizes Franklin's erudition, his electrical experiments, and his honorary degrees.[68]

LEFT: *Franklin, by Benjamin Wilson, c. 1759*
RIGHT: *Franklin, mezzotint by James McArdell, 1761*

LEFT: *Franklin, by Mason Chamberlain, 1762*
RIGHT: *Franklin, mezzotint by Edward Fisher, 1763*

In 1759 Franklin toured Scotland, was made a burgess and guild brother of Edinburgh and Glasgow, and met such Scottish luminaries as William Robertson, David Hume, and Adam Smith. Honors from Harvard, Yale, William and Mary, and the American provinces were one thing; but this acclaim and these honors were coming from the enlightened centers of the British world. His friend Richard Jackson, who would also become an agent or lobbyist for Pennsylvania, even proposed to get him elected to Parliament. But Franklin said he was "too old to think of changing Countries." He would soon have second thoughts about that possibility. He was as happy as he had ever been in his life.[69]

DEBORAH

Time flew by and the months turned into years. Negotiations with the proprietors, especially with the principal proprietor, Thomas Penn, turned

Deborah Franklin, by Benjamin Wilson, c. 1759

out to be slower and more difficult than he expected. But, more important, he soon found that he enjoyed London more and more and was now as much at home in the huge metropolis as he had been in Philadelphia. As early as January 1758, he told his wife that he could not possibly return for at least a year from then. His work, he said, required "both time and patience."[70] By 1760 he had given up even bothering to mention to Deborah when he might return. Although he repeatedly told his wife that he missed her and his daughter, Sally, his letters home soon became more and more perfunctory. Perhaps to ease his conscience over his long absence from his family, he showered gifts on Deborah and Sally. Crate after crate of fine goods were shipped to Philadelphia—carpeting, bedding, tablecloths, blankets, glassware, silverware, shoes, gloves, and curiosities of all sorts. Franklin, who earlier in his life had been happy with his simple pewter spoon and earthen bowl, now spared no expense in spreading luxury over his absent family.

Franklin's friend William Strahan wrote a strange and convoluted letter to Deborah and tried to persuade her and Sally to join Franklin in London. He even hinted that there were ladies in London who would sail twice the ocean to get her illustrious husband. But Deborah knew better than to try to enter Franklin's ever widening London world. She refused Strahan's appeal, pleading her fear of the ocean, and stayed in Philadelphia.

Franklin was not surprised by Deborah's refusal to heed Strahan's clever and cunning pleas to come over to London. In fact, he told her, he "was much pleas'd" with her answer to Strahan's "Rhetoric and Art." He certainly would not have been comfortable with the loud and plain Mrs. Franklin accompanying him on all his calls, dinners, and sojourns. Although Franklin continued to call Deborah his "dear child" and never voiced any feelings about her lack of sophistication, most of his letters to her from London have all the intimacy of a business manager talking to his employee—in sharp contrast to the warm and chatty letters Franklin wrote to his sister Jane Mecom. Deborah was not like John Adams's Abigail: although she was an efficient and doting wife—"a good and faithful Helpmate," Franklin called her—she was scarcely an intellectual companion. It is hard, for example, to envision Deborah fully appreciating the charming humor of *The Craven Street Gazette*, a parody of newspaper gossip about the court that Franklin wrote for the amusement of the Stevensons and their friends.[71]

Deborah's situation was awkward, to say the least. When Strahan told Deborah that Mrs. Stevenson, "a very discreet good gentlewoman," had nursed Franklin through a two-month illness "with an assiduity, concern, and tenderness, which perhaps, only yourself could equal," she had no answer. What could she say?[72] As a Quaker friend in Philadelphia noted, Deborah and Sally bore Franklin's "long absence with a more resign'd and Christian Spirit than could be expected." In fact, the friend added, many Philadelphians were also wondering when Franklin was coming back home.[73]

But Franklin, like many other colonists, had always thought of England as "home." Now he was beginning to identify with Britain even more closely than he had earlier and was actually thinking of following Strahan's advice and settling in England permanently. He and his son visited his ancestral home in Northampton and discovered roots and relatives they had not known. When Franklin looked up Deborah's relatives in Birmingham, he found that "they are industrious, ingenious, working people and think themselves vastly happy that they live in dear old England."[74] The more he thought about the differences between the mother country and the colonies, the more impressed he was with Britain and with the British government.

THE ROYALIST FRANKLIN

By the early 1760s Franklin had become a thoroughgoing imperialist and royalist. He had developed an emotional commitment to the Crown's empire, a vision of a pan-British world that was rivaled in its grandeur only by that of William Pitt. Few Englishmen in 1760 were more proud of being English, and few were more devoted to the English monarchy and the greatness of the British Empire. Although he remained sensitive to criticism of the colonists, he sought at every turn to affirm his own and his fellow Americans' "respect for the mother country, and admiration of everything that is British."[75]

With the British conquest of Canada, Franklin's long existing dream of establishing new colonies in the West seemed closer to realization, and he himself now became involved in several land schemes, first in Nova Scotia and later in the American West. Although he believed that "the Foundations of the future Grandeur and Stability of the British Empire" lay in America, he spoke, as he said, "not merely as I am a Colonist, but as I am a Briton."[76] The New World might be the source of "the greatest Political Structure Human Wisdom ever yet erected," but this structure, this empire, would remain British.

Although some Britons in the mother country continued to suggest that the colonists at some future date might get together and break up this empire, Franklin, like most colonists in 1760, would have none of it. There was no danger whatsoever, he said, of the Americans' "uniting against their own nation, which protects and encourages them, with which they have so many connections and ties of blood, interest, and affection, and which 'tis well known they all love much more than they love one another. . . . I will venture to say, an union amongst them for such a purpose is not merely improbable, it is impossible." Of course, "the most grievous tyranny and oppression" could drive any people to rebellion, but in 1760 Franklin could not conceive of the British government's becoming tyrannical.[77]

At the outset of his mission Franklin had been so confident of his reputation in the world that he had tried to go right to the top of the British government and meet with the Crown's chief minister, William Pitt. But Pitt refused to see him. "He was then too great a Man," Franklin later explained, "or too much occupy'd in Affairs of greater Moment," and Franklin had to settle for meeting with secretaries and ultimately with Thomas Penn, the principal proprietor.[78]

As he became increasingly frustrated negotiating with Penn, his dislike of the man deepened. When Franklin suggested to Penn in January 1758 that the 1682 charter granted to Penn's father to establish the colony gave the General Assembly all the rights of a parliamentary legislature, Penn disagreed. Penn said that the royal charter was not empowered to make such a grant and that if his father had granted any privileges to the assembly, it was not by authority of the charter. Franklin replied that if William Penn had no right to grant these privileges and yet had promised the many settlers who came to the province that they would have them, then the colonists had been "deceived, cheated and betrayed."

Penn's answer infuriated Franklin. The colonists themselves, Penn said, "should have looked" into the royal charter; it "was no Secret; . . . if they were deceiv'd, it was their own fault." According to Franklin, Penn said all this "with a Kind of triumphing laughing Insolence, such as a low Jockey might do when a Purchaser complained that He had cheated him in a Horse." At that moment, said Franklin, he conceived "a more cordial and thorough Contempt for him than I ever before felt for any Man living."[79]

As a consequence, Franklin became more certain than ever that the king's government in Pennsylvania would be far preferable to rule by such a man. Friends cautioned him that his enthusiasm for turning Pennsylvania into a royal province might be disastrous for the colony. They suggested that only Parliament could take away the proprietors' charter, and Parliament might in the process decrease the power of the assembly and some of the province's liberties. But in his passion and with his confidence in royal authority, Franklin ignored such warnings and pressed ahead, much to the bewilderment of some of his contemporaries and some modern historians. He urged the General Assembly to petition "the Crown to take the Province under its immediate Government and Protection." Although he had little evidence that the Crown was interested in taking the colony under its protection, he told the legislature that such a petition "would be even now very favourably heard" and "might without much Difficulty be carried."[80]

In light of what eventually happened to the empire in 1776, Franklin's efforts to turn Pennsylvania into a royal colony may seem as futile and foolish as some contemporaries and some subsequent historians have asserted.[81] But at the time they did not seem so to Franklin and to others who were enamored of crown authority. Franklin was not simply driven by his hatred of Thomas Penn. He was in fact a good royalist, a crown officeholder, after all, who was completely devoted to the king and to the king's empire. Therefore, despite considerable opposition within Pennsylvania itself to changing the charter, it was not at all strange or irrational for him to want to enhance royal authority and tighten the bonds of the empire by eliminating an anachronistic private interest like that of the Penn proprietors.

Knowing what happened in 1776 as we do makes it difficult for us to interpret American thinking in 1760. There were many Americans who were as excited over the accession of George III to the throne in 1760 as Englishmen and many who were as deeply loyal to the British Empire as anyone in the mother country. Franklin was one of the most excited and most loyal of all.[82]

Although in his mission of 1757 Franklin ostensibly had been the agent of the Pennsylvania Assembly, he had become in reality the king's man. No one in 1760 could have been more respectful of royal authority. Royalty fascinated him, and he cut short a trip to the Continent so that he could attend the new king's coronation.[83] Like most colonists that year, he had no inkling of any impending imperial crisis, but, unlike most colonists, he had no sense either of any real disparity of interests between Britain and her colonies. In fact, his confidence in the virtue and good sense of politicians at the highest levels of the British government was so great that it bewildered and amazed even some of his British friends. He could not share their "melancholly Apprehensions" and "Fears for the

Nation," and he castigated "the stupid brutal Opposition" that the new young king and his measures were receiving. Far from declining, English virtue, he wrote in 1763, "bids fair for Increasing," especially "if the old Saying be true, as it certainly is, Ad Exemplum Regis, &c." Ahead he saw only a "happy and truly glorious" reign for George III.[84]

Franklin used his influence with Dr. Pringle and perhaps Peter Collinson to meet George III's "dearest friend" and chief minister, Lord Bute. Bute was a great patron of the arts and sciences, very interested in botany and electricity, and would have wanted to meet the celebrated Dr. Franklin. At any rate Franklin bragged of his acquaintance with his lordship. He bought two engravings of Allan Ramsay's portrait of the chief minister and even sent one of them back to Pennsylvania to be prominently displayed in his Philadelphia home, along with a picture of the king and queen. Indeed, he had enough influence with Lord Bute in 1762 to get his thirty-one-year-old son appointed royal governor of New Jersey.[85]

Although William possessed his own charm and connections, having Franklin as his father was undoubtedly his most important attribute, which William was more than willing to acknowledge. Since Franklin had found posts for his son back in Philadelphia—first the clerkship of the Pennsylvania Assembly and later the office of postmaster of Philadelphia—it was natural that he would try to help William in London. William first asked Bute for the office of secretary of the colony of South Carolina, but when he learned that that position had gone to another, he asked Bute for the governorship of New Jersey, which had recently become vacant. In his memorial to Bute, the Scottish lord, William shrewdly appealed to their mutual non-Englishness. If "your Lordship," he said, had not "given such repeated Proofs of your having no local Attachments, that you consider all His Majesty's Subjects, however distant, if of equal Virtue and Loyalty, on an equal Footing, I who am an American, should scarce have had the Boldness to solicit your Patronage and Assistance on this Occasion." Although we do not have all the details relating to the appointment, Lord Bute satisfied William's desire to be "particularly serviceable to Government."[86]

Since New Jersey was a relatively poor colony and its governor's salary was not large, not everyone wanted the position; indeed, Thomas

Pownall, who had returned to England after several administrative positions in the colonies, was reported to have refused it. Still, there were usually more candidates for colonial governorships than could be satisfied. Thus William's appointment, especially since he was a native American and, in John Adams's later caustic phrase, "a base born Brat," was no small achievement. In fact, as one observer noted in September 1762, "many Scruples were raised on account of [William's] *being Illegitimate,* which we were Strangers to till very lately."[87] The entire process of William's appointment as governor of New Jersey reveals not only the peculiar nature of that patronage-dominated world but also the desires and the ability of the two Franklins, father as well as son, to move in that world and to be "serviceable to Government." It was thought that Franklin himself had an eye on an imperial office. Some of his enemies accused him of wanting to turn proprietary Pennsylvania into a crown colony so that he could become its first royal governor.

Franklin had long accepted the cultural inferiority of the New World to the Old World without embarrassment or complaint. In 1745 he had told his correspondent Strahan that he and his fellow colonists were eager to gobble up anything and everything written in the mother country, whether good or bad. Indeed, he said, the British authors had so much "Fame . . . on this Side [of] the Ocean" that the colonists had become "a kind of Posterity with respect to them. We read their Works with perfect Impartiality, being at too great a Distance to be bypassed by the Fashions, Parties, and Prejudices that prevail among you. We know nothing of their personal Failings; the Blemishes in their character never reach us, and therefore . . . we praise and admire them without Restraint."[88]

Sometimes the distance from the center of British civilization seemed so great to Franklin that his imagination ran wild. In his 1749 pamphlet *Proposals Relating to the Education of Youth in Pensilvania,* Franklin had noted that "Something seems wanting in America to incite and stimulate Youth to Study." He thought that "the Encouragements to Learning" were much greater in Europe than in America. "Whoever distinguishes himself there, in either of the three learned Professions, gains Fame, and often Wealth and Power: A poor Man's Son, has a Chance, if he studies hard, to rise . . . to an extraordinary Pitch of Grandeur; to have a Voice in

Parliament, a Seat among the Peers; as a Statesman or first Minister to govern Nations, and even to mix his Blood with Princes." No wonder he wanted to get to England.[89]

His experience when he arrived in England in the late 1750s was very different from that of many other Americans. Wealthy colonists such as John Dickinson of Delaware or Charles Carroll of Maryland who lived in London in these years were overawed by the city's sophistication and grandeur and in response seemed to need to justify the deficiencies and provinciality of colonial America by expressing disgust with the luxury and corruption of English life. As a young law student at the Inns of Court in 1754, Dickinson was shocked at the notorious ways in which hundreds of thousands of pounds were being spent to buy elections. This "most unbounded licentiousness and utter disregard of virtue," he told his parents, could end, as it always had, only in the destruction of the empire. Young Carroll in 1760, despite his worldliness from having studied and traveled abroad for twelve years, agreed with this dire prediction of England's fate. "Our dear-bought liberty," he told his father, "stands upon the brink of destruction." These became increasingly widely held views among the colonists.[90]

Franklin felt little of this American provincial need to denigrate English life. Of course, he had long recognized that the English themselves were continually complaining in their public papers of their own "prevailing corruption and degeneracy." But he himself had always known, as he had told Peter Collinson back in 1753, that "you have a great deal of Virtue still subsisting among you" and that the English constitution was "not so near a dissolution, as some seem to apprehend." Upon his arrival in England he had met up with the same mood of England's feeling "itself so universally corrupt and rotten from Head to Foot, that it has little Confidence in any publick Men or publick Measures."[91] Yet his experience in London soon convinced him that much of that English self-criticism was mistaken.

He began filling his letters with disparaging comments about the provinciality and vulgarity of America in contrast with the sophistication and worthiness of England. Britain, "that little Island," he wrote in 1763, enjoyed "in almost every Neighbourhood, more sensible, virtuous and elegant Minds, than we can collect in ranging 100 Leagues of our vast Forests."[92] No one brought up in England, he said, could ever be happy in America. In fact, it was not England that was corrupt and luxury-loving, it was America; and the great danger was that the English nation, if it did not draw off some of its wealth, "would, like ours, have a Plethora in its Veins, productive of the same Sloth, and the same feverish Extravagance."[93] Everywhere in the Old World he saw contrasts with provincial America that mortified him. The Sunday gaiety of the people of Flanders, together with their ordered prosperity, for example, only reminded him, by contrast, of how narrow and straitlaced, and how silly, was Puritan New England.[94] In these years Franklin scarcely seems to have regarded himself as an American.

So happy was he during his five years in Britain that he very nearly did not return to America. When his friend Strahan urged him to stay and run for Parliament, he was tempted. Although he talked of growing "weary" of his long "Banishment" and of his desiring to return to "the happy Society of my Friends and Family in Philadelphia," he repeatedly put off leaving. Finally, in 1762, the need to settle his affairs in America, especially the business of the post office (the royal office that he much valued), compelled his return. But he knew he would come back to England. "The Attraction of *Reason*," he told Strahan on the eve of his departure for America, "is at present for the other Side of the Water, but that of *Inclination* will be for this side. You know which usually prevails. I shall probably make but this one Vibration and settle here for ever."[95]

FRANKLIN'S BRIEF RETURN TO AMERICA

When he arrived in America in the fall of 1762, Franklin found that it had changed. The streets of Philadelphia seemed "thinner of People, owing perhaps to my being so long accustom'd to the bustling crowded Streets of London." But, more alarming, there was too much money everywhere, and the Philadelphia artisans were not what they used to be when he was one of them. "Our Tradesmen are grown as idle, and as extravagant in their Demands when you would prevail on them to work, as so many Spaniards."[96]

He was no sooner back in America than he began thinking of returning to England. "No Friend can wish me more in England than I do my self," he told Strahan in August 1763. "But before I go, every thing I am concern'd in must be so settled here as to make another Return to America unnecessary." First, he had to settle the business of the North American post office. He spent seven months of 1763 on postal inspection tours that took him from Virginia to New England, totaling, he said, some 1,780 miles. He sought to improve service between the major cities and to extend it to the newly acquired territory of Canada. He tried to talk Deborah into accompanying him on these trips, but she refused.

While he was away on these tours he did give Deborah permission to open all the mail that would arrive from England. He told her, in a sentence as revealing of their relationship as any, "It must give you Pleasure to see that People who knew me there so long and so intimately, retain so sincere a Regard for me." Knowing that his wife would never leave Philadelphia, he now laid plans to build a new three-story brick house on Market Street, just a few feet from the spot where Deborah had first spied him in 1723. Since he began building it at the same time he was telling his friends in England that he would soon be with them, the home, which he never saw completed until 1775, may have been for Deborah alone. Maybe it was another part of the business he had to settle so he would not have to come back to America again—another salve for his conscience perhaps.[97]

Before he could return to England, Franklin had to deal with an uprising of some Scotch-Irish settlers from the Paxton region on the Pennsylvania frontier who were angry at Indian violence and neglect by the eastern-dominated assembly. Franklin had no sympathy with "armed Mobs" and was happy to have the governor call on him for help in putting them down. He wrote a pamphlet, he said, "to render the Rioters unpopular; promoted an Association to support the Authority of the Government and defend the Governor by taking Arms, sign'd it first myself, and was followed by several Hundreds, who took Arms accordingly."

The governor flattered him with an offer of the command of the militia, but he "chose to carry a Musket." More flattering still, with the so-called Paxton Boys threatening to march on Philadelphia, the governor ran "to my House at midnight, with his Counsellors at his Heels, for

Advice, and made it his Head Quarters for some time." The governor then appointed him and several others to negotiate with the rioters; the delegation met with the armed frontiersmen and persuaded them to return home. Although he made fun of the colony's desperate need for him, Franklin could barely suppress his glee at his renewed authority in Pennsylvania politics. Think of it, he said to Dr. John Fothergill back in London, "within four and twenty Hours, your old Friend was a common soldier, a Counsellor, a kind of Dictator, an Ambassador to the Country Mob, and on [the governor's and his counsellors'] Returning home, *Nobody*, again."

In Franklin's mind the mobs and rioting had some good results. It suggested that the colony was "running fast into Anarchy and Confusion," and that "our only Hopes are, that the Crown will see the Necessity of taking the Government into its own hands, without which we shall soon have no Government at all." Franklin was able to get the assembly to pass a number of resolves blaming the proprietors for all of Pennsylvania's troubles.[98]

With the help of his young political lieutenant Joseph Galloway, Franklin next sought to organize a popular petition urging that Pennsylvania be turned into a royal colony. He hoped that such a show of popular support would win over doubters in the assembly and in the colony. In order to convince Pennsylvanians of the benefits of substituting royal for proprietary authority, he, Galloway, and their allies launched a propaganda campaign of unprecedented intensity and scale. Franklin and Galloway organized a mass meeting in Philadelphia at which Galloway, known as the "Demosthenes of Pennsylvania," harangued the crowd, arguing that "the way from Proprietary Slavery to Royal Liberty was easy." The proponents of making Pennsylvania a royal colony not only plied potential signers with liquor; they got many people to sign their names to blank sheets of paper with no knowledge of what they were signing. At the same time Franklin's press poured forth thousands of pieces of propaganda, including the assembly's resolves and "Explanatory Remarks" on them, newspaper articles, and broadsides, all promoting the cause of royal government, with Franklin writing much of the material. Both Galloway and Franklin wrote pamphlets as well and "by the thousands" gave them away free. In his own pamphlet, entitled *Cool*

Thoughts on the Present Situation of Our Public Affairs, Franklin tried to assure the people that Pennsylvania would lose none of its privileges by becoming a royal colony. Only an act of Parliament could take those privileges away, he said, "and we may rely on the united Justice of King, Lords, and Commons, that no such Act will ever pass, while we continue loyal and dutiful Subjects."[99]

But his persuasive powers were not very effective with the public: the petition to replace the proprietary government gained only 3500 signatures, and those were mostly from Philadelphia. At the same time Franklin faced a determined opponent of his plans in the assembly, John Dickinson, the well-to-do lawyer, originally from Delaware, who had trained in England and who would later become famous in the colonies with the publication of his *Letters from a Farmer in Pennsylvania* in 1767–68. In an impressive speech in May 1764, Dickinson argued that revoking the charter and turning Pennsylvania into a royal colony might endanger the colony's liberties, especially its religious freedom. "Have we not *sufficiently felt* the effects of royal resentment?" Dickinson asked. "Is not the authority of the Crown fully enough exerted over us?"[100] Equally damaging to Franklin's cause was the defection of the Speaker of the assembly, Isaac Norris. Although Norris had earlier encouraged making Pennsylvania a royal colony, he now followed Dickinson, his son-in-law, and spoke against a crown takeover; then, pleading ill health, he abruptly resigned from the assembly.

Franklin and Galloway were not used to opposition from members of the Quaker party. Dickinson had no sooner finished his speech in the assembly than the arrogant young Galloway was on his feet to answer him. Galloway was proud of his oratorical abilities, and in a vigorous extemporaneous rebuttal to Dickinson he defended the disinterestedness of the Crown in contrast to the private interest of the proprietors—a position with which Franklin completely agreed. This encounter and the subsequent publication of the speeches, with Dickinson claiming that Galloway's printed version was "a *pretended speech,*" created bad blood between the two men, leading to a fistfight and a challenge to a duel that never came off.[101] Despite the opposition of Dickinson and Norris, however, Franklin and Galloway still had nearly all the votes in the legislature. Franklin was elected Speaker in place of Norris, and the assembly overwhelmingly voted to request that the Crown take over the government of the colony.

The supporters of the proprietors decided to emulate Franklin and solicit people's signatures on petitions opposing the scheme to turn Pennsylvania into a royal colony. By September 1764 they had garnered 15,000 signatures, over four times the number Franklin had raised for his petition. Under the leadership of William Smith, Anglican clergyman and provost of the College of Pennsylvania, and William Allen, chief justice of the colony, both of whom had just returned from England, the proprietary cause rapidly gained strength. More and more Pennsylvanians were having second thoughts about abandoning the charter of William Penn, which had brought them so many privileges, so much religious freedom, and so much prosperity.

The campaign for elections to the Pennsylvania Assembly in October 1764 was one of the most scurrilous in American colonial history, and both Franklin and Galloway lost their seats. Franklin was accused of a host of sins—of lechery, of having humble origins, of abandoning the mother of his bastard son, of stealing his ideas of electricity from another electrician, of embezzling colony funds, and of buying his honorary degrees. But what ultimately cost Franklin his seat was the number of Germans who voted against him, angry at his earlier ethnic slur about "Palatine Boors."[102]

Franklin was stunned by his defeat. He had completely misjudged the sentiments of his fellow colonists, something he would continue to do over the succeeding decade. Nevertheless, even though he was now out of the assembly, his political influence remained strong, and his Quaker party still controlled a majority of the legislature. At least some members of the assembly wanted to continue threatening the Penns with royalization in order to extract taxes and other privileges from them.[103] Hence in late October the assembly voted to send Franklin once again to England to request the Crown to end proprietary rule in Pennsylvania. Although some legislators may have intended to use Franklin's mission simply to intimidate the proprietors into reforms, Franklin himself was as serious as ever in his desire to bring royal government to the colony. No doubt he was equally desirous of getting back to London, where he was more appreciated.

"A LONDONER FOR THE REST OF MY DAYS"

His two years back in America had not diluted in any way his love of London and his faith in the beneficence of royal authority, a faith that exceeded not only that of his fellow Americans but that of his British friends in London. He told his friend Strahan that if the proprietary party with which he was at war was able to destroy him and prevent his bringing royal government to Pennsylvania, then he would become "a Londoner for the rest of my Days."[104] He was as fervent a royalist as he had ever been. In defending his reputation among His Majesty's ministers and his ability to bring royal government to Pennsylvania, he emphasized his "constantly and uniformly promoting the Measures of the Crown." In fact, he told his fellow Pennsylvanians, as "a Man who holds a profitable Office under the Crown," he could be counted on to behave "with the Fidelity and Duty that becomes every good Subject."[105]

Most colonists in the early 1760s were not yet thinking of rebellion, but they were certainly no lovers of crown prerogative as exercised by their royal governors. They prided themselves on the ability of their colonial assemblies—the "democratic" part of their mixed constitutions—to defend their English rights and liberties against what was always thought to be the continually encroaching power of the Crown. From the beginning of the eighteenth century, colonial politics had been marked by greater degrees of popular participation than people in the mother country experienced. Not only could two out of three adult white males vote in most colonies, compared with one out of six in England, but the royal patronage and political power necessary to control the people and their legislative representatives were much weaker in the colonies than in Britain itself. Coupled with this popular participation was a confusion over who precisely the leaders of the society were, a situation that made authority in the colonies repeatedly vulnerable to challenge. Eighteenth-century royal governors continually complained of the fury and madness of the people in the colonies and the extent to which republican principles were eroding proper respect for royal authority. Thomas Penn himself warned that the power of the contentious colonial assemblies must be curbed or "the constitution will be changed to a perfect Democracy."[106]

Although Franklin at one time had been one of those colonial demagogues whom British officials frequently complained about, he was now on the other side of the water and the other side of the political fence. Just at the moment when many of his fellow colonists were becoming ever more fearful that Great Britain was becoming corrupt and losing its liberty, just at that moment that many Americans were becoming more mistrustful of the intentions of the British government, Franklin was becoming ever more confident of its benevolence and the future of the British Empire. Far from seeing the British nation sinking in luxury and corruption, he was seriously considering settling there forever. He had an excessive faith in the British Crown, and he had many friends and acquaintances in the colonies who shared his faith and who encouraged his mission to change Pennsylvania into a royal colony. Indeed, it is remarkable how many of his American friends in the early 1760s were future Tories and loyalists.

In 1764 Rhode Islander Martin Howard Jr. asked Franklin, whom he had known from the Albany Congress, to support a secret petition already on the way to England requesting the transformation of his colony's popular government into a crown colony. Rhode Islanders, complained Howard, who would eventually become a prominent loyalist, had "now Nothing but a Burlesque upon Order and Government, and will never get right without the Constitution is altered." The Anglican clergyman Samuel Johnson of Connecticut was likewise disgusted with his colony's government. It was, he said, "so monstrously popular, that all our Judges and the other officers depend intirely on the people, so that they are under the strongest Temptation in many Cases to consider not so much what is Law or Equity, as what may please their Constituents." He told Franklin on the eve of Franklin's departure for England, "Would to God you were charged with pleading the same Cause in behalf of all the Governments, that they might all alike be taken into the Kings more immediate Protection."

Only because Franklin's royalist friends and acquaintances expected a sympathetic hearing from him did they dare to voice such sentiments to him, sentiments that, if they should be revealed, these men realized would "bring a popular Odium" on those who held them. They had heard Franklin's views on the king and the empire, and they knew that he was a crown officer and that his son was the royal governor of New Jersey. Consequently, they had every reason to believe that he was one with them. In fact, Howard said as much. He told Franklin that he had "not time to enlarge [on the issue of becoming a royal colony] and indeed your thorough Knowledge of the Subject would anticipate all and more than I could say."[107]

Franklin's Pennsylvania supporters who saw him off on November 7, 1764, now openly linked his fate with that of King George III, hoping that they would soon have cause "to sing with Heart and Voice, GEORGE AND FRANKLIN."[108] Before the year was over, Franklin was back in London in his old lodgings with Mrs. Stevenson on Craven Street. This time also Franklin thought his mission in England would be brief. Instead, it lasted over a decade. Deborah Franklin remained in Philadelphia and never saw her husband again.

THREE

BECOMING A PATRIOT

THE STAMP ACT

In 1763 Great Britain emerged from the Seven Years War as the most powerful empire the world had ever seen. Its armies and navies had been victorious from India to the Mississippi River. The Treaty of Paris that concluded the war gave Britain undisputed dominance over the northeastern half of North America. From the defeated powers, France and Spain, Britain acquired all of Canada, East and West Florida, and millions of fertile acres between the Appalachian Mountains and the Mississippi River. France turned over to Spain the territory of Louisiana in compensation for Spain's loss of the Floridas; and thus this most fearsome of Britain's enemies was completely removed from the North American continent.

But all this new land had to be policed, and that would cost money, lots of it. Lord Jeffrey Amherst, commander in chief in North America, estimated that he would need 10,000 troops to keep the peace with the French settlers in Quebec and the Indians and to deal with squatters, smugglers, and bandits in the West. The costs of maintaining this army would well exceed £300,000 a year. Where was the money to come from? Britain's war debt already totaled £137 million; interest payments on that debt were running £5 million a year, a huge figure when compared with an ordinary annual British peacetime budget of £8 million. Since British subjects in the home islands felt pressed to the wall by taxes, it seemed reasonable to the government to seek new sources of revenue in the colonies.

The first step in this program of reform and taxation was to replace the 1733 Molasses Act with the Sugar Act of 1764. The earlier Molasses Act had levied a sixpence per gallon duty on French and Spanish West Indian molasses, a by-product of sugar refining, that the colonists sought to import in order to make rum. In deference to the rum industry maintained by the British West Indian planters, the extremely high duty of 1733 had been designed not to raise revenue but to prohibit the importation of any foreign West Indian molasses into the colonies. In other words, the prohibitory duty was meant to prevent the colonists from developing their own rum industry that would rival that of the British West Indian sugar planters. But the Molasses Act had not been effectively enforced, and despite the prohibitory duty the New Englanders had created a flourishing and prosperous rum industry. Through bribery and smuggling, New Englanders continued to import foreign, especially French, West Indian molasses. (France had forbidden its colonial sugar planters to use their own surplus molasses to make rum in the way the British planters did because it would compete with its brandy and wine industry.)

In 1764 British officials decided that the need for revenue was now more important than protecting the British West Indian planters' rum industry. They thus lowered the prohibitory duty of sixpence a gallon on foreign molasses to what seemed to be a more affordable threepence a gallon (later lowered to a single pence). By rigidly enforcing this lower duty's collection, however, British officials hoped to stop the colonists' bribery and the smuggling of foreign molasses and encourage its legal importation instead, which in turn would earn revenue for the Crown. In addition to this lower duty on foreign molasses, the Sugar Act levied duties on foreign wine and certain other goods imported into the colonies.

Although most colonists, especially New Englanders, were angered by the Sugar Act, Franklin was not. If revenue had to be raised to support the troops, then so be it. Empires cost money. "A moderate Duty on Foreign Mellasses may be collected; when a high one could not," he said. "The same on Foreign Wines; a Duty not only on Tea but on all East India Goods might perhaps not be amiss, as they are generally rather

Luxuries than Necessities."[1] This was a reasonable, pragmatic view, but only if seen by someone looking at the empire from Whitehall.

Of course, Franklin assumed that the British government would do nothing to hurt the empire. Even a rumor of Parliament's directly taxing the colonists did not bother him. "I am not much alarm'd about your Schemes of raising Money on us," he told Richard Jackson in January 1764. "You will take care for your own sakes not to lay greater Burthens on us than we can bear; for you cannot hurt us without hurting your selves. All our Profits center with you, and the more you take from us, the less we can lay out with you."[2] His trust in the good sense of British officials was remarkable. "We are in your Hands as Clay in the Hands of the Potter," he told Collinson, and "as the Potter cannot waste or spoil his Clay without injuring himself; so I think there is scarce anything you can do that may be hurtful to us, but what will be as much or more so to you. This must be our chief Security."[3]

But the British government needed more revenue to maintain the army in the colonies, and under the leadership of George Grenville, who replaced Bute as chief minister, it proposed levying a stamp tax on legal documents, almanacs, newspapers, playing cards, and nearly every form of paper used in the colonies. Before the government acted, however, Grenville asked the colonial agents in London, including Franklin, what they thought should be done. The agents, of course, were opposed to a stamp tax, as were many colonial officials, including even Lieutenant Governor Thomas Hutchinson of Massachusetts. (As the partner in printing firms, Franklin had a special reason to object to the stamp tax. "It will affect the Printers more than anybody," he told his Philadelphia partner, David Hall.)[4]

But could the agents come up with an alternative plan for raising revenue? Grenville asked. The other agents had nothing to offer, but Franklin, inventive as always, naturally proposed something: that Parliament authorize the issuing of paper currency at interest—in effect, imposing a tax on paper money. Franklin thought this tax would be more acceptable to the colonists than a stamp tax. Although "it will operate as a general Tax on the Colonies," it would not be "an unpleasing one," for it would burden mostly "the rich who handle most money."[5] That Franklin could think that any sort of tax would be acceptable to his fellow

Americans in 1765 suggests that his commitment to the empire was seriously clouding his political judgment. But Grenville was "Besotted with his Stamp Scheme," said Franklin, and he rejected his proposal.[6]

Once Parliament did pass the Stamp Act in March 1765, Franklin decided to make the best of the situation. He did so even though two of his partners—David Hall and James Parker—warned him that this tax would likely put them out of business. He could not have prevented its passage, Franklin reported to his Philadelphia friend Charles Thomson that July; that would have been like hindering the setting of the sun. The stamp tax did not amount to a lot of money anyhow, and Americans could work it off. "Frugallity and Industry will go a great way towards indemnifying us," he said. "Idleness and Pride Tax with a heavier Hand than Kings and Parliaments; If we can get rid of the former we may easily bear the Latter."[7] He could not have been more out of touch with American opinion.

Grenville decided that the tax would go down easier in the colonies if Americans were appointed to collect the tax and receive a commission for doing so. He asked the agents in London to nominate stamp commissioners for each colony, men who would distribute the stamps. Franklin jumped at the opportunity to patronize an ally and friend in Pennsylvania, and he named as stamp distributor John Hughes, one of his most fervent supporters in his struggle with the colony's proprietors. It was a huge mistake. The appointment almost ruined Franklin's position with the American public and nearly cost Hughes his life.

The Stamp Act sparked a firestorm of protest that swept up and down the American continent.[8] The colonists knew only too well from European history that monarchies that could take their subjects' money without their subjects' consent would become absolute and tyrannical. They knew too from history that direct taxes, like that of the stamp tax, had always been regarded as a form of subjection.[9] American resistance was thus inevitable. Merchants in the principal ports formed protest associations and pledged to stop importing British goods in order to bring economic pressure on the British government. Newspapers and pamphlets, the number and like of which had never appeared in America before, seethed with resentment against what one New Yorker called "these designing parricides" who had "invited despotism to cross the ocean, and fix her abode in this once happy land."[10] At hastily convened meetings of towns, counties, and legislative assemblies, the colonists' anger boiled over into fiery declarations.

This torrent of angry words could not help but bring the constitutional relationship between Britain and its colonies into question. In the spring of 1765, the Virginia House of Burgesses adopted a series of resolves denouncing the parliamentary taxation and asserting the colonists' right to be taxed only by their elected representatives. These were introduced by Patrick Henry, who at age twenty-nine had just been elected to the legislature. In the dignified setting of the House of Burgesses, Henry dared to challenge crown authority directly. Just as Julius Caesar had had his Brutus and King Charles I his Oliver Cromwell, so, he declared, he did not doubt that some American would now stand up for his country against this new tyranny. The Speaker of the House stopped Henry for suggesting treason; and some of Henry's resolves (including one proclaiming the right of Virginians to disobey any law that had not been enacted by the Virginia assembly) were too inflammatory to be accepted by the legislature. Nevertheless, colonial newspapers printed the resolves as though the Virginia House of Burgesses had endorsed them all. Many Americans became convinced that Virginians had virtually asserted their legislative independence from Great Britain.

Henry's boldness was contagious. The Rhode Island Assembly declared the Stamp Act "unconstitutional" and authorized the colony's officials to ignore it. In October 1765 thirty-seven delegates from nine colonies met in New York in a Stamp Act Congress and drew up a set of formal declarations and petitions denying Parliament's right to tax them. Overnight the Stamp Act brought about the colonial union that Franklin and Hutchinson's Albany Plan had failed to bring about a decade earlier. But as remarkable as this unprecedented display of colonial unity was, the Stamp Act Congress could not fully express American anger and hostility.

Ultimately it was mob violence that destroyed the Stamp Act in America. On August 14, 1765, a crowd tore apart the office and attacked the home of Andrew Oliver, the stamp distributor for Massachusetts. The next day Oliver promised not to enforce the Stamp Act. A week and a half later mobs attacked Lieutenant Governor Thomas Hutchinson's elegant mansion, scattered and destroyed many of his papers, completely wrecked the interior of the building, and tore down much of its exterior.

At the very moment that the fiery thirty-year-old John Adams was pouring out his suspicions and loathing of Hutchinson—calling him a man of "very ambitious and avaricious Disposition" who was exciting "Jealousies among the People"—Hutchinson's contemporary, Franklin, was sharing thoughts and commiserating with his old friend.[11] In October and November 1765 Hutchinson, who would eventually become the arch-loyalist and the most hated man in all of North America, wrote Franklin in despair. Since the two men had collaborated earlier at the Albany Congress and were both royal officeholders, Hutchinson identified with Franklin and he assumed, correctly, that Franklin identified with him. Franklin hated mobs as much as anyone, and he could only sympathize with Hutchinson over what the Massachusetts mobs had done to him. Franklin had earlier told Hutchinson of his doubts that Parliament would repeal the Stamp Act, but Hutchinson dared not pass on to the people of Boston these doubts. Bostonians expected an early repeal, and "it is not safe there to advance any thing contrary to any popular opinions whatsoever. Every body who used to have virtue enough to oppose them," Hutchinson said, "is now afraid of my fate." Hutchinson could not help pointing out that opponents of the Stamp Act were now using Franklin's motto from the time of the Albany Congress, "join or die." "When you and I were at Albany ten years ago," he noted ruefully, "we did not Propose an union for such Purposes as these."[12]

As news of the rioting in Massachusetts spread to other colonies, similar violence and threats of violence spread with it. From Newport, Rhode Island, to Charleston, South Carolina, local groups organized for resistance. In many places fire and artillery companies, artisan associations, and other fraternal bodies formed the bases for these emerging local organizations, which commonly called themselves Sons of Liberty. Led mostly by shopkeepers, printers, master mechanics, and small merchants—the middling sort that Franklin had once been part of—the Sons of Liberty burned effigies of royal officials, forced stamp agents to resign, compelled businessmen and judges to carry on without stamps, developed an intercolonial network of correspondence, generally enforced nonimportation of British goods, and managed antistamp activities throughout the colonies. The governor of Pennsylvania thought that "we are not more than one degree from open Rebellion."[13] In no colony were stamps ever issued.

The stamp tax seemed to Americans such a direct and unprecedented threat to their constitutional right not to be taxed without their own consent that resistance was immediate, spontaneous, and widespread. Even Thomas Hutchinson had known that such a stamp tax was a terrible mistake and had vigorously disapproved of the Stamp Act from the moment he first heard of it—speaking against it and writing letters to English correspondents, and then formally sending a treatise opposing the act to England for circulation there.[14] That Franklin condoned the Stamp Act in the manner he did clearly reveals just how little he understood American opinion.

As soon as Hughes, the appointed stamp distributor for Pennsylvania, learned of the mob violence and destruction that had occurred in the colonies north of Pennsylvania, he wrote Franklin a series of anguished letters, which he thought might be his last. "The Spirit or Flame of Rebellion is got to a high Pitch amongst the North Americans," he said; "and it seems to me that a Sort of Frenzy or Madness has got such hold of the People of all Ranks that I fancy some Lives will be lost before this Fire is put out." Fearing that the mobs would try to pull down his house, Hughes vowed that he would defend his home "at the Risque of my Life." He armed himself and prepared for a siege, but eventually a large numbers of friends came to his aid and his house was saved.[15]

Since many people in Pennsylvania actually blamed Franklin for bringing about the Stamp Act, the mobs threatened to level his newly built Philadelphia house as well. His partner David Hall wished that Franklin were in Philadelphia to deal with the events, but then added, "I should be afraid for your Safety."[16] His wife, Deborah, and several of her relatives resolved to defend the new house, and that determination encouraged friends to protect her and the house successfully. But Franklin's reputation in America was not so easily defended. His enemies in Pennsylvania accused him not only of framing the Stamp Act but also of profiting from it. "*O Franklin, Franklin,* thou curse to Pennsylvania and America, may the most accumulated vengeance burst speedily on thy guilty head!" exclaimed the young Benjamin Rush, not yet the famous Philadelphia physician and friend of Franklin. Some warned that Franklin might be hanged in effigy.[17]

FRANKLIN'S RESPONSE TO THE STAMP ACT CRISIS

At first Franklin dismissed these charges and dismissed the possibility of popular rioting as well. He could not believe that Americans had become so worked up over the Stamp Act. "The Rashness of the Assembly of Virginia is amazing!" He could only hope that the Pennsylvania Assembly would act with "Prudence and Moderation; for that is the only way to lighten or get clear of our Burthens." His printing partners—David Hall in Philadelphia, James Parker in New York, and Peter Timothy in Charleston—tried to maintain Franklin's traditional policy of neutrality in their newspapers, with disastrous results. "All the Papers on the Continent, ours excepted," Hall told Franklin, "were full of Spirited Papers against the Stamp Law, and that because I did not publish those Papers likewise, I was much blamed, got a great Deal of Ill-will, and that some of our Customers had dropt on that Account." For his part, Parker, despite sometimes feeling "the true Old English Spirit of Liberty," had become resigned to "acquiesce in the Chains laid upon me." By trying to avoid the heated controversy aroused by the Stamp Act, he had lost his business to a more Whiggish rival newspaper and was even charged with being "no Friend to Liberty." In South Carolina, Timothy discovered that his declining to engage in violent opposition to the Stamp Act in his newspaper had "so exasperated every Body" that a rival paper was set up in order to destroy him. He found himself "from the most *popular* reduced to the most *unpopular* Man in the Province." It was fast becoming clear to his printing partners, if not to Franklin himself, that his policy of impartiality, which he had set forth in his 1731 "Apology for Printers," no longer made sense at a time when "the People are all running Mad." It did not help matters that both Parker and Timothy had been appointed local crown officers through the influence of Franklin.[18]

As for John Hughes and his apprehensions, Franklin told him to keep calm and persevere in executing the Stamp Act. It might make Hughes "unpopular for a time," but if Hughes acted "with Coolness and Steadiness," the people would slowly come round to accept the stamp tax. "In the meantime, a firm Loyalty to the Crown and faithful Adherence to the Government of this Nation, which it is the Safety as well as the Honour of the Colonies to be connected with, will always be the wisest Course for you and I to take, whatever may be the Madness of the Populace or their blind Leaders, who can only bring themselves and Country into Trouble, and draw on greater Burthens by Acts of rebellious Tendency."[19]

Franklin had long wanted Britain and its colonies to be "considered as one Whole, and not as different States with separate Interests," and he had thought that American representation in Parliament might be a way of bringing that union about.[20] But representation took on a new urgency as he sensed a change in the relationship between Britain and its colonies.

ENGLISH ARROGANCE

Far from coming to think of the colonists more and more as their fellow subjects, the mid-eighteenth-century English had become increasingly distanced from them. With their military successes over France, the English (not the British, for the Scots were unable to sustain any strong sense of nationhood) developed an ever keener sense of their own Englishness—a sense of nationality distinct from that of the Scots, the Irish, and the Americans who lived on the outer edges of the empire. The very success of the English in the Seven Years War, in which the British Empire became a world empire, increased this sense of English distinctiveness. The English now began to regard the North American colonists less as fellow Englishmen across the Atlantic and more as another set of people to be ruled. Indeed, in 1763 the Earl of Halifax, former head of the Board of Trade and secretary of state for the southern department in charge of the colonies during the Grenville ministry, went so far as to say that "the people of England" considered the Americans, "though H.M.'s subjects, as foreigners."[21]

As Franklin began to discover more and more during the Stamp Act crisis, Englishmen in the realm no longer regarded colonists three thousand miles away as equal to themselves. In fact, it was the English on the home island who first and most often invoked the term "Americans" to refer to the far-removed colonists. For sophisticated Englishmen, the term "American" often conjured up images of unrefined, if not barbarous, persons, degenerate and racially debased, who lived in close proximity to African slaves and Indian savages thousands of miles from civilization. They liked to emphasize that, as the eighteenth-century colonies had become a dumping ground for English criminals, one should not be surprised that the Americans were coarse, rowdy, and prone to breaking the law. Dr. Johnson was reported to have labeled the colonists "a race of convicts."[22]

Most Americans reacted to these midcentury expressions of English arrogance with defensive outrage. "Are the inhabitants of British America," asked the fiery Boston lawyer James Otis in 1765 ("our great incendiary," Hutchinson called him), "all a parcel of transported thieves, robbers, and rebels, or descended from such?"[23] Did the English think most people in North America were Negroes and mulattoes? "Are you not of the same stock?" asked a Pennsylvanian of his fellow colonists in 1760. "Was the blood of your ancestors polluted by a change of soil? Were they freemen in England and did they become slaves by a six-weeks' voyage to America?" By the 1760s and especially after 1765, the colonial press was full of these kinds of statements of indignation and fury. "Are not the People of America, BRITISH Subjects? Are they not *Englishmen*?" These were the angry and anguished cries of people who felt snubbed and deeply humiliated by their supposed cousins back home.[24]

Franklin's response was inevitably different. As a distinguished scientist and world celebrity and the recipient of several British honorary degrees, he naturally possessed a self-confidence and a sense of equality with most Britons that few of his fellow colonists could match. When he heard or read the aspersions that the English were casting upon his countrymen, he generally reacted, at least at first, not with self-protective outrage, but with reason, humor, and satire.

In the many newspaper pieces he wrote in 1765-1766 in answer to the "frequent invectives" and the "angry reflections on the Americans in the public papers," he appealed to British reasonableness and self-interest. The colonists, he pointed out, were an important source of British prosperity, both by supplying needed goods and by purchasing British manufactures. And they loved the British monarch as much as any Englishman at home. What was the purpose of all the railing against the Americans?

he asked in an anonymous piece published in a London paper in December 1765. Was all this denunciation supposed to persuade the colonists to accept the Stamp Act? "The gentle terms of *republican race, mixed rabble of Scotch, Irish and foreign vagabonds, descendants of convicts, ungrateful rebels,* &c.," he said, "are some of the sweet flowers of English rhetorick, with which our colonists have of late been regaled. Surely, if we are so much their superiors, we should shew the superiority of our breeding by our better manners!"[25]

Sarcastic responses like this—indeed, satire in general—supposed commonly understood standards of rightness and reasonableness. Since a satirist like Franklin could expose to instantaneous ridicule only what was readily considered ridiculous by his readers, he necessarily believed he was on intimate terms with them and could count on their sharing his tastes and viewpoint.[26] In 1766, writing as "Pacifus" in the English press, Franklin proposed a solution to the Stamp Act crisis that Jonathan Swift would have loved. Britain, wrote Franklin, should impose overwhelming military force on the colonists, burn all their capitals, cut the throats of every man, woman, and child in the capitals, and destroy all their trade. "No Man in his Wits, after such terrible Military Execution, will refuse to purchase stamp'd Paper," he concluded. "If any one should hesitate, five or six Hundred Lashes in a cold frosty Morning would soon bring him to Reason."[27] Naturally Franklin believed that his modest proposal was so harsh, so oppressive, and presumably so un-English that no Englishman in his right mind would contemplate it. With such satirical exaggeration Franklin assumed that he and his London readership were participating in the same moral universe—something his fellow Americans were coming increasingly to doubt. Stamp Act or no Stamp Act, Franklin had not lost hope, in other words, that the magnificent empire he admired so much could be made whole.

AMERICAN REPRESENTATION IN PARLIAMENT

But he knew things had changed. England and America seemed to be more and more two separate countries. The sense that the empire was a single community could no longer be taken for granted. If there were to be a union, it would now have to be a constructed one, more or less in the way the Act of Union of 1707 had bound together the two countries of Scotland and England to create Great Britain, and that meant American representation in Parliament. In August 1765 Franklin asked Thomas Hutchinson whether the colonists ought to apply for representation in the House of Commons. Through the fall he continued to think of colonial representation in Parliament as a solution to the imperial problems of taxation.[28] In February 1766 he published in Strahan's *London Chronicle* the letters he presumably had written to Massachusetts governor William Shirley twelve years earlier arguing the need for colonial representation in Parliament. In these letters Franklin had reminded Shirley that it was the right of Englishmen not to be taxed without their own consent and had agreed with Shirley that perhaps that consent could be satisfied by American representation in the House of Commons. It was certainly in Franklin's interest to have such letters come out in this tense moment when colonial suspicions of him were widespread.[29]

Franklin gradually came to realize that neither Americans nor Englishmen liked the idea of colonial representation in Parliament. Since Americans were becoming more and more resentful of English arrogance, he believed they would not now ask for representation in the House of Commons. But he thought the colonists would accept it if it were offered. If a union similar to that with Scotland was established with America, "which methinks it highly imports this Country to establish, it would probably subsist as long as Britain shall continue a Nation." Yet he feared that the English had become too proud and despised the Americans too much "to bear the Thought of admitting them to such an equitable Participation in the Government of the whole." Nevertheless, he clung to the idea in desperation; even as late as 1767 he thought that American representation in Parliament was the only firm basis on which the empire's "political Grandeur and Stability can be founded."[30]

In fact, the time for colonial representation in Parliament had long since passed, if it had ever existed. After the Stamp Act, Congress had pointed out in 1765 that the colonists "are not, and from their local Circumstances" could never be, represented in the House of Commons, those few patriots like James Otis who had earlier suggested colonial representation in Parliament ceased doing so. Franklin remained the great exception.[31]

FRANKLIN'S EXAMINATION BEFORE THE HOUSE OF COMMONS

Three thousand miles away, and with many of his allies royal officials, Franklin had no great ear for American public opinion, and he struggled to understand what Americans were saying. He had no liking whatsoever for mobs and rioting, but he slowly came to appreciate that even reasonable Americans would not support a stamp tax under any conditions. True to his practical nature, he searched for some sort of compromise that would hold the two countries in the empire together. He was busy everywhere, as he told the Scottish philosopher Lord Kames, "attending Members of both Houses, informing, explaining, consulting, disputing, in a continual Hurry from Morning to Night."[32] Under a variety of pseudonyms he wrote more articles for the London newspapers, reminding his English readers that the colonies and Britain had a common interest in the empire. If he were to rescue his reputation in America, he had much catching up to do.

In an interview in November 1765 with the Earl of Dartmouth, newly appointed head of the Board of Trade, Franklin declared that enforcing the Stamp Act would create more mischief than it was worth. Franklin realized that Parliament would find it difficult to back down in the face of mobbing and violence. But if the act were merely suspended for a few years, he told Dartmouth, it could eventually be dropped "on some other decent Pretence without ever bringing the question of Right to a Decision." Any attempt to enforce the act with troops, he warned, would have the effect, "by mutual Violences, Excesses and Severities, of creating a deep-rooted Aversion between the two Countries, and laying the Foundation of a future total Separation." If suspension of the tax were not possible, then, Franklin suggested to Dartmouth his usual solution to complicated political problems: "three or four wise and good Men, Personages of some Rank and Dignity, should be sent over to America, with a Royal Commission to enquire into Grievances, hear Complaints, learn the true State of Affairs, giving Expectations of Redress where they found the People really aggriev'd, and endeavouring to convince and reclaim them by Reason, where they found them in the Wrong." Perhaps such a royal commission could save the British government from its present perplexity. It was reluctant to send troops to enforce the Stamp Act, but neither did it want to repeal the act, "as it will be deem'd a tacit giving up the Sovereignty of Parliament."[33]

The sovereignty of Parliament! An awesome concept and the one over which the empire was finally broken. It is difficult for us today to appreciate the respect and wonder with which nearly all Englishmen held Parliament in the eighteenth century, certainly all Englishmen who thought of themselves as Whigs and defenders of liberty and the Glorious Revolution of 1688–1689. For all good Whigs—and indeed for all those who rejected the seventeenth-century Tory beliefs in absolute monarchy, indefeasible hereditary succession, and passive obedience—Parliament was the great defender against tyranny. It was the august author of the Bill of Rights of 1689, the historical protector of the people's property, and the eternal bulwark of their liberties against the encroachments of the Crown. The eighteenth-century Parliament may not have represented the British people in any modern democratic sense, but it certainly stood for the nation and embodied its Britishness as no other institution did.[34] In fact, Parliament was superior to the people it supposedly represented, which is why its members referred to visitors to its proceedings as "strangers," a practice still in effect today. Because Parliament was what had always stood between the power of the Crown and the liberty of the subject, to oppose Parliament in the name of liberty was incomprehensible to most Englishmen.

Once the British brought in Parliament as the instrument of reforming the empire in the 1760s, the stakes were raised to an entirely different level. Many Englishmen more or less expected the colonists to resist the power of the royal governors in the king's empire, and they were not deeply disturbed by such resistance. Indeed, during the first half of the eighteenth century, many members of Parliament with Whiggish and anticrown sympathies had themselves tended to restrain the desire of royal bureaucrats to expand the king's empire. This was in fact where the "salutary neglect" that Edmund Burke later spoke of came from. Resisting crown power was what good Whigs did. So colonial opposition to the power of the king was one thing. But opposition to the acts of Parliament was quite another thing altogether. For the Americans to oppose Parliament was unconscionable. It was Toryish and alien to the Whig understanding of politics, and it struck at all that the Glorious Revolution had been about.

Franklin was faced with the need to explain American opposition to this sacred British bastion of liberty to Englishmen in London. A lengthy examination before the House of Commons in February 1766 gave him an opportunity to begin this explanation and at the same time to recover some of his lost reputation in America. A new ministry led by Lord Rockingham had replaced the Grenville government for reasons that had nothing to do with American affairs. Nonetheless, the new ministry was eager to repeal the Stamp Act enacted by its predecessor. American boycotts of British goods were hurting British merchants, and pressure from the merchant community had convinced many members of Parliament that repeal of the Stamp Act was necessary. But the Rockingham government needed reasons for doing so and found in Franklin a means of explaining why the government had to retreat. Dr. Franklin was the celebrated American philosopher and scientist, noted everywhere for his practicality and reasonableness. If any one of the forty-odd persons called to testify on the harmful consequences of the Stamp Act could convince the House of Commons to repeal it, he could.

In four hours of testimony, Franklin performed brilliantly. Some of the questions were friendly and they gave him the opportunity to show what a mistake the Stamp Act had been. But when hostile questions were raised, he deftly parried them. Since many of his fellow Americans thought he had planned the Stamp Act, Franklin was most eager to establish his sympathy with American opposition to it. So when he was asked whether some modified stamp tax would be acceptable to Americans, his response was sharp: "No; they will never submit to it." He shot back just as quickly with "They would not pay it" when asked whether any tax similar to the stamp tax would be acceptable to the colonists. When asked, "If the stamp-act should be repealed, would it induce the assemblies of America to acknowledge the rights of parliament to tax them?" his answer was as direct as it could be: "No, never." He made it as clear as possible that Parliament had no right to lay a stamp tax on the colonists, and his pointed responses probably saved his reputation in America.

Yet when he was confronted with the question of whether Americans denied the right of Parliament to levy any kind of tax or duty whatsoever, he unwittingly revealed his distance from his fellow Americans. He said that he had "never heard any objection to the right of laying duties to regulate commerce; but a right to lay internal taxes was never supposed to be in parliament, as we are not represented there."[35] With this distinction between internal taxes, such as the stamp tax, and external taxes, such as the duties on molasses and other colonial imports, Franklin had opened up a can of worms.

Within days the repeal of the Stamp Act was moved in the House of Commons, and on March 8, 1766, the king reluctantly assented to the bill. Franklin's friend William Strahan thought that Franklin had brought about the repeal all by himself, and many in America thought so too, which was just as well, since they also thought he was responsible for the Stamp Act in the first place. His examination in the House of Commons had been taken down verbatim and was immediately published in London and later in Boston, New London, New York, Philadelphia, and Williamsburg. Charles Thomson congratulated Franklin for the repeal and told him of all the joy that was in the hearts of the colonists—"a Joy not expressed in triumph but with the warmest sentiments of Loyalty to our King and a grateful acknowledgement of the Justice and tenderness of the mother Country."[36]

Amid all the excitement few colonists noticed the price the British government had to pay to get the repeal through a reluctant House of Commons. Some opposition members had wanted to maintain what Franklin called a token tax "merely to keep up the Claim of Right."[37] But instead the government passed a Declaratory Act that asserted, in case anyone thought otherwise, that Parliament had the right to legislate for the colonies "in all cases whatsoever." This claim of Parliamentary sovereignty—the claim that there must exist in each state one final, indivisible, supreme lawmaking power—would ultimately destroy the empire.[38]

FRANKLIN'S NEW CONCEPTION OF EMPIRE

Franklin, like nearly every American, was thrilled by the repeal of the Stamp Act. He thought that it demonstrated that the empire was a working structure and that, if only the passionate irrational mobs could be ignored, reasonable men could work out their differences in an amicable manner. "We now see that tho' the Parliament may sometimes possibly thro' Misinformation be mislead to do a wrong Thing towards America, yet," he told his partner David Hall, "as soon as they are rightly inform'd, they will immediately rectify it, which ought to confirm our Veneration for that most august Body, and Confidence in its Justice and Equity." On the surface at least, he remained sanguine about the future of the British Empire—as long as all the rioting in America would "totally cease" and the colonists now behave in "a decent, dutiful, grateful" manner and show the mother country that its repeal of the Stamp Act had not been a mistake.[39]

He knew too that he personally had been through a rough patch, but life had its ups and downs. He wasn't going to let "the unthinking undiscerning Multitude" determine his mood. Sometimes it rains, sometimes it hails, he told his sister in March 1766, but then "again 'tis clear and pleasant, and the Sun shines on us." All in all, he said in his best Panglossian manner, "the World is a pretty good sort of a World; and 'tis our Duty to make the best of it and be thankful."[40]

He had lost none of his faith in the British Crown, and he was determined to get back to the reason for his mission to London—to oust the proprietors and establish Pennsylvania as a royal colony. However many doubts he may have had of Parliament's authority, the king was still the king, and of his authority over the colonies Franklin had no doubt whatsoever. During his examination in the House of Commons, Franklin had been asked how the various colonial assemblies could levy taxes for the Crown in violation of the 1688 Declaration of Rights, which stated that only the consent of Parliament could raise money for the Crown. He answered that however august a body Parliament was, its consent in matters of taxation applied only to the realm, and "the Colonies are not supposed to be within the realm; they have assemblies of their own, which are their parliaments."[41] Whether he fully realized it or not at the time, this statement suggested an entirely new way of looking at the empire.

After the repeal of the Stamp Act, thirty-three dissenting members of the House of Lords published a protest against the way the riotous colonists had been appeased. In his copy of the protest Franklin entered in the margins his retorts to the statements of the Lords. In the process he further clarified his thinking about the structure of the empire. More and more he tended to see the Crown as the benign center of the empire and Parliament as the malevolent source of tyranny.

This was not how most English Whigs then saw things. With the accession to the throne of the twenty-two-year-old George III in 1760, many Whigs sensed the signs of a revival of crown tyranny, more subtle than the Stuart tyranny of the seventeenth century because it was using influence and corruption in place of brute force. George III tried to heed his mother's wishes that he be a strong king; he ousted the Old Corps of Whig ministers and appointed his own "friends" to office, including his favorite Lord Bute, even though these friends did not have the support of the House of Commons. These actions aroused traditional Whig fears of crown influence and tyranny, which is why Edmund Burke, a good Whig and champion of Parliament, eventually became such a fervent defender of American rights against George III's despotism.

Franklin did not at all share this view of matters. As a crown officer Franklin seemed to think the king could do no wrong. The Whigs believed that Bute was the insidious and invisible power behind the throne, and that even after his dismissal from office in 1764 he was still pulling secret strings and causing all current political disturbances. But Franklin admired Bute; the king's favorite was the patron who was principally responsible for his son's being appointed royal governor of New Jersey. Given these circumstances, Franklin could not help being an enthusiast for the monarch against the tyrannical Parliament that had passed the Stamp Act, and he assumed his fellow Americans were with him. In the political context of the time his was actually an extreme Tory position, the Tories being traditionally noted for their support for broad and extensive crown authority.

When the Lords in their 1766 protest suggested that the colonists had insulted the honor of the king, Franklin was quick to reply, Not true. "All acknowledge their Subjection to his Majesty." He resented the Lords' calling the colonists "OUR North American subjects." They were not the Lords' subjects, but "the King's." In comment after comment Franklin made it clear that Parliament had no business dealing with the colonies. Indeed, throughout his comments Franklin accused the Lords, as members of Parliament, of "thrust[ing] themselves in with the Crown in the Government of the Colonies." When the Lords declared that the repeal of the Stamp Act would make the authority of Great Britain *"contemptible,"* Franklin said Great Britain's authority perhaps, but "Not the King's." When the Lords referred to the legislative authority of Great Britain over the colonies, he pointed out that "this is encroaching on the Royal Power." And when they said that Parliament's power to tax extended to all members of the state, he responded, "Right, but we are different States, subject to the King." When the Lords expressed fear that the colonists would in time claim to be "free from any obedience to the power of the British Legislature," Franklin pointedly added, "but not to the Power of the Crown." When the Lords complained that the colonists had showed "so much contempt of the Sovereignty of the British Legislature," Franklin answered, "The Sovereignty of the Crown I understand. The Sovereignty of the British Legislature out of Britain I do not understand."[42]

Following the repeal of the Stamp Act, Franklin had begun to imagine an empire in which all the colonies were tied to Great Britain solely through the king, at least until some sort of fair and equal representation of the colonies in Parliament could be worked out. "In this View they seem so many separate little States, subject to the Same Prince."[43] Modern historians have called this a "commonwealth" theory of the empire because it anticipated the idea of the empire expressed in the Statute of Westminster of 1931, which established the modern Commonwealth of Nations in which the independent dominions are tied together solely by their common allegiance to the Crown. Franklin's view was precocious. Other Revolutionary leaders, such as Thomas Jefferson, John Adams, and James Wilson, did not reach such a conception of the empire until some years later—for most of them, not until the 1770s. In the mid-1760s most of these leaders continued to accept some parliamentary authority; they, like John Dickinson in his *Letters from a Farmer in Pennsylvania,* tried to divide Parliament's power, arguing that it could not tax the colonists but could regulate their trade.[11]

These attempts to divide Parliament's power eventually proved futile.

The British argued relentlessly and unyieldingly that Parliament was sovereign and that its power was supreme, indivisible, and final. All British subjects, British officials said over and over in the years after 1766, were either totally under this supreme Parliamentary authority or totally outside it; there could be no middle ground. This was the view that lay behind Parliament's Declaratory Act of 1766. Confronted with these powerful arguments for the complete sovereignty of Parliament, Franklin in 1768 found himself increasingly confirmed in his opinion "that no middle doctrine can be well maintained.... Something might be made of either of the extremes; that Parliament has a power to make *all laws* for us, or that it has a power to make *no laws* for us."[45] Given this choice, most Americans decided that Parliament had no power to make any laws for them. Of course, this position, reached by nearly all American leaders by 1774, did not satisfactorily explain previous colonial experience in the empire, since the colonists had obeyed many Parliamentary statutes in the past.

Still, Franklin was anxious to stifle "publick Discussion of Questions that had better never have been started," and thus he hesitated to follow out the logic of this doctrine of sovereignty.[46] Instead, he continued to cling to the hope of uniting the two countries, Britain and America, through parliamentary representation in the way Scotland and England had been united in 1707. In the meantime, as a royal officeholder, he continued to celebrate his personal connection to the king. "I am a Subject of the Crown of Great Britain," he wrote at the end of the Lords' protest. "[I] have ever been a loyal one, have partaken of its Favours."[47] His king and queen, he told Polly Stevenson in 1767, remained "the very best in the World and the most amiable."[48] The crisis over the Stamp Act had eroded none of his earlier confidence in the king. Even now he continued to work hard to destroy the Penns' charter and bring royal government to Pennsylvania.

TOO ENGLISH IN AMERICA AND TOO AMERICAN IN ENGLAND

For the next four or five years after 1766 Franklin was ambivalent about the nature of England's relation to America. He felt himself caught in a widening gulf, one that he tried desperately to bridge. "Being born and bred in one of the countries, and having lived long and made many agreeable connections of friendship in the other," he could only "wish all prosperity to both." Being unideological in an intensely ideological age made him seem a man apart and out of touch with his times. He talked and wrote and sought to explain each side to the other until he was weary with the effort—especially since he seemed to have no effect in either country, "except that of rendering myself suspected by my impartiality." The English thought him too American, while the Americans thought him too English.[49] Inevitably he was accused of having "no fixed principles at all."[50]

He continued to write dozens of pieces for the British press, posing sometimes as a colonist, many other times as an Englishman. Far from being simply the experimenter in electricity, he was fast becoming known as a thinker and publicist—as a writer, something he always valued as "a principal Means of my Advancement" in the world.[51] The famous portrait of him by David Martin, exhibited in 1767, makes no reference to electricity but shows him merely as a learned man deeply involved in reading and writing (see page 126). Franklin liked the painting so much that he had a copy made at his own expense and sent it to Deborah in Philadelphia. In his will he left the portrait to the executive council of Pennsylvania; it was how he wanted to be remembered.[52]

In his many writings for the press he tried to be evenhanded, and he did all he could to calm the passions of both sides. Perhaps, as has been suggested, he was conditioned to act impartially by his earlier experience as a printer—an experience that he had tried to codify in his "Apology for Printers."[53] Just as he had tried to avoid libel and abuse in his newspaper, so did he try to smooth over the political debate between Britain and its colonies. Scurrilous attacks in the press, he said, were not helping the situation at all. He told his partner David Hall that he agreed wholeheartedly with Hall's decision to avoid printing inflammatory pieces in the *Pennsylvania Gazette* at the time of the Stamp Act crisis. He would have done the same, even if he had held no crown office. The colonists had to realize that such incendiary writing was only making matters worse. "At the same time that we Americans wish not to be judged of, in the gross by particular papers written by anonymous scribblers and published in the

Franklin, by David Martin, 1766

colonies," Franklin wrote to his son, William, in 1767, "it would be well if we could avoid falling into the same mistake in America in judging of ministers here by the libels printed against them." He saw his role as a reporter of the arguments of both sides. He had an obligation to lower the heat and lessen the passions of opinion—"to extenuate matters a little," he said.[54]

CONSPIRACIES ON BOTH SIDES

Franklin was especially appalled by all the talk of conspiracy and hidden designs that existed on both sides of the Atlantic. It was not that seeing conspiracies and plots was unusual; in fact, such conspiratorial interpretations—attributing events to the concerted designs of willful individuals—were common to the age. This pre-modern society lacked our modern repertory of impersonal forces such as "industrialization," "urbanization," or the "stream of history," which we so blithely invoke to explain complicated combinations of events. It had as yet little understanding of the indeliberate and unintended processes of history. It tended to ask of events not "How did they happen?" but "Who did them?" The moral order of the world depended on answering the latter question correctly. Although the world was becoming more and more complicated and was outrunning people's capacity to explain it in personal terms, many Englishmen on both sides of the Atlantic still sought to hold particular individuals morally responsible for all that happened. Since, as one colonial clergyman declared in 1770, "every moral event must have . . . a moral cause," by which he meant a motive, then every immoral event must have an immoral cause, which could be found in the evil motives of dissembling and designing individuals.[55]

Thus English officials thought that some of the colonial leaders were rebellious and were conspiring to throw off British rule and become independent. Events in Massachusetts in 1768 convinced the House of Lords, for example, that "wicked and designing men" in the colonies were "evidently manifesting a design . . . to set up a new and unconstitutional authority independent of the crown of England." The answer to such plots was to send fleets and troops to the colonies and bring the principal rebels back to England to be hanged. The Americans, for their part, could only conclude that what was happening to them was the result of the concerted designs of purposeful individuals, and thus they were prone to see ministerial plots everywhere against their liberties—indeed, against English liberty in general. Someone as sophisticated as Thomas Jefferson, for example, might ascribe "single acts of tyranny . . . to the accidental opinion of a day; but a series of oppressions, begun at a distinguished period and pursued unalterably thro' every change of ministers, too plainly prove a deliberate and systematical plan of reducing us to slavery." In such a frame of mind everything that happened in England took on a heightened meaning. The colonists came to believe, for instance, that the fate of the English radical John Wilkes and his riotous supporters was intimately involved with their own; he and they were both fighting for English liberty against an oppressive establishment.[56]

John Wilkes, the man the Americans came to champion in the 1760s, was one of the greatest demagogues in English history. He was an impoverished gentleman and journalist with a seedy reputation, but he had the patronage of Lord Temple and had become a member of Parliament. In 1763 he had been imprisoned for publishing a libel against the king in No. 45 of his newspaper the *North Briton*. The House of Commons ordered the offending issue of the paper publicly burned. Wilkes fled to France, and the English courts declared him an outlaw. In 1768 Wilkes returned to England and was several times elected to the House of Commons, but each time Parliament denied him his seat. Huge London crowds, crying "Wilkes and liberty" and backed by thousands of the kinds of middling people from whom Franklin himself had sprung—shopkeepers, tradesmen, petty merchants, and others denied a substantial role in English politics—took to the streets in tumultuous riots that the authorities were unable to contain. The windows of the Lord Mayor's Mansion House as well as those of every house that refused "to put out lights for Mr. Wilkes" were smashed. Finally, on May 10, 1768, troops fired on the Wilkesite mobs in St. George's Fields in London, killing eleven and wounding a dozen others, including several bystanders. This "massacre," as it was called, provoked even more disturbances and rioting over the following months.[57]

When the colonists learned of these events, they turned Wilkes into an American hero. "Wilkes and liberty" was toasted up and down the coast of North America. The colonists made the No. 45 into a symbol of liberty; they named towns and children after Wilkes, raised money for his cause, and opened up communications with him. The suppression of Wilkes and his repeated exclusion from Parliament seemed to the Americans to represent all that was wrong with Britain's corrupt and oligarchic politics. To most Americans, Wilkes was not a rioter and demagogue but a victim of British tyranny.[58]

Experiencing the Wilkesite mobs firsthand, Franklin had a very different view. He hated mobs, all mobs, but the "drunken mad mobs" stirred up by Wilkes were the worst anyone had ever witnessed. "The scenes," he told his son, the royal governor of New Jersey, "have been horrible." For the life of him he could not understand how Americans could turn Wilkes into a hero. As far as he was concerned, Wilkes was "an outlaw and an exile, of bad personal character, not worth a farthing." He was appalled to learn that some Americans were applauding Wilkes's

No. 45, "which I suppose they do not know was a Paper in which their King was personally affronted, whom I am sure they love and honour." When "sober sensible Men" in England saw the colonists "so easily infected with the Madness of English Mobs," America's reputation was seriously hurt.

But the mobbing suggested to Franklin that Britain itself was in trouble. How could someone of Wilkes's reputation even dare to come over from France and set himself up for election to the House of Commons? The country seemed to be going to the dogs. "All respect to law and government," he told Galloway, "seems to be lost among the common people, who are moreover continually enflamed by seditious scribblers to trample on authority and every thing that used to keep them in order." The action of the troops in the "massacre" at St. George's Fields infuriated some English leaders, especially, he said, since a Scottish regiment had done the shooting. As a result, several soldiers were imprisoned. "If they are not hanged," he said, "it is feared there will be more and greater mobs; and if they are [hanged], that no soldier will assist in suppressing any mob hereafter. The prospect either way is gloomy." Something had to be done. Instead of "angry declaimers on both sides the water" blowing up the flames of discord, Franklin wanted a few prudent men promoting concord and harmony.[59]

With all their talk of deliberate designs and conspiracies, both British officials and American leaders, he concluded, seemed to have lost their senses. "To be apprehensive of chimerical dangers, to be alarmed at trifles, to suspect plots and deep designs where none exist, to regard as mortal enemies those who are really our nearest and best friends, and to be very abusive"—what could such ideas be but a kind of insanity? Perhaps because he saw the disarray of the British government close up—the officials' lack of any intimate knowledge of America, the shuffling of men in and out of office for reasons that had nothing to do with America—he saw confusion, passion, stupidity, and arrogance, but no plots and designs. Amid all the conspiratorial thinking on both sides he could only sigh and shake his head at the foolishness of people. He spent most of his energy in these years of the imperial crisis trying "to palliate matters" and to mitigate the "Railing and reviling" of zealots and dissidents who were only widening the breach between England and her colonies.[60]

THE TOWNSHEND DUTIES AS EXTERNAL TAXES

Living in London, Franklin was often able to sense what the English were up to, but he had a much harder time gauging American opinion. In June 1767, Chancellor of the Exchequer Charles Townshend seemed to take to heart Franklin's earlier distinction between external and internal taxes voiced during his examination in Parliament, and decided to levy customs duties, or external taxes, on a number of British products shipped to the colonies, including paper, glass, paint, and tea. Perhaps Townshend, like many in London, believed that Franklin represented American opinion. If so, Townshend would have thought he was doing the right thing: as late as that April, Franklin stated categorically in the London press that "the colonies submit to pay all external taxes laid on them by way of duty on merchandizes imported into their country, and never disputed the authority of parliament to lay such duties."[61]

Such statements again reveal Franklin's difficulty in catching up with American opinion. Even after the Townshend duties were passed, he continued to describe them as *external* taxes and therefore in his opinion well within Parliament's authority to levy. When he learned of the colonists' outcry against the duties and the American nonimportation agreements boycotting British goods, his first impulse was not to deny the constitutionality of the duties but to try to placate the English and quiet the Americans. He tried to explain to the English the various sources of the colonists' anger, including the prohibitions on their manufacturing hats and iron products. Above all, he wanted to assure the English that the colonists, "notwithstanding the reproaches thrown out against us," were "truly a loyal people." Indeed, he wrote in the *London Chronicle* in 1768, "there is not a single native of our country who is not firmly attached to his King by principle and by affection."[62] At the same time he urged his fellow Americans to be patient and quiet, avoid tumults, and "hold fast [our] Loyalty to our King, (who has the best Disposition towards us, and has a Family Interest in our Prosperity)." Above all, he said to his countrymen, do not do anything that would lose the sympathy of the English people, who were not at fault, their being of "a noble and generous Nature."[63]

FRANKLIN AND HIS PHILADELPHIA FAMILY

By 1768 his original mission had become less and less meaningful. Little hope of Pennsylvania's becoming a royal colony remained. Yet Franklin lingered on in London. He had lived, he said, "so great a Part of my Life in Britain," and had "formed so many Friendships in it," that he could not help loving the mother country.[64] He was enjoying the city, going to his clubs, meeting people, not just ordinary people but royalty. He was flattered that the king of Denmark, Christian VII, who was visiting England in 1768, expressed a desire to meet and converse with him. And so he dined with the king, as he explained in an effusive letter to William in which he proudly drew the table to show where each dinner guest sat.[65] There was nothing in Philadelphia to match that. Although he told people in Pennsylvania—including his wife, who kept pleading with him to come back home—that he would soon return, he kept putting off the move.

Franklin seemed virtually to have put Deborah out of his mind as a wife and lover; instead, he more and more regarded her as an informant about the lives and deaths of people they knew in America and the manager of his business affairs back in Philadelphia. For her part Deborah remained, as she often signed herself, his "a feck shonet wife," who continued to supply him with long and rambling letters that were difficult to read. They were full of her chaotic spellings and unpunctuated streams of thoughts, but wonderfully warm and detailed, crammed with the everyday routines of life in Philadelphia and with minute descriptions of the new house Franklin had never seen. Despite the jealousy she must have felt toward her husband's Craven Street family, she always managed to end her letters by sending her "love" and "Compleymentes" to "good Mrs. Stephenson" and her daughter. As with many wives in that patriarchal age, her love was mingled with respect and even awe of her husband, doubly so because of Franklin's fame. She hesitated to say "anything to you that will give you aney uneseynes" and feared constantly to do the smallest thing, "leste it shold not be write." She particularly hesitated to inform him of the engagement of their daughter, Sally, to Richard Bache, who ran a dry goods store in Philadelphia. "Obliged to be father and mother," she had agreed to the engagement. "I hope I ackte to your Satisfackshon."[66]

Franklin was not happy with a storekeeper for a son-in-law, and despite Deborah's continual expectation of his imminent return, told his wife that he wouldn't be coming back that year, 1767, either. He made no comment about missing his only daughter's wedding and instead warned Deborah not to spend too much money on the occasion. He emphasized that he was living in London "as frugally as possible not to be destitute of the Comforts of Life." Life on Craven Street may not have been luxurious but it was certainly comfortable, comfortable enough for him to take in the children of distant relatives and the illegitimate son of William, whom William passed off as the son of a poor relation. His surrogate London family on Craven Street seemed in many ways preferable to his real one back in Philadelphia. Mrs. Stevenson catered to all of his needs as well as Deborah could have, and Mrs. Stevenson's daughter Polly was more lively and intelligent than Sally Franklin. No wonder that a friend visiting him in 1769 reported that "Doctor Franklin looks heartier than I ever knew him in America."[67]

Deborah became more and more discouraged over Franklin's absence. Some were telling her in 1767 that Franklin was coming home that summer, but others said he was not. As for her, she could not say, "as I am in the darke and my life of old age is one Contineuwd State of suspens." In 1768 she complained for the first time that all her responsibilities were "very harde" on her, since she was now more than sixty. A year later she suffered a stroke, from which she only slowly recovered. She blamed the stroke on her distress over Franklin's "staying so much longer" than she had expected. Franklin never replied to this remark but instead kept on her about her accounts. When in 1771 she overran her expenses he cruelly admonished her: "You were not very attentive to Money-matters in your best Days," he told her, "and I apprehend that your Memory is too much impair'd for the Management of unlimited Sums, without injuring the future Fortune of your Daughter and Grandson." At the same time as Deborah was telling him that she was "growing verey febel verey faste," he was informing her that he had just returned from a monthlong journey, "which has given a new Spring to my Health and Spirits." As her mind and health deteriorated, Franklin's letters to her became more and more perfunctory: he asked nothing about her condition and told her very little about his life. She never stopped asking when he was coming home. In 1773, nine years from the time he had last seen her, Franklin told his wife that he hesitated to return to America for fear "I shall find myself a Stranger in my Own Country; and leaving so many Friends here, it will seem leaving Home to go there."[68] She wrote her last letter to him on October 29, 1773. She died a year later, in December 1774.

TO BE USEFUL TO GOVERNMENT

In 1768 Franklin had a new reason for making London his permanent home. The English government finally decided that American affairs merited their own executive department, and rumor spread that the government might even draw on American expertise to help run it. That January, Franklin told his son that there was talk of his being appointed an undersecretary in the new department. Since he thought the government considered him to be "too much of an American," he was skeptical of the rumors. Besides, with the constant change of ministers nothing was certain anymore.[69]

By the late spring of 1768, however, Franklin had something more concrete than rumors to excite him. The secretary to the Treasury, Grey Cooper—"my fast friend," Franklin called him—dangled before him the possibility of Franklin's having a subministerial position in the Grafton government. This would settle the matter once and for all of returning home. One of the reasons Franklin had contemplated going home to Philadelphia was to protect his position as deputy postmaster, a royal office that his enemies threatened to take from him and one he did not want to lose. Indeed, he was convinced that because he had made the office profitable he "had some kind of Right to it."[70] The Earl of Sandwich, the postmaster general and Franklin's boss, thought that Franklin ought either to return to America and run his post office there or resign the office. Cooper (who, in Sir John Pringle's opinion, was "the honestest man of a courtier that he ever knew") informed Franklin that the Duke of Grafton, the head of the Treasury and chief minister, might have a solution to his dilemma. If Franklin wanted to maintain his post office position, fine, said Grafton, then he could return to America. "Yet," as Franklin relayed what

Grafton had said, "if I chose rather to remain in England, my merit was such in [Grafton's] opinion, as to entitle me to something better here, and it should not be his fault if I was not well provided for."

Franklin was obviously excited by this possibility, but he did not want to show it. He did tell Cooper, however, that he had lived so long in England and had so many friends here that "it could not but be agreeable to me to remain among them some time longer, if not for the rest of my life." He added in the best courtier fashion that "there was no nobleman to whom I could from sincere respect for his great abilities and amiable qualities, so cordially attach myself, or to whom I should so willingly be obliged for the provision he mentioned, as to the Duke of Grafton, if his Grace should think I could, in any station where he might place me, be serviceable to him and to the public."[71]

At Cooper's urging Franklin called on Grafton in the early summer of 1768, but Grafton apologetically broke several appointments. Franklin, however, did get to meet with Frederick North, the Earl of Guildford, who was chancellor of the exchequer and Grafton's close colleague. North told Franklin that if he could be persuaded to stay in England, the government hoped to "find some way of making it worth your while." Franklin replied that he would "stay with pleasure if I could any ways be useful to government." Franklin believed that if a post were offered him he could not turn it down. It would be a terrible mistake, he told his son, "to decline any favour so great a man expressed an inclination to do me, because at court if one shews an unwillingness to be obliged it is often construed as a mark of mental hostility, and one makes an enemy." Of course, Franklin told everybody that he was going to go home to America, but, as he confided to his son, this was just in case the offer of a position fell through. Although he did not want to lose face by being rejected, he very much wanted an office in the government. This "flattering expectation" was a dream come true. At last, he might be able to bring some reason to bear on the imperial crisis and help to save the empire that he had loved so much.[72]

Cooper introduced Franklin to other members of the government, whom he thoroughly charmed—at least he said he did. He made friends with the secretary to the post office, Anthony Todd, and, as he told his son, he completely won over Lord Clare, the former head of the Board of Trade. Clare, he said, had liked him ever since his examination before the House of Commons "for the spirit I showed in defence of my country. . . . At parting, after we had drank a bottle and half of claret each, he hugged and kissed me, protesting he never in his life met with a man he was so much in love with." Although Franklin self-protectively played down the possibility of an office in the ministry, he was very much dazzled by the prospect.[73]

THE CONFRONTATION WITH LORD HILLSBOROUGH

Already, Franklin was concocting land schemes in the North American West that would help to realize some of his dreams for the British Empire and make some money for him besides. As governor of New Jersey, his son William had participated in treaty negotiations with the Indians in 1768 and had arranged land deals involving hundreds of thousands of acres in the West. In order to get the scheme approved by the Crown, the American speculators made Franklin a partner and asked him for help in recruiting support. Franklin brought in a number of his friends and pressured others, including Grey Cooper, secretary to the Treasury, to join. The Franklins were important, but the real heavyweights in the company were Thomas and Richard Walpole, nephews of the great former chief minister, Sir Robert Walpole. Although the company was officially called the Grand Ohio Company, everyone referred to it as the Walpole Company.[74]

Lord Hillsborough was the head of the new American Department and not at all happy with this Walpole Company. As an Anglo-Irish landlord with nearly 20,000 tenants on his huge estates in County Down, he was very much opposed to any land schemes that would encourage settlers to migrate from the British Isles to North America, especially tenants in search of freehold land. Already some Britons were becoming apprehensive that too many of their countrymen were depopulating the British Isles, creating deserted villages and half-empty estates. During these years leading up to the Revolution there was talk everywhere in Britain of desperate measures, including parliamentary legislation, to curb the emigration of Britons to America.[75]

When the Walpole partners first approached Hillsborough as secretary of the American Department, they asked for a grant of only 2.5 million acres for their company. Hillsborough told them that they were too modest: ask for 20 million acres, he suggested. This was a duplicitous suggestion, as Franklin later realized, but the Walpole speculators bought it and upped their request to 20 million acres—one of the biggest land grabs in world history. Hillsborough actually hoped that such a grandiose claim would discredit the whole project and prevent its getting a royal charter. He wanted to diminish the power of the colonies, not help them grow.

Hillsborough had emerged as very much a hard-liner on American affairs, eager to put the rebellious colonists in their place. When in February 1768 the Massachusetts assembly issued to the other colonies a "Circular Letter" denouncing the Townshend duties as unconstitutional, Hillsborough ordered the legislature to rescind its action. Once the assembly refused and mobbing broke out in Boston, Hillsborough dispatched two regiments of troops to Massachusetts. With nearly 4000 armed redcoats in the crowded seaport of 15,000 inhabitants, Boston was set up for a confrontation, and with the "massacre" of March 1770, in which five civilians were killed by British soldiers, it got one.

Franklin expressed a great deal of sympathy with Massachusetts, which he now regarded as his homeland as much as Pennsylvania. In letters that reached the Massachusetts patriots, he described the colonies as distinct states in the empire, under no parliamentary authority whatsoever. Even before he learned of the Boston Massacre, he told the colony's patriots that the Duke of Bedford's party, which dominated the government, was full of malice toward the colonists and was just looking for a pretext to order soldiers "to make a Massacre among us." By identifying himself with his countrymen in this way and by referring to the soldiers in Boston as "detestable Murderers," Franklin won over enough sympathizers in the Massachusetts assembly to be named its agent in London.[76] He was already agent of Pennsylvania, New Jersey, and Georgia—an indication that the colonists were finding it difficult to locate anyone in London who could lobby on their behalf. But though the Massachusetts assembly agreed to Franklin's appointment as its agent, some important patriots in the colony, including Samuel Adams, had been opposed to appointing him, being unsure that he was really one of them.

In January 1771 Franklin went to see Hillsborough, the secretary of state for American affairs, to present his credentials as the agent for the Massachusetts assembly. The confrontation was an important experience for Franklin, so important, in fact, that he immediately went home and wrote it all down in the form of a dramatic dialogue—the better to demonstrate to some of his skeptical Massachusetts constituents his devotion to American interests.

On the day of the meeting he was surprised to be ushered in to see the secretary ahead of others who were waiting. He apologized to Lord Hillsborough, saying he had only wanted to pay his respects and acquaint the secretary with his appointment by the Massachusetts House of Representatives. Upon hearing the name "Massachusetts," Hillsborough cut Franklin short and told him, "with something between a Smile and a Sneer," that he would not accept his appointment, since the assembly had no right to appoint an agent without the consent of the governor. The dialogue went on for a number of minutes until Hillsborough, *"with a mix'd look of Anger and Contempt,"* declared that he would not dispute the matter further with Franklin. After a few more exchanges, Franklin finally withdrew. But not without a parting shot: "It is I believe of no great Importance whether the Appointment is acknowledged or not," he told Hillsborough, "for I have not the least Conception that an Agent can *at present* be of any Use, to any of the Colonies."[77]

Although this remark infuriated Hillsborough, Franklin at first did not care. He had only contempt for Hillsborough's abilities and defined his character as a combination of "Conceit, Wrongheadedness, Obstinacy and Passion." If it came to a knockdown political struggle between the two of them, Franklin thought that he had sufficient influence with prominent men in the government to win and that Hillsborough would be removed from office. "One Encouragement I have, the Knowledge that he is not a Whit better lik'd by his Colleagues in the Ministry than he is by me, and that he cannot probably continue where he is much longer, and that he can scarce be succeeded by anybody who will not like me the better for his having been at Variance with me."[78]

But Franklin was mistaken, and once he realized that Hillsborough did indeed have the backing of the government, he was shocked and became deeply depressed. He realized, as Strahan explained to William Franklin, that he was "not only on bad Terms with Lord Hillsborough, but with the *Ministry in general*."[79] All the flattering expectations that he had had over the previous three years of his becoming an important player in imperial affairs were suddenly shattered.

THE *AUTOBIOGRAPHY*

It was in the aftermath of this dramatic failure in 1771 that Franklin began reflecting upon his remarkable life. For the next six months he was confused, irritable, and dispirited. He thought himself useless and seemed to lose all his zest and ambition. He was angry at the system that he had tried and failed to conquer. No longer did he refer to England as "home." America became the "home" he increasingly began to long for.[80]

Poor Richard Bache, Franklin's new son-in-law, came to England seeking Franklin's help in acquiring a government position at this moment, which was just the wrong time. In his anger and depression Franklin told his son-in-law to go back to Philadelphia, become a businessman, and "by Industry and Frugality" and a hardworking wife "get forward in the World"—in other words, follow the early career of his famous father-in-law. "Almost any Profession a Man has been educated in," said Franklin, "is preferable to an Office held at Pleasure, as rendering him more independent, more a Freeman [and] less subject to the Caprices of Superiors."[81] This from a man who had held a crown office at pleasure for eighteen years and who recently had been ardently hoping for another one.

To ease his bitterness and his depression Franklin set out on a series of journeys around the British Isles, and on one of these visits in the summer of 1771, to the country house of his friend Jonathan Shipley, Bishop of St. Asaph, he began writing his *Autobiography*.

The first part of his life, up to age twenty-five—the best part, most critics have agreed—was thus written in a mood of frustration, nostalgia, and defiance. Look, he suggested in this first part of his memoir, he was not really a dependent courtier seeking office at some superior's pleasure; he was a free man who against overwhelming odds had made it as a hardworking and independent tradesman. This first section of his *Autobiography* thus became a salve for his wounds and a justification for his apparent failure in British politics.

Franklin explicitly addressed the *Autobiography* to his son William, stating at one point that it had been written with the intention "of gratifying the suppos'd Curiosity of my Son." Some scholars have suggested that this was simply a literary device common to memoirs in the early modern period, but it is more likely that Franklin actually did intend the first part of his memoir for his son, perhaps partly as an admonishment to William to cut his expenses and do as his father had done.[82] As early as 1750, Franklin had worried that his son might not be as industrious as he had been; and he had warned the young man that he intended to spend his money before he died. Not for Franklin the "absurd" English practice of leaving a huge estate.[83]

Of course, in at least one respect William had done exactly what his father had done. In 1760 he had indulged "that hard-to-be-govern'd Passion of Youth" with an unknown woman and, like the young Benjamin Franklin, had fathered an illegitimate son, whom he named William Temple. But, unlike his father, William Franklin had been raised as a gentleman from birth and had taken that for granted. Certainly the first part of Franklin's memoir reminded William that his father had not had William's privileged upbringing and implied that the best course for a young man was to make his own way in the world. In a letter to William telling him about the advice Franklin had recently given his son-in-law, Richard Bache, Franklin could not help stressing his desire "to see all I am connected with in an Independent Situation supported by their own Industry."[84]

THE AFFAIR OF THE HUTCHINSON LETTERS

Suddenly, however, the signals from the British government shifted and became more positive. During travels in Ireland that fall, Franklin met Lord Hillsborough, who to his amazement changed his tone toward him.

His lordship even invited him to his Irish estates, where Franklin was "detain'd by a 1000 Civilities from Tuesday to Sunday."[85] Franklin was bewildered and wondered what this shift of attitude meant. Even better, in August 1772 Hillsborough was finally ousted from the ministry, and Lord Dartmouth, whom Franklin knew and liked, was appointed in his place.

Franklin recovered some of his earlier sense of his importance in English politics and actually thought he himself might have had something to do with Hillsborough's resignation and Dartmouth's appointment. Since Dartmouth was sympathetic to America and western expansion and land speculation, and had "express'd some personal Regard for me," Franklin hoped it would now be much easier to transact imperial business.[86] And who knows, maybe a subministerial position might materialize after all? With his earlier expectations renewed, he immediately dropped the writing of his *Autobiography*, which he would not resume until 1784 in France, following the successful negotiation of the treaty establishing American independence.

By August 1772 Franklin was as optimistic as he had ever been. He once more felt immune to the slings and arrows of his enemies, who had tried to injure him and take away his crown office. For years popular images of him, including medallions made by Josiah Wedgwood, had circulated throughout the British Isles, and he had become by far the most famous American in Britain and indeed in the world. He bragged to his son of how much the intellectual community respected him and how many friends he had in Britain—"my company so much desired that I seldom dine at home in winter, and could spend the whole summer in the country houses of inviting friends, if I chose it." Even the king "too has lately been heard to speak of me with great regard."[87]

With this heightened sense that he once again could be a significant figure in imperial politics and might be able finally to reconcile the colonies and the mother country, Franklin became involved in the affair of the Hutchinson letters. This affair was the most extraordinary and revealing incident in his political life. It effectively destroyed his position in England and ultimately made him a patriot.[88]

In the late 1760s, Thomas Hutchinson, then lieutenant governor of Massachusetts, as part of a small group that included Andrew Oliver,

Franklin, porcelain medallion by Josiah Wedgwood, 1778

Hutchinson's brother-in-law, had written some letters to a British undersecretary, Thomas Whately. In these letters Hutchinson especially urged that stern measures, including "an abridgment of what are called English liberties," were needed in America to maintain the colonies' dependency on Great Britain. If nothing was done, "or nothing more than some declaratory acts or resolves," Hutchinson had written in January 1769, "*it is all over with us.* The friends . . . of anarchy will be afraid of nothing be it ever so extravagant."[89]

After Thomas Whately's death in 1772, Franklin was given these letters, which included some from Andrew Oliver, by "a Gentleman of Character and Distinction" (no one knows who).[90] That December he sent them to Massachusetts in order, as he said, to convince key persons in the colony that blame for the imperial crisis lay solely with a few mischievous colonial officials like Hutchinson, who was now the royal governor of the colony.[91] These native officials, and not the British government in London, were the ones who had bartered "away the Liberties of their native Country for Posts" and betrayed the interest of not only Massachusetts but the Crown they pretended to serve, and indeed, the interest of "the whole English Empire." The ministry in England, Franklin suggested, was not conspiring against American liberty after all. It had been misled by the evil counsel of these "mere Time-servers" whose letters back to London "laid the Foundation of most if not all our present Grievances." These local American officials were the persons who actually created the "Enmities between the different Countries of which the Empire consists."[92]

By this action Franklin was willing to make Thomas Hutchinson, his former friend and colleague at the Albany Congress, a scapegoat for the whole imperial crisis. Indeed, he actually had the nerve to say of Hutchinson and Oliver that "if they are good Men, and agree that all good Men wish a good Understanding and Harmony to subsist between the Colonies and their Mother Country, they ought the less to regret, that at the small Expence of their Reputation for Sincerity and Publick Spirit among their Compatriots, so desirable an Event may in some degree be forwarded." In other words, said Franklin, perhaps with as much naïveté as cynicism, if Hutchinson and Oliver, Hutchinson's successor as lieutenant governor, truly cared about the empire, they ought to be willing to be scapegoats and accept the sacrifice of their reputations for the sake of bringing about an Anglo-American reconciliation.[93]

With the Hutchinson letters as evidence, Franklin believed that the present government in London would be cleared of responsibility for the crisis in the empire and the way would be opened for rational settlement of the differences between the mother country and her colonies. Once the colonists saw where blame for the imperial crisis truly lay, then their hostility toward the British ministry would eventually subside. As Lord Dartmouth, the new pro-American secretary of the American Department, told Franklin, time was needed for passions to cool. Besides, Franklin noted, time was on America's side. "Our growing Strength both in Wealth and Numbers . . . will make us more respectable, our Friendship more valued, and our Enmity feared; thence it will soon be thought proper to treat us, not with Justice only, but with Kindness." Thus Franklin advised the Massachusetts patriots "to be quiet," and give "no fresh Offence to Government." By all means, stick up for "our Rights" in resolutions and memorials, but, he said, bear "patiently the little present Notice that is taken of them." In the meantime Lord Dartmouth, with Franklin's help, would have an opportunity to straighten things out and save the empire.[94]

This was a spectacular miscalculation, so spectacular a miscalculation in fact that it raises questions once again about Franklin's political judgment and his understanding of the emotions involved in the imperial crisis.[95] Franklin actually thought that he and a few men of goodwill could head off the crisis. As late as 1775 he was still persuaded that the issues separating Britain and the colonies were merely "a Matter of Punctilio, which Two or three reasonable People might settle in half an Hour."[96] In fact, as his earlier mistakes over trying to make Pennsylvania a royal colony and getting Americans to accept the Stamp Act indicate, Franklin was not always a shrewd politician, at least not when it came to judging popular passions.

To be sure, he was free of the wild suspicions and conspiratorial notions that beguiled many on both sides of the imperial conflict. But he suffered from a naïve confidence in the power of reason and a few sensible men to arrange complicated and impassioned matters. He always thanked God for giving him "a reasonable Mind . . . with moderate Passions, or so much of his gracious Assistance in governing them," that freed him, he said, from much of the "Uneasiness" that afflicted other men. He was by nature a conciliator. Just as "every Affront is not worth a Duel," and "every Injury not worth a War," so too, he was fond of saying, "every Mistake in Government, every Incroachment on Rights is not worth a Rebellion."[97] It was as if he were temperamentally incapable of comprehending popular emotions in America, emotions whose extent and intensity severely limited the ability of a small number of individuals to manipulate events and reach compromises. It had been his problem ever since at least the time of the Stamp Act, if not of the Albany Plan.

The consequences of Franklin's sending the Hutchinson letters to Massachusetts could not have been worse, both to him personally and to the relationship between Britain and her colonies. Although Franklin had stipulated that the Hutchinson–Oliver letters not be published but instead be circulated among only a few "Men of Worth" in Massachusetts, he should not have been surprised that by June 1773 they were published as a pamphlet and distributed throughout the colony. The title page of this pamphlet told its readers that they would discover "the fatal source of the confusion and bloodshed in which this province especially has been involved and which threatened total destruction to the liberties of all *America.*"[98]

The published letters created an uproar in Massachusetts. The House of Representatives immediately petitioned the Crown to recall Hutchinson and Oliver. In presenting the Massachusetts petition to Lord Dartmouth, Franklin thought his plan had worked. He tried to persuade the secretary for American affairs that the people of Massachusetts, "having lately discovered, as they think, the authors of their grievances to be some of their own people, their resentment against Britain is thence much abated."[99]

Franklin could not have been more wrong. Rather than becoming less resentful of Britain, the Massachusetts colonists were angrier than ever at the mother country. The revelation of the letters seemed to confirm the conspiracy against their liberty that Americans earlier had only feared and suspected. Those letters gave proof, declared the Boston Committee of Correspondence, that God had "wonderfully interposed to bring to light the plot that has been laid for us by our malicious and invidious enemies."[100] The Massachusetts radicals looked for an opportunity to renew the struggle, and on December 16, 1773, taking advantage of that year's British Tea Act, which gave a monopoly to the East India Company to sell tea in America, they dumped £10,000 of British tea into Boston harbor.

When the Hutchinson letters were published in England that August, everyone wanted to know how they had been obtained. William Whately, the brother of the deceased Thomas Whately, thought that an imperial bureaucrat, John Temple, was the culprit and challenged him to a duel, in which Whately was wounded. When a second challenge followed, Franklin felt he could no longer keep silent, and in December 1773 he publicly confessed to having sent the letters to Boston, but he never revealed how he had obtained them. Although he scarcely anticipated the remarkable British reaction to this confession, his confidence in his ability to calm the imperial crisis was already fast eroding.

BULLBAITING IN THE COCKPIT

Within weeks of the publication of the Hutchinson letters in England, Franklin sensed that his efforts to absolve the ministry for the imperial crisis were not turning out as he had hoped. When he realized that British officials were not cooperating to save the empire, he composed two of his most brilliant satires, "Rules by Which a Great Empire May Be Reduced to a Small One" and "An Edict by the King of Prussia," both published in the London *Public Advertiser* in September 1773.[101]

When his sister expressed hope that he would become the means of restoring harmony between Britain and its colonies, he responded that he had grown tired of "Meekness" and had written the two "saucy" papers in order to hold up "a Looking-Glass in which some Ministers may see their ugly Faces, and the Nation its Injustice." Although Franklin preferred "Rules for Reducing a Great Empire" because of the spirited endings of the paragraphs, all of which promised that the suggested rules would make the people "more disaffected, *and at length desperate*," most people liked the "Edict" piece better. This essay purported to be a decree of the king of Prussia, Frederick II, pointing out to the English that Britain had originally been settled by Germans, and informing them that they had not sufficiently compensated Prussia for its aid in the Seven Years War. For these reasons the English in the future would have to pay taxes to the German kingdom and suffer other impositions on their trade and manufacturing—taxes and impositions that were precisely those the colonists were suffering at the hands of Great Britain. Franklin delighted in telling his son how many people were *"taken in"* by the hoax, "and imagined it a real edict," until they got to the end and found out that all of the Prussian regulations had been copied from acts of the English Parliament dealing with the colonies.

Although Franklin realized that the satires would probably backfire by angering the government and by encouraging the colonists in their resistance, he did not seem to care anymore. All that writing he had done over the previous decade trying to explain the nature of the colonies to successive British ministries had come to naught. Perhaps the time for conciliation was over. "A little Sturdiness when Superiors are much in the Wrong," he told his sister, "sometimes occasions Consideration. And there is truth in the Old Saying, *That if you make yourself a Sheep, the Wolves will eat you.*"[102]

Franklin's admission that it was he who had sent the Hutchinson letters to Massachusetts touched off a bitter British newspaper assault against him. This rhymed denunciation was a good sample.

To D——r F——n

Thou base, ungrateful, cunning, upstart thing!
False to thy country first, then to thy King:
To gain thy selfish and ambitious ends,
Betraying secret letters writ to friends:
May no more letters through thy hands be past,
But may thy last year's office be thy last.[103]

In the eyes of the British government Franklin had now come to represent all the guile and treachery of the unruly colonists. On January 20, 1774, news of the Boston Tea Party arrived in London, a few days before the Privy Council was to meet to decide the fate of the Massachusetts petition to have Hutchinson removed from office. Instead of focusing on the Massachusetts petition, the meeting of the Privy Council turned into a full-scale indictment of Franklin, who now seemed responsible for everything that had gone wrong in the empire, including the recent Tea Party.

On January 29, in an amphitheater in Whitehall aptly called the Cockpit, and before the entire king's council, many members of the court, and scores of curious spectators in the gallery, Solicitor General Alexander Wedderburn viciously attacked Franklin, in what Franklin compared to a "Bull-baiting."[104] For nearly an hour Wedderburn poured abuse on Franklin the likes of which many had never heard before. Much of it was even too scurrilous for the press to publish. Franklin, Wedderburn declared, was "the true incendiary" and "the first mover and prime conductor" behind all of the troubles in Massachusetts. He had "forfeited all the respect of societies and of men," for he was not a gentleman; he was in fact nothing less than a thief.[105]

Through the entire tirade, with the crowd cheering and laughing,

Franklin stood silent, his face frozen, determined to show the audience no emotion whatsoever. At the end the Privy Council rejected the Massachusetts petition as groundless—designed only "for the Seditious Purpose of keeping up a Spirit of Clamour and Discontent."[106]

As Franklin told his Pennsylvania colleague Galloway three weeks later, he had hoped that his sending the Hutchinson letters to Massachusetts would have convinced the colonial leaders there that the "Blame" for the breakdown in imperial relations ought to lie with their own native officials. This, he had hoped, would "remove much of their Resentment against Britain as a harsh unkind Mother, . . . and by that means promote a Reconciliation." For its part the Massachusetts assembly did indeed resolve that all its grievances were the responsibility of Hutchinson and Oliver. "If the Ministry here had been disposed to a Reconciliation, as they sometimes pretend to be, this," said Franklin, "was giving a fair Opening, which they might have thanked me for; but they chuse rather to abuse me," who was really only a public messenger. Once again he invoked the old notion based on his earlier experience as a printer that he was merely an impartial relater of information and news.[107]

Everything had turned out the opposite of what he had intended. Rather than Thomas Hutchinson's becoming a scapegoat for the imperial crisis, Franklin himself had become in British eyes the single person most responsible for American resistance. By publicly humiliating Franklin in this brutal manner, the British government may have vented some of its rising hostility toward its rebellious colonists, but at the same time it virtually destroyed the affections of the only colonist in England who might have brought about reconciliation. Whether true or not, the story later circulated that Franklin upon leaving the Cockpit whispered in Wedderburn's ear, "I will make your master a LITTLE KING for this."[108] Two days later the government fired Franklin as deputy postmaster general of North America.

LAST EFFORTS TO SAVE THE EMPIRE

Despite his humiliation and his anger, Franklin had not given up all hope. He continued for a year more to try to save the empire. At one point he even offered to pay out of his own pocket the cost of the tea thrown into Boston harbor. He lobbied desperately against the passage in 1774 of the Coercive Acts, which closed the port of Boston and altered the Massachusetts charter, and he sought by a variety of avenues to convey the American position to the British government. But he knew his situation was becoming hazardous. "If by some Accident the Troops and People of N[ew] E[ngland] should come to Blows," he told Galloway in October 1774, "I should probably be taken up [that is, arrested], the ministerial People affecting every where to represent me as the Cause of all the Misunderstanding."[109]

His friends advised him to leave England, but he stayed on. Confident of his innocence, he thought "the worst which can happen to me will be an Imprisonment on Suspicion, tho' that is a thing I should desire to avoid, as it may be expensive and vexatious, as well as dangerous to my Health."[110] Besides he was anxious to see what the Continental Congress meeting in Philadelphia in September 1774 would do. Perhaps it could use nonimportation of British goods to bring pressure to bear on the British government and result in the present ministers' going out and giving "Place to Men of juster and more generous Principles." In response to rumors that he was returned to royal favor and would be promoted to a better position than his former one, Franklin declared he was no longer interested in any offices that the government might offer him. Indeed, he informed his sister several times that year, "I would not accept the best Office the King has to bestow, while such Tyrannic Measures are taking against my Country." He was becoming ever more convinced, as he told his son in August, that "Posts and Places are precarious Dependencies," not fit for someone who would be "a Freeman." Nevertheless, he still thought he had some influence in England and was reluctant to leave if there was the slightest possibility of his helping to prevent the destruction of that "great political Building," the British Empire.[111]

When the Earl of Chatham, who as the untitled William Pitt had led the government to victory in the Seven Years War, approached Franklin that same month in hopes of saving the empire Pitt had done so much to create, Franklin was guardedly optimistic. He saw new British "Advocates" for America's cause "daily arising." If the Americans could stop importing and consuming British goods, he said, "this Ministry must be ruined." But as he gained a greater hold on American opinion he lost touch with British opinion. The nonimportation and nonconsumption agreements that the First Continental Congress approved in 1774 did not ruin the ministry. He could not have been more mistaken in telling Thomas Cushing of Massachusetts that the new Parliament to be elected in October would likely be more favorable to America. Once the British people saw the Continental Congress's resolve, he told Cushing, he was persuaded that "our Friends will be multiplied, and our Enemies diminish'd, so as to bring on an Accommodation in which our undoubted rights shall be acknowledg'd and establish'd." Unless, of course, said Franklin, the court was able to bribe its way to a majority in the new Parliament.[112]

Although Franklin had no authority to negotiate for America, some peace-seeking Englishmen assumed he had and tried to use him as an intermediary in their desperate efforts to head off the breakup of the empire. Since Franklin was persona non grata with the king and with Whitehall, Franklin never talked directly with any member of the government. But others who consulted Franklin, including two prominent Quakers, David Barclay and John Fothergill, and Admiral Lord Richard Howe, did carry on some sort of secret negotiations with several members of the government. By December 1774 Franklin tried to make it clear to the negotiators that above all else Americans would never agree to the right of Parliament to legislate on the internal affairs of any colony—a denial of Parliamentary sovereignty that the British government would never accept. Two months later, in February 1775, the negotiators had virtually given up hope that the American and ministerial positions could be reconciled.

In the meantime Lord Chatham had approached Franklin once again with hopes for conciliation. At the end of December 1774 and throughout January 1775 they met and talked about what might be done. On January 29, Chatham actually called on Franklin at Craven Street—an event, Franklin told his son, "much taken notice of and talk'd of.... Such a Visit from so great a Man, on so important Business, flattered not a little my Vanity; and the Honour of it gave me the more Pleasure, as it happen'd on the very Day 12 month, that the Ministry had taken so much pains to disgrace me before the Privy Council." Then without giving Franklin any time to make any final suggestions, Chatham on February 1,

1775, went ahead and introduced his comprehensive plan for conciliation in the House of Lords. Lord Sandwich, the First Lord of the Admiralty, rose and declared that the plan ought to be rejected with the contempt it deserved. The plan, he said, could never have been drafted by a British peer; it had to be the work of an American. Sandwich then looked at Franklin, who was present in the gallery, and said that he fancied it was the work of "one of the bitterest and most mischievous Enemies this Country had ever known." Chatham's proposal was hooted down and soundly rejected without a second reading by the House of Lords. The Lords treated it, said Franklin, "with as much Contempt as they could have shown to a Ballad offered by a drunken Porter."[113]

For Franklin this was virtually the last straw. The Lords' rejection of Chatham's proposal in such a hasty and frivolous manner stunned him. Their ignominious action, he said, revealed only the depth of their ignorance, passion, and prejudice. It gave him "an exceeding mean Opinion of their Abilities, and made their Claim of Sovereignty over three Millions of virtuous sensible People in America, seem the greatest of Absurdities." "Hereditary Legislators!" he exclaimed. They were not fit "to govern a Herd of Swine."[114]

Listening in Parliament during the following weeks to the arrogant dismissals of Americans "as the lowest of Mankind and almost of a different Species from the English of Britain," Franklin became more and more irate. Not only were the Americans said to be dishonest knaves, but they were called dastardly cowards who were no match for His Majesty's soldiers. He later recalled hearing one British general say "that with a Thousand British Grenadiers he would undertake to go from one end of America to the other and geld all the Males partly by force and partly by a little Coaxing." Never had he been so angry; indeed, he was so furious that one friend feared that he might be "a little out of [his] Senses." England, Franklin told his American confidants, had become rotten to the core; in fact, continuation of the union with England might infect America and destroy "the glorious publick Virtue so predominant in our rising Country."[115]

At last he knew that his mediating role in the imperial crisis was over. He had learned that his wife had died, and he had to go home. He thought he had done his best, but British officials had made his task impossible. He was now convinced that the glorious empire to which he had devoted so much of his life was "destroyed by the mangling hands of a few blundering ministers."[116] He felt his Americanness as never before. His emotional separation from England was now final and complete. On March 19, 1775, he and his friend Joseph Priestley read over some American newspapers that had just arrived, looking for propaganda pieces. When Franklin came to the stories about the addresses sent by the neighboring towns to the closed port of Boston, recalled Priestley, his emotions gave way and "the tears trickled down his cheeks."[117] The next day the man whom Dr. Johnson called a "maker of mischief" sailed for America and became a passionate patriot, more passionate in fact than nearly all the other patriot leaders.[118]

FOUR

BECOMING A DIPLOMAT

UNDER SUSPICION

By the time Franklin arrived in Philadelphia on May 5, 1775, fighting between the colonists and British soldiers had already broken out in Lexington and Concord. The year before, in order to enforce the Coercive Acts, the British Crown had replaced the much abused governor of Massachusetts, Thomas Hutchinson, with a military commander in chief, Thomas Gage. Hutchinson went to England in exile, full of despair over what was happening in his beloved Massachusetts, just as his former royalist colleague was returning to the land of his birth. Because Franklin had become an international celebrity, he was interviewed by a newspaper editor upon his return—perhaps the first person in American history to be so greeted at the dock. In the news account Franklin urged Americans to stand firm and prepare for the struggle ahead. "He says we have no favours to expect from the Ministry; nothing but submission will satisfy them." Only a "spirited opposition" could save Americans from "the most abject slavery and destruction."[1]

Franklin brought with him from London his fifteen-year-old illegitimate grandson, William Temple Franklin, at last openly acknowledged as William's son and called Temple by his family.[2] Franklin moved into the Market Street house, which he had never before seen completed and which Deborah had labored to furnish in accordance with his precise instructions. He seems to have completely forgotten about Deborah, even though she had been dead for less than half a year. In no surviving document of this period does Franklin ever mention her. In fact, not a single friend or relative ever wrote him a note of sympathy or even referred to the death of his wife.[3]

The day after Franklin landed, May 6, the Pennsylvania Assembly elected him as one of its delegates to the Second Continental Congress, which was to meet in Philadelphia on May 10. At first Franklin tried to maintain a low profile. When he was not engaged in public business, he spent his time at home. Never a great speaker at best, he was unusually silent during the debates in the Congress. John Adams wondered what Franklin was doing in there, since "from day to day, sitting in silence, [he was] a great part of his time fast asleep in his chair."[4]

Despite Franklin's efforts to keep out of the limelight, however, he was the most famous American in the world and someone who presumably knew British officials and British ways as no other American did, and naturally everyone wanted to exploit his expertise and inventiveness for a variety of tasks. He was immediately appointed postmaster general and then assigned to a multitude of congressional committees. In between working on a petition to the king, the manufacture of saltpeter for gunpowder, and devices for protecting American trade, he found time to design the face of the proposed new currency and a model for pikes for the soldiers. He even drew up a revised version of his Albany Plan of Union for the colonies, which the Congress listened to but refused to record officially.

What impressed most delegates, however, was the intensity of Franklin's commitment to the patriot cause. He seemed deeply angry at the Crown and British officialdom and was impatient with all efforts at reconciliation. He thought the various colonial petitions to the king were a waste of time; he fully expected a long, drawn-out war; and he believed that independence was inevitable. All this was startling to Americans who had come to believe that Franklin, because of his long residence in London, had to be more English than American. The degree of Franklin's Revolutionary fervor and his loathing of the king surprised even John Adams, who was no slouch himself when it came to hating.[5] Adams told his wife, Abigail, in July that Franklin had now shown himself to be "entirely American"; indeed, he had become the bitterest enemy of Great Britain, the firmest spokesman for separation. "He does not hesitate at our boldest Measures," said Adams, "but rather seems to think us, too irresolute, and backward."[6] His passion for independence was all the more impressive coming from a Pennsylvanian, since that colony's leadership was especially divided and hesitant in 1775. In fact, many Americans in the other colonies had not yet lost hope of reconciliation with Britain.

It was actually left to a former English artisan and twice-dismissed excise officer named Thomas Paine, who had only recently arrived in the colonies, to voice openly and unequivocally the hitherto often unspoken desire to be done with Britain once and for all. In his pamphlet *Common Sense,* published anonymously in January 1776, Paine dismissed George III as the "Royal Brute" and called for immediate American independence. When this radical pamphlet appeared anonymously, Franklin's reputation for being an eager and passionate advocate for immediate separation from Britain was so well-known that some people attributed it to Franklin.[7]

No doubt some of Franklin's displays of anger and antagonism toward Britain were calculated. There were many Americans in 1775 suspicious of Franklin's dedication to the American cause, and he needed to overcome these suspicions. As early as 1771 Arthur Lee, a member of the well-known Lee family of Virginia, had written to Samuel Adams that Franklin was a "false" friend and should not be counted on to be a faithful agent of the Massachusetts assembly. Franklin, said Lee, who was in London at the time, was a crown officeholder whose son was royal governor of New Jersey. He had come to London to convert Pennsylvania into a royal province, which necessarily had made him something of a courtier. All these circumstances, "joined with the temporising conduct he has always held in American affairs," meant, Lee concluded, that in any contest between British oppression and a free people Franklin could not be trusted to support America. Lee, whom Franklin would tangle with later in Paris, possessed an innately suspicious mind, and on top of that he was jealous of Franklin. Not only did he and his powerful Virginia family have land claims in the West that rivaled those of the

Franklins, but he also wanted the Massachusetts agency for himself. He even offered to serve as agent without pay rather than have the American cause betrayed.[8]

The Massachusetts legislature did not accept Lee's charges, but Lee's suspicions of Franklin did not go away. He passed them on to his Virginia family, including his brother Richard Henry Lee, who became very influential in the Second Continental Congress. Samuel Adams and some other patriots still thought that Franklin had "a suspicious doubtful character," and wrote to people who knew something of Franklin and asked about his political leanings.[9] Shortly after the Congress convened, William Bradford, son of Franklin's old printing rival and publisher of the *Pennsylvania Journal*, wrote his Virginia friend James Madison of the doubts some of the delegates had of Franklin's patriotism, largely, it seems, because of rumors spread by Richard Henry Lee. "They begin to entertain a great Suspicion that Dr. Franklin came rather as a spy than as a friend," said Bradford, "& that he means to discover our weak side & make his peace with the minister by discovering it to him."

Madison had no way of knowing the truth of all the rumors that were floating about, "but the times are so remarkable for strange events," he thought, "that their improbability is almost become an argument for their truth." Even though he was hundreds of miles from Philadelphia, he was pretty certain about Franklin. "Indeed," said Madison, "it appears to me that the bare suspicion of his guilt amounts very nearly to a proof of its reality. If he were the man he formerly was, & has even of late pretended to be, his conduct in Philada. on this critical occasion could have left no room for surmise or distrust. He certainly would have been both a faithful informer & an active member of the Congress. His behaviour would have been explicit & his Zeal warm and conspicuous."[10] That this especially clever and sagacious future framer of the Constitution could think this way tells us a great deal about the atmosphere at the time.

Franklin's need to counter these rumors and suspicions that he was less than a patriot and maybe even a spy explains some of his Revolutionary fervor. It explains his decision to donate his entire salary as postmaster general to the assistance of disabled soldiers. He did this, he told his friend Strahan, so "that I might not have, or be suspected to have the least interested Motive for keeping the Breach [between Britain and America] open."[11] He knew that many Americans were thinking as Madison was, and he realized that he would have to make his patriotic zeal as "warm and conspicuous" as possible.

Over forty years earlier Franklin had reflected on why converts to a belief tended to be more zealous than those bred up in it. Converts, he noted in 1732, were either sincere or not sincere; that is, they changed positions either because they truly believed or because of interest. If the convert was sincere, he would necessarily consider how much ill will he would engender from those he abandoned and how much suspicion he would incite among those he was to go among. Given these considerations, he would never convert unless he were a true believer. "Therefore [he] must be zealous if he does declare." On the other hand, "if he is not sincere, He is oblig'd at least to put on an Appearance of great Zeal, to convince the better, his New Friends that he is heartily in earnest, for his old ones he knows dislike him. And as few Acts of Zeal will be more taken Notice of than such as are done against the Party he has left, he is inclin'd to injure or malign them, because he knows they contemn and despise him."[12]

Some such thinking as this explains the bizarre letter Franklin wrote on July 5, 1775, to his lifelong English friend William Strahan.

> Mr. Strahan,
>
> You are a Member of Parliament and one of that Majority which has doomed my Country to Destruction. You have begun to burn our Towns, and murder our People. Look upon your Hands! They are stained with the Blood of your Relations! You and I were long Friends: You are now my Enemy, and I am, Yours,
>
> B. Franklin

Of course, he never sent this outrageous letter, the like of which he never wrote to any of his other British friends and correspondents. He wrote to Strahan, one of his oldest English friends, for local effect only. Since he was trying to convince his fellow Americans of his patriotism, he let people in Philadelphia see the letter, and then quietly laid it away.[13] Within days he was writing his usual warm letters to Strahan.

But his fake letter to Strahan and his other displays of patriotism were effective. Bradford was soon writing Madison that the suspicions against Franklin had died away. "Whatever was his design at coming over here," Bradford wrote on July 18, 1775, "I believe he has now chosen his side, and favors our cause." Franklin had made his zeal for the cause very conspicuous indeed.[14]

A VERY PERSONAL AFFAIR

Some of Franklin's anger and passion against British officialdom may have been calculated, but not all by any means. The Revolution was a very personal matter for Franklin, more personal perhaps than it was for any other Revolutionary leader. Because of the pride he took in his reasonableness and in his ability to control his passions, his deep anger at the British government becomes all the more remarkable, but ultimately understandable. Franklin had invested much more of himself in the British Empire than the other patriot leaders. He had had all his hopes of becoming an important player in that empire thwarted by the officials of the British government, and he had been personally humiliated by them as none of the other patriots had been. Although he kept telling his correspondents that he made "it a Rule not to mix personal Resentments with Public Business," there is little doubt that his participation in the Revolution was an unusually private affair.[15]

Because he had identified himself so closely with the empire, he took every attack by the British government on the American part of that empire as a personal affront. He was hurt and bitter over the way the British ministers had treated him. He blamed them for prosecuting him "with a frivolous Chancery suit" in the name of William Whately over his role in the affair of the Hutchinson letters, a suit that his lawyer told him would certainly lead to his imprisonment if he appeared again in England. He believed that Britain's bombardment of Falmouth (Portland), Maine, and its apparent intention to do the same to America's other coastal towns were designed to hurt him personally; for "my American Property," he reminded his English friends, "consists chiefly of Houses in our Seaport Towns."[16]

Although legally he was still a member of the British Empire in 1775, emotionally he was not. He was way out ahead of many of his countrymen in his belief in the certainty of independence. And he had left his English friends even farther behind. Although his English friends kept imploring him to work out some kind of reconciliation, he now knew that all such efforts were futile. Of course, he continued to write warm and tender letters to Britain, yet he jarringly juxtaposed statements of affection toward his correspondents with severe criticisms of the nation of which they were a part. He began a letter to John Sargent, his banker in London, with accounts of the ways "your Ministry" had begun to burn "our Seaport Towns"; but he ended the letter with "My Love to Mrs. Sargent and your Sons . . . [and] with sincere Esteem, and the most grateful Sense of your long continu'd Friendship." For all his English friends it was now "your Nation," "your Ministers," and "your Ships of War" and for his fellow Americans and himself "our Seaport Towns," "our Sea Coast," and "our Liberties."[17]

One senses the mixed feelings he had in writing to some of his best friends about the impossibility of reconciliation. He was sad and angry at the same time, with the anger being more palpable. He saw clearly, as he said to one of his British friends in October 1775, that Britain and America were "on the high road to mutual enmity, hatred, and detestation," and that "separation will of course be inevitable." He had loved the empire as few Americans had. He had always thought that the fast-growing population of America meant "the Foundations of the future Grandeur and Stability of the British Empire [would] lie in America," but he had never doubted that the empire would remain British. Now that was no longer the case. And he could not help reminding his British friends what the mother country was losing. Although "the greatest Political Structure Human Wisdom ever yet erected" was being destroyed by the stupidity of a few ministers, the most important part of that empire, America, he told his English friend and member of Parliament David Hartley, "will not be destroyed: God will protect and prosper it: You will only exclude yourselves from any share in it."[18]

Since he had been personally rejected by English officialdom, he could no longer view England as the center of all civilization and virtue. Everything was now reversed. The Americans had become "a new virtuous People, who have Publick Spirit," while the English were "an old corrupt one, who have not so much as an Idea that such a thing exists in Nature." He was especially impressed by the devotion his fellow delegates gave to the work of the Continental Congress. Unlike the members of Parliament, the congressional delegates "attend closely without being bribed to it, by either Salary, Place or Pension, or the hopes of any." Everywhere ordinary people were "busily employed in learning the Use of Arms. . . . The Unanimity is amazing."[19]

He could scarcely believe that his formerly beloved England was waging such a ferocious war against America. In one of his most passionate exaggerations, he told his friend Jonathan Shipley that General Gage caused more destruction to Charlestown, Massachusetts, in one day than "the Indian *Savages*" had caused in all our wars, "from our first settlement in America, to the present time." Dr. Johnson (who was nothing but "a Court Pensioner") infuriated him by urging that English officials seek to excite the slaves to cut their masters' throats and to hire the Indians to fight the Americans. "When I consider that all this Mischief is done my Country, by Englishmen and Protestant Christians, of a Nation among whom I have so many personal Friends," he told Shipley, "I am ashamed to feel any Consolation in a prospect of Revenge." Ashamed or not, he very much wanted revenge.

"You see I am warm," he said, but he could not help it. Although he possessed "a Temper naturally cool and phlegmatic," he was only responding to the temper of his fellow Americans, "which is now little short of Madness."[20] Years later, even as the peace negotiations with Britain were taking place in 1782, Franklin circulated a fictitious document describing a package sent by a Seneca Indian chief to the governor of Canada listing all the American men, women, and children his tribesmen had killed on behalf of the English. The list, together with hundreds of scalps, was to be sent to King George for his refreshment. Franklin saw nothing wrong with his hoax: "The *Form* may perhaps not be genuine," he told a French friend, "but the *Substance* is truth."[21]

Just how personal the Revolution was for Franklin is vividly revealed in his treatment of his son. Up to now Franklin and William had had the closest possible relationship. They had been partners in Franklin's electrical experiments; in fact, William had been the only person Franklin had involved in his famous kite experiment. William had shared his

William Franklin, by Mather Brown, c. 1790

father's dreams for the British Empire and his hopes of a fortune in western land speculation. He had accompanied him to Albany in 1754 and had collaborated with him during the Seven Years War. He traveled with his father to London in 1757. They had journeyed to his father's ancestral homes at Ecton and Banbury and collected genealogical information together. And like his father, William had become a royal officeholder and a keen supporter of royal authority. When they weren't together, the father and son had kept constantly in touch and had looked after each other's family. Few eighteenth-century fathers and sons had ever been closer or more intimate with one another.

Now all this intimacy came to an end. Several days after Franklin had his office of deputy postmaster taken from him, he urged his son to give up his office as royal governor and retire to his farm. "'Tis an honester and a more honourable because a more independent Employment." With barely concealed anger he told William that he would "hear from others the Treatment I have receiv'd." Although he left William to his "own Reflections and Determinations upon it," it was clear from a subsequent letter that he expected his son to give up his crown office in support of his father. Shortly after his return to America in 1775 Franklin met with William at the home of Joseph Galloway, who had just resigned from politics in disgust with the patriot direction of affairs. Franklin was surprised to discover that his old friend and close confidant Galloway was such a committed royalist, but it was he, not Galloway, who had changed. Franklin tried to persuade both Galloway and his son to join him in the patriot cause. When they refused, Franklin sought to cut his communications with both of them to the barest minimum. He gave up completely on William, but he kept trying with Galloway; as late as the fall of 1776 he assumed that Galloway would at least remain neutral in the conflict. As royal governor of New Jersey, William had no opportunity to remain neutral. The two times Franklin met his son again in the summer of 1775 ended in shouting matches loud enough to disturb the neighbors.[22]

Franklin was naturally embarrassed by the fact that his son was royal governor of New Jersey—indeed, by 1776 the only royal governor still in office in America—but his anger at his son went beyond his need to display his own American patriotism. When Governor Franklin was arrested in June 1776 and sent as a prisoner to Connecticut, Franklin said and did nothing, unaffected even by a poignant plea for help from William's wife. After William violated his parole and made contact with the British commanders in New York, General William Howe and his brother, Admiral Lord Richard Howe, George Washington had him placed in solitary confinement in Litchfield, Connecticut, and deprived him of all writing materials. Even the pleadings of Strahan could not move Franklin to ease the conditions of his son's confinement. "Whatever his Demerits may be in the Opinion of the reigning Powers in America," Strahan told Franklin in 1778, "the Son of Dr. Franklin ought not to receive such Usage from them."[23] Franklin refused to lift a finger to aid his son, but others did, including Franklin's son-in-law, Richard Bache. Eventually Congress arranged for William's exchange, and William became a fervent loyalist leader in New York.

Because rumors abounded during the Revolutionary War that Franklin and his son were actually in collusion, Franklin perhaps had some reason to avoid all contact with his loyalist son. But after the peace treaty recognizing American independence was signed in September 1783, the situation was different and William wrote his father requesting reconciliation. Franklin's reply was cool, to say the least. While he suggested that reconciliation might be possible, he wanted William to know how personal the Revolution had been to him. "Indeed," he said, "nothing has ever hurt me so much and affected me with such keen Sensations, as to find my self deserted in my old Age by my only Son; and not only deserted, but to find him taking up Arms against me, in a Cause wherein my good Fame, fortune and Life were all at Stake." Although Franklin acknowledged William's claim that duty to king and country accounted for his loyalism, he really wasn't persuaded. *"There are,"* he emphasized, *"Natural Duties which precede political Ones, and cannot be extinguished by them."*[24]

In July 1785 the father and son met for several days in Southampton, England, but Franklin, anxious to protect William's son Temple from any taint of loyalism, was in no mood for reconciliation. All he wanted was for William to sell him all his unconfiscated property in New Jersey, which would then be passed on to Temple. Franklin was all business, and he bargained hard to get the property at a price far below its current value. He also demanded that William cede to him some property in New York as compensation for a debt of £1500 that William owed him. That was the end of the matter. He never communicated with William again and indeed rarely ever mentioned him and then only coldly. In his will he left his son some worthless lands in Nova Scotia and some books and papers that William already possessed—in effect, nothing. "The part he acted against me in the late war, which is of public Notoriety," he wrote in his will, "will account for my leaving him no more of an Estate he endeavored to deprive me of."[25]

During the peace negotiations with Britain in 1782, Franklin was passionate and implacable on only one issue—that of compensation for the loyalists. If the loyalists were to be indemnified for their losses, he said, then the patriots had to be similarly compensated for all the lootings, burnings, and scalpings carried out by the British and their Indian allies. Even his two colleagues during the peace negotiations, John Adams and John Jay, were surprised at the intensity of Franklin's bitterness toward the loyalists. It was far greater than their own.[26]

THE PASSIONATE REVOLUTIONARY

Franklin identified the American cause as his own, and he spared no energy on its behalf, even though he was the oldest member of the Second Continental Congress. In October 1775 as a member of a committee to investigate the military needs of the army, he traveled from Philadelphia to Cambridge to meet with George Washington, who had been appointed commander in chief. In March 1776, at the age of seventy, Franklin and several other commissioners trekked up the Hudson Valley to Canada in a fruitless effort to bring the Canadians in on the American side. No sooner had he finished serving on the committee that drafted the Declaration of Independence than he became president of the Pennsylvania convention called to write a new constitution for the state. Through the summer of 1776 he alternated his time between the Pennsylvania convention and the Congress. His most important contribution to the new state constitution was his urging the creation of a plural executive and a single-house legislature, which to many smacked of simple democracy and popular radicalism. One article of the constitution he specifically claimed. It expressed a view of government that his witnessing corrupt English politicians seeking lucrative royal offices had taught him. The article declared that there was no need in the government for "offices of profit, the usual effects of which are dependence and servility unbecoming freemen, in the possessors and expectants; faction, contention, corruption, and disorder among the people."[27]

Although as a colony Pennsylvania had possessed only a single-house legislature, a government with a plural executive and a unicameral legislature was such an anomaly among all the other Revolutionary state constitutions created in 1776, nearly all of which had single governors and senates as well as houses of representatives, that it turned the radical Pennsylvania constitution into an object of heated controversy over the succeeding decade. It was "intolerable," a monster "singular in its kind, confused, inconsistent, deficient in sense and grammar, and the ridicule of all *America* but ourselves, who blush too much to laugh." Benjamin Rush thought the Pennsylvania convention must have been drunk with liberty to have produced such an "absurd" constitution, which, he said, "substituted a mob government to one of the happiest governments in the world." But the charge that was most often hurled at the Pennsylvania constitution was that it was "an execrable democracy—a Beast without a head."[28] For most Americans in 1776 to be a simple democracy was not a good thing, which is why nearly all the state constitutions formed at the time created governors and senates to offset the democracy embodied in their houses of representatives.

Democracy in the eighteenth century was not yet the article of faith that it would become in the decades following the American Revolution. It was still a technical term of political science, meaning simply rule by the people. In traditional political thinking going back to the ancient Greeks, rule by the people alone was never highly regarded, for it could easily slip into anarchy and a takeover by a tyrant. The best constitution was one that was mixed or balanced, where the people's rule was offset by the rule of the aristocracy and monarchy. Eighteenth-century intellectuals admired the English constitution so much because it seemed to have nicely mixed and balanced the three simple forms of government, monarchy, aristocracy, and democracy, in the Crown, House of Lords, and House of Commons.

Of course, Americans in 1776 thought that the Crown had used money and influence to buy up the House of Commons and had corrupted the English constitution. They meant to prevent that corruption in their own new republican state constitutions. But most American constitution makers did not intend to abandon the idea of mixed and balanced government. John Adams, whose writings probably had the greatest influence on constitution-making in most of the states, but certainly not Pennsylvania, put the conventional wisdom best: "Liberty," he said, "depends upon an exact Ballance, a nice Counterpoise of all the Powers of the state.... The best Governments of the World have been mixed."[29]

Perhaps as much as anything it was Franklin's identification with the simple, unmixed democratic constitution of Pennsylvania that sowed the seeds of John Adams's growing enmity toward Franklin. Franklin's later identification with France only made matters worse. When French intellectuals saw in the bicameral legislatures of the other constitutions an effort to retain an aristocratic social order in the senates, they were astonished. They asked how "the same equilibrium of powers which has been necessary to balance the enormous preponderance of royalty, could be of any use in republics, formed upon the equality of all the citizens." For the French *philosophes* a state could have but a single interest. In fact, they said, that was what republicanism was all about. Believing as they did that "the representatives of a single nation naturally form a single body" and that there was no place for senates in the new egalitarian republics of the United States, the French *philosophes* celebrated the Pennsylvania Constitution as the only one that had refused to imitate the English House of Lords. John Adams, of course, reacted angrily to this French criticism and insisted all the more strenuously on the need for a mixed government with a single governor and a two-house legislature. Indeed, his magnum opus, the sprawling three-volume *Defence of the Constitutions of the United States,* was written in the white heat of his fury with this French, criticism of America's balanced state constitutions. In his anger with the French, Adams never forgot that Franklin had favored a simple unbalanced government with a unicameral legislature. This is what gave Franklin his reputation for being a "democrat," which for most eighteenth-century Americans remained a disparaging term.[30]

REBUFFING BRITISH PEACE OFFERINGS

Franklin had to interrupt his constitution-making in 1776 to deal with a peace offering brought by the British commanders, General William Howe and Admiral Lord Richard Howe. Lord Howe had been a friend of Franklin in England, and he wrote Franklin an amicable letter in July 1776 in hopes of finding the means of reconciling America and Great Britain. With the authorization of Congress, Franklin responded in the most passionate and blunt terms. It was impossible, he told Howe, that Americans would think of submission to a government that had carried on an unjust and unwise war against them "with the most wanton Barbarity and Cruelty." He knew only too well the "abounding Pride and deficient Wisdom" of the former mother country. Britain could never see her own true interests, for she was blinded by "her Fondness for Conquest as a Warlike Nation, her Lust of Dominion as an Ambitious one, and her Thirst for a gainful Monopoly as a Commercial one."

Even in this quasi-official dispatch, Franklin could not help thinking of the breakdown of the empire in personal terms. He recalled that only a year and a half earlier, at Howe's sister's house in London, Lord Howe had given him expectations that reconciliation between Britain and her colonies might soon take place. Not only did Franklin have "the Misfortune to find those Expectations disappointed," but he was soon "treated as the Cause of the Mischief I was labouring to prevent." Franklin's only "Consolation under that groundless and malevolent Treatment" was that he had "retained the Friendship of many Wise and Good Men in that Country." His advice to Lord Howe was to resign his command and "return to a more honourable private Station." Franklin's angry letter shocked Howe. This was a very different Franklin from the one Howe had known eighteen months earlier in London.[31]

Thinking the Americans might be more open to a reconciliation following their defeat in the battle of Long Island in August 1776, Lord Howe tried once again. He asked the Continental Congress for some of its members to meet with him in a private conference on September 11. The Congress selected Franklin, John Adams, and Edward Rutledge to attend the meeting under a flag of truce. It was a loaded committee, since all three had signed the Declaration of Independence and were unlikely to retract that momentous decision. Franklin proposed that the committee meet Howe either at the New Jersey governor's mansion at Perth Amboy, from which William had been forcibly removed as a prisoner of the patriots (a curious suggestion), or at Staten Island, which was occupied by British forces. Howe chose the latter.

On the way from Philadelphia to the meeting, the committee found the roads and inns crowded with troops and stragglers fleeing from the British forces in New York. In New Brunswick, Franklin and Adams were forced to share a room with a tiny window and a bed not much smaller than the room. This famous incident, recounted by Adams in his diary many years later, was one of Adams's more benign memories of Franklin. The account reveals Adams's talent as a storyteller, which under other circumstances might have made him a superb novelist.

Adams, who was just recovering from an illness, feared the night air blowing on him and shut the window. "Oh!" said Franklin, "Dont shut the window. We shall be suffocated."

Adams answered that he was afraid of the evening air.

"The Air within this Chamber will soon be, and indeed is now worse than that without Doors," replied Franklin. "Come! Open the Window and come to bed, and I will convince you: I believe you are not acquainted with my Theory of Colds."

Adams opened the window and leaped into bed. He told Franklin that he had read his theory that no one ever got a cold going into a church or any other cold place. But "the Theory was so little consistent with my experience," he said, "that I thought it a Paradox." Adams was willing, however, to have it explained. "The Doctor then began a harangue, upon Air and cold and Respiration and Perspiration, with which I was so much amused that I soon fell asleep."

Having the last laugh, Adams went on to point out that Franklin's theory of colds ultimately did him in. "By sitting for some hours at a Window, with the cool Air blowing upon him," in 1790 the eighty-four-year-old Franklin had "caught the violent Cold, which finally choaked him," recalled Adams with more malice than he had expressed earlier in the story.[32]

At the meeting with Howe, the admiral explained that he could not officially treat with Franklin, Adams, and Rutledge as a committee of Congress, but he could confer with them "merely as Gentlemen of great Ability, and Influence in the Country" on the means of restoring peace between Britain and the colonies. Franklin said that his lordship could regard the committee as he wished, but he and his colleagues knew only too well what they represented. This was not a very auspicious beginning, revealing as it did how much catching up to American opinion the British government still had to do. Howe went on to say that he could not admit the idea of the colonies' independence "in the smallest degree." He suggested that Britain and America might return to the situation prior to 1763. But the committee, with Franklin passionately and sometimes sneeringly in the lead, declared emphatically that it was too late. "Forces had been sent out, and Towns destroyed," said Franklin. America had already declared its independence, he concluded, and "could not return again to the Domination of Great Britain."[33]

THE MISSION TO FRANCE

That independence, however, still had to be won, and most Americans thought they would need help from abroad to achieve it. In several letters to English friends, Franklin suggested the possibility of America's appealing to a foreign power for assistance. In November 1775 the Continental Congress had appointed Franklin to a Committee of Secret Correspondence, which was to seek foreign support for the war. In December, Franklin asked a European *philosophe* in the Netherlands to find out whether some European state might be willing to aid the Americans. At the same time France, the greatest of the continental powers, had sent an agent to America to see whether the rebels were worth supporting. On behalf of the Committee of Secret Correspondence, Franklin wrote Connecticut merchant Silas Deane in March 1776 to engage him in secretly approaching the French government in order to secure money and arms.

After the Declaration of Independence that July, America's situation was clarified and its search for foreign aid could be more open. Congress now realized that a formal commission of delegates was needed in Paris if the United States was to persuade France to join the war as America's ally. Unlike Adams and Jefferson, who declined to become one of the commissioners to be sent to France, Franklin had no hesitation in accepting and, in fact, may have pushed to get the appointment. In October, Congress appointed Franklin to join Deane and Arthur Lee of Virginia, who was still in London, as a three-man commission to obtain arms and an alliance. The choice of Franklin was obvious. He was an international celebrity who knew the world better than any other American.

Franklin seems to have yearned to get back to the other side of the Atlantic. Perhaps he felt he was the stranger in his own country that he predicted he might be. In a sketch written shortly after the meeting with Howe he outlined various conditions for peace that might be negotiated with Great Britain—including, of course, unconditional independence, but also Britain's ceding to the United States for some sum of money all of Canada, the Floridas, Bermuda, and the Bahamas. One reason why such negotiations for peace with Britain were timely now, wrote Franklin, was that they might pressure the French into signing an alliance. But he added that such negotiations would also "furnish a pretence for BF's going to England where he has many friends and acquaintance, particularly among the best writers and ablest speakers in both Houses of Parliament." If the British balked at the terms of settlement, he wrote, then he was influential enough "to work up such a division of sentiments in the nation as greatly to weaken its exertions against the United States and lessen its credit in foreign countries."[34] Any excuse, it seemed, to get back across the Atlantic.

When people learned of Franklin's planned mission to France, some were deeply suspicious of his motives. He was blamed once again for bringing about the Revolution, making people of the same empire "strangers and enemies of each other." The British ambassador to France and many American loyalists thought that he was escaping America in order to avoid the inevitable collapse of the rebellion. Even his old friend Edmund Burke could not accept the news that Franklin was going on a mission to France. "I refuse to believe," Burke wrote, "that he is going to conclude a long life which he brightened every hour it continued, with so foul and dishonorable [a] flight."[35] But Franklin was not fleeing America out of any fears for the success of the Revolution; he merely wanted to return to the Old World, where he felt more at home.

On October 26, 1776, Franklin sailed with his two grandsons, sixteen-year-old Temple, William's illegitimate son, and seven-year-old Benjamin Franklin Bache, Sally's boy. They arrived in France in December—after a bold and risky voyage, for, as Lord Rockingham noted, Franklin might have been captured at sea and "once more brought before an implacable tribunal."[36] That he took the voyage says a great deal about Franklin's anger and his determination to defeat the British. It also says a great deal about his desire to experience once again the larger European world, where he had spent so much of his adult life. It would be nearly nine years before he returned to the United States.

Even before he reached France, Franklin was emotionally prepared for his new role as America's representative to the world. Back in 1757, Thomas Penn had predicted that the highest levels of English politics would eventually be closed to Franklin. Whatever Franklin's scientific reputation meant to the intellectual members of the Royal Society or the Club of Honest Whigs, Penn said, it would count for very little in the eyes of the ruling aristocracy, the "great People" who actually exercised political power.[37] As Franklin himself came to this realization by the early 1770s, he began to see the English stage on which he had been operating as more and more limited. Suddenly his reputation "in foreign courts" as a kind of ambassador of America seemed to compensate for his loss of influence in England.

During his last years in London he proudly told his son that "learned and ingenious foreigners that come to England, almost all make a point of visiting me, for my reputation is still higher abroad than here." He pointed out that "several of the foreign ambassadors have assiduously cultivated my acquaintance, treating me as one of their *corps*." Some of them wanted to learn something about America, mainly out of the hope that troubles with the American colonies might diminish some of Britain's "alarming power." Others merely desired to introduce Franklin to their fellow countrymen. Whatever the reasons for his extraordinary international reputation as the representative American, Franklin was well aware of it and was prepared to use it to help America.[38]

THE SYMBOLIC AMERICAN

In 1776 Franklin was the most potent weapon the United States possessed in its struggle with the greatest power on earth. Lord Rockingham observed at the time that the British ministers would publicly play down Franklin's mission to France, but "inwardly they will tremble at it."[39] The British government had good reason to tremble. Franklin was eventually able not only to bring the French monarchy into the war against Britain on behalf of the new republic of the United States but also to sustain the alliance for almost a half-dozen years. Without his presence in Paris throughout that tumultuous time, the French would never have been as supportive of the American Revolution as they were. And without that French support, the War for Independence might never have been won.

The French knew about Franklin well before he arrived in 1776. The great French naturalist Comte de Buffon read his *Experiments and Observations on Electricity* in 1751 and urged a translation. The next year King Louis XV endorsed the publication of a translated edition of Franklin's work and personally congratulated the author. In the years that followed, Franklin received letter after letter from French admirers of his electrical experiments. One of these admirers, Dr. Jacques Barbeu-Dubourg, began exchanging writings with Franklin. He translated many of Franklin's essays and works, including his testimony before the House of Commons in 1766, and had them reprinted in the French monthly *Ephémérides du citoyen*. Readers of the journal were told that from Franklin's statements "they will see what constitutes the superiority of intelligence, the presence of mind and the nobility of character of this illustrious philosopher, appearing before an assembly of legislators."[40] His testimony in the House of Commons was eventually published in five separate French editions.

In 1767 and again in 1769 Franklin visited France, was presented to the king, and dined with the royal family. He was especially impressed with the politeness and urbanity of the French and, as he wrote in a playful letter to Polly Stevenson, he had started to become French himself. "I had not been here Six Days before my Taylor and Peruquier had transform'd me into a Frenchman. Only think what a Figure I make in a little Bag Wig and naked Ears! They told me I was become 20 Years younger, and look'd very galante; so being in Paris where the Mode is to be sacredly follow'd, I was once very near making Love to my Friend's Wife."[41]

During his visits to France, Franklin made many friends among French intellectuals. Dubourg described him in print as "one of the greatest and the most enlightened and the noblest men the new world had seen born and the old world has ever admired."[42] In 1772 Franklin was elected a foreign associate to the French Royal Academy of Science, one of only eight foreigners so honored. The next year Dubourg published two volumes of the *Oeuvres de M. Franklin*, prefixed with a print of Franklin that made him look like a Frenchman, together with the line "He stole the fire of the Heavens and caused the arts to flourish in savage climes."[43] In the preface Dubourg further sharpened the image of the backwoods philosopher emerging from the land of the peaceful Quakers.

The French, of course, already had an image of America as the land of plain Quakers. Voltaire in his *Lettres philosophiques* (1734) had identified Pennsylvania with the Society of Friends, who were celebrated for their equality, pacifism, religious freedom, and, naturally, their absence of priests. It was as if nobody but Quakers lived in Pennsylvania. With three

Franklin as a Frenchman, engraving by François Martinet, 1773

articles on Pennsylvania, Philadelphia, and the Quakers, Diderot's *Encyclopédie* further contributed to this picture of Pennsylvania as the land of freedom, simplicity, and benevolence—an image that gradually was expanded to the New World in general.[44]

Many of the French *philosophes* like Voltaire were struggling to reform the *ancien régime,* and they turned the New World into a weapon in their struggle. America in their eyes came to stand for all that eighteenth-century France lacked—natural simplicity, social equality, religious freedom, and rustic enlightenment. Not that the reformers expected France to become like America. But they wanted to contrast this romantic image of the New World with the aristocratic corruption, priestly tyranny, and luxurious materialism they saw in the *ancien régime.* A popular debate that arose in France—over the issue of whether the climate of the New World was harmful to all living creatures and caused them to degenerate—was fed by these political concerns.[45] With this issue in mind, many of the liberal reformers were eager to emphasize the positive qualities of America. Idealizing all that was different from the luxury and corruption they saw around them, many of the liberal French *philosophes* created "a Mirage in the West," a countercultural image of America with which to criticize their own society.

In addition to the *philosophes,* many French aristocrats were themselves critics of their society, involved in what today we might call "radical chic." They were eager to celebrate the new enlightened values of the eighteenth century, many of which were drawn from the classical republican writings of the ancient world. French nobles invoked classical antiquity and especially republican Rome to create imagined alternatives to the decadence of the *ancien régime.* Of course, they did not appreciate the explosive nature of the materials they were playing with. They sang songs in praise of liberty and republicanism, praised the spartan simplicity of the ancients, and extolled the republican equality of antiquity—all without any intention of actually destroying the monarchy on which their status as aristocrats depended. The French nobles applauded Beaumarchais's *Le Barbier de Séville* and *Le Mariage de Figaro,* and later Mozart's operatic version, *Le Nozze di Figaro,* with their celebration of egalitarian and anti-aristocratic values, without any sense they were contributing to their own demise. They flocked to Paris salons to ooh and aah over republican paintings such as Jacques-Louis David's severe classical work *The Oath of the Horatii,* without foreseeing that they were eroding the values that made monarchy and their dominance possible. Many of these French aristocrats, such as the Duc de La Rochefoucauld, a friend and admirer of Franklin, were passionate advocates of abolishing the very privileges to which they owed their positions and fortunes. They had no idea where all their radical chic would lead. In 1792 La Rochefoucauld was stoned to death by a frenzied revolutionary mob.[46]

Franklin was part of this radical chic from the beginning. The French aristocrats were prepared for Franklin, and they contributed greatly to the process of his Americanization. They helped to create Franklin the symbolic American. In this sense Franklin as the representative American belonged to France before he belonged to America itself. Because

The Oath of the Horatii,
by Jacques-Louis David, 1785

the French had a need of the symbol before the Americans did, they first began to create the images of Franklin that we today are familiar with—the Poor Richard moralist, the symbol of rustic democracy, and the simple backwoods philosopher.

He was the celebrated Dr. Franklin from the moment of his arrival in France in 1776. He was invited by a wealthy merchant, Jacques Donatien Le Ray, the Comte de Chaumont, to live in the garden pavilion of his elegant Hôtel de Valentinois located on his spacious estate in Passy, a small village outside of Paris on the route to Versailles. Unlike Franklin's London home, which had been in the midst of the crowds and bustle of the city, this house was a half mile from Paris, sitting on a bluff with terraces leading down to the Seine, with views overlooking the city. Franklin enjoyed this suburban existence; when pressed by his colleagues to move into Paris in order to save money, he refused. Chaumont was a government

LEFT: *Franklin, engraving by Augustin de Saint-Aubin, 1777, after a drawing by Charles-Nicholas Cochin*
RIGHT: To the Genius of Franklin, *etching by Marguerite Gérard, after a design by Jean-Honoré Fragonard, 1778*

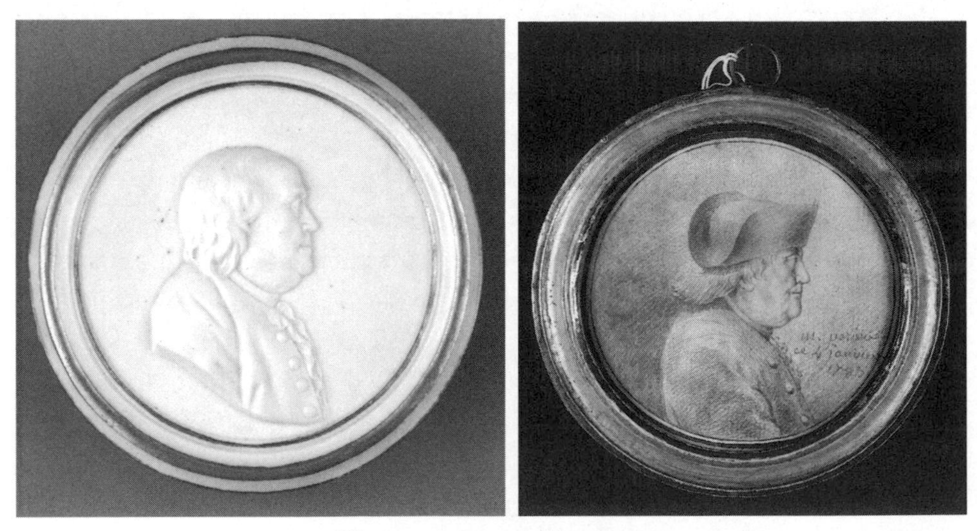

LEFT: *Franklin, porcelain medallion, Sèvres ware, 1778*
RIGHT: *Franklin, French school, c. 1783*

contractor. As an enthusiastic partisan of the United States, he refused any rent from Franklin, at least at first, and saw to it that the great man lived in relative luxury, serviced by a liveried staff of a half-dozen or more servants. In addition to the large formal gardens in which Franklin enjoyed walking, Franklin's house had a lightning rod on the roof and a printing press in the basement. He spent his entire time in France quite comfortably ensconced in these plush surroundings. His food was ample and his wine cellar was well stocked with over a thousand bottles. He needed all these supplies, for he had a steady stream of guests.

The great man is "much sought after and entertained," noted an observer, "not only by his learned colleagues, but by everyone who can gain access to him." The nobility lionized him. They addressed him simply as "Doctor Franklin, as one would have addressed Plato or Socrates."[47] The French placed crowns upon his head at ceremonial occasions, wrote poems in his honor, and did their hair à la Franklin. Wherever he traveled in his carriage, crowds gathered and, amid acclamations, gave way to him in the most respectful manner, "an honour," noted Silas Deane, "seldom paid to the first princes of the blood." Only three weeks after his arrival, it was already the mode of the day, said another commentator, "for everyone to have an engraving of M. Franklin over the mantelpiece."[48] Indeed, the number of Franklin images that were produced is astonishing. His face appeared everywhere—on statues and prints and on medallions, snuffboxes, candy boxes, rings, clocks, vases, dishes, handkerchiefs, and pocketknives. Franklin told his daughter that the "incredible" numbers of images spread everywhere "have made your father's face as well known as that of the moon."[49]

Not only did Jean-Antoine Houdon and Jean-Jacques Caffiéri mold busts of Franklin, in marble, bronze, and plaster, but every artist, it seemed, wanted to do his portrait. Jean-Baptiste Greuze and J. F. de L'Hospital painted him, and Joseph-Siffred Duplessis did at least a dozen portraits of him (see pages 178–79). The Duplessis portrait of 1778 portrayed Franklin in a fur collar and was repeatedly engraved and copied by numerous other artists; it became the most widely recognizable image of Franklin.[50] "I have at the request of friends," Franklin complained, "sat so much and so often to painters and Statuaries, that I am perfectly sick of it."[51] No man before Franklin, it has been suggested, ever had his likeness

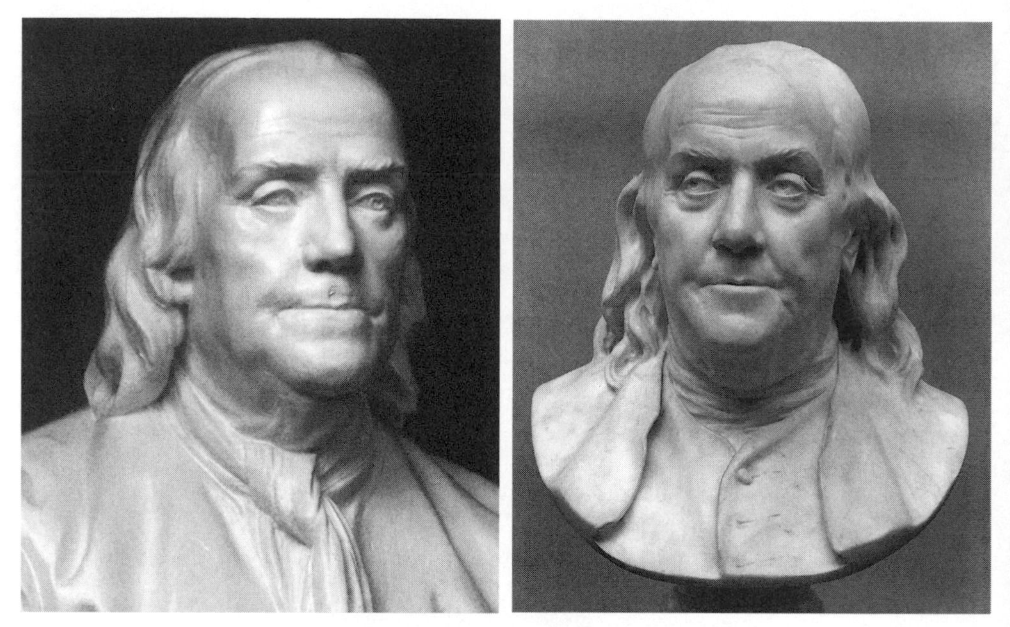

LEFT: *Franklin, bust by Jean-Jacques Caffiéri, 1777*
RIGHT: *Franklin, bust by Jean-Antoine Houdon, 1778*

LEFT: *Franklin, by Joseph-Siffred Duplessis, 1778*
RIGHT: *Franklin, by Jean-Baptiste Greuze, 1777*

Franklin, by J. F. de L'Hospital, 1778

reproduced at one time in so many different forms.[52] Apparently King Louis XVI became so irritated with Franklin's image everywhere that he presented one of Franklin's admirers in his court with a porcelain chamber pot with the American hero's face adorning the bottom.[53]

To the French, Franklin personified not only republican America but the Enlightenment as well. As a Freemason, he was a member of that eighteenth-century international fraternity that transcended national boundaries. In 1777 he was made a member, and later grand master, of the Masonic Lodge of the Nine Sisters, the most eminent lodge in France. Although many monarchists were suspicious of Freemasonry and discouraged their friends from joining the order, the lodge nevertheless contained many distinguished artists and intellectuals. Franklin used his association with them to further the American cause. He suggested to a fellow lodge member, La Rochefoucauld, for example, that he translate the American state constitutions into French. When this was done, Franklin presented copies to every ambassador in Paris and spread copies throughout Europe.

Since he was the American Enlightenment personified, it was necessary that he meet his European counterpart—Voltaire. When Voltaire returned to France in 1778 after twenty-eight years in exile, he met with Franklin several times. The most public of these meetings took place at the Academy of Science in April 1778. Since both the old *philosophes* were at the meeting, the rest of those in attendance called for them to be introduced. But, according to John Adams, who witnessed the occasion, bowing to one another was not enough. Even after Franklin and Voltaire took each other's hands, the crowd cried for more. They must embrace "à la francoise." "The two Aged Actors upon this great Theater of Philosophy and frivolity," recalled Adams sardonically, "then embraced each other by hugging one another in their Arms and kissing each other's cheeks, and then the tumult subsided. And the Cry immediately spread through the whole Kingdom and I suppose over all Europe.... How charming it was! Oh! it was enchanting to see Solon and Sophocles embracing!"[54]

Franklin's genius was to understand how the French saw him and to exploit that image on behalf of the American cause. Since Franklin was from Pennsylvania, people assumed he was a simple Quaker, and he played the part to perfection. He dressed plainly in white and brown linen, declared one observer, "glasses on his head, a fur cap, which he always wears on his head, no powder, but a neat appearance." Instead of the short sword worn by most aristocrats, "he carries as his only defense a cane in his hand."[55] Franklin knew very well the political significance of what he was doing. After describing to an English friend his simple dress with his "thin grey strait Hair, that peeps out under my only Coiffure, a fine Fur Cap which comes down my Forehead almost to my Spectacles," he remarked, "Think how this must appear among the Powder'd Heads of Paris."[56]

In French eyes Franklin came to symbolize America as no single person in history ever has. He realized that he was "much respected, complimented and caress'd by the [French] People in general," and that "some in Power" paid him a particular "Deference," which, he said, was probably why his colleagues "cordially hated and detested" him so much.[57] Indeed, it seemed he could do no wrong in France.

When Franklin was received by Louis XVI at Versailles, he violated almost every rule of this, the most ornate and ritual-bound court in all of Europe. While his American colleagues wore the elaborate court dress prescribed by the royal chamberlain, Franklin appeared in his simple rustic dress; and the French courtiers loved it. He could have been taken "for a big farmer," said one observer, "so great was his contrast with the other diplomats, who were all powdered, in full dress, and splashed all over with gold and ribbons."[58] The French turned everything about Franklin into a sign of Quaker or republican simplicity. They fell over themselves in enthusiasm for this village philosopher. To his French admirers even Franklin's deficiencies became great virtues. Was he quiet in large gatherings? This only demonstrated his republican reticence. Did he speak and write rather poor ungrammatical French? This only showed that he spoke and wrote from the heart.

Even when he fooled the best of the French intellectuals with one of his literary tricks, he was celebrated. No less a personage than the *philosophe* Abbé Raynal, for example, fell for Franklin's famous Polly Baker hoax, which was first published in a London paper in 1747. In his account Franklin had Polly, a prostitute, defend herself in a speech before a court in Connecticut for giving birth to five successive illegitimate children. She was doing nothing more, she said, than her duty—"the Duty of the first and great Command of Nature, and of Nature's God, *Encrease and Multiply.* A Duty, from the steady Performance of which, nothing has ever been able to deter me; but for its Sake, I have hazarded the Loss of the Publick Esteem, and frequently incurr'd Publick Disgrace and Punishment; and therefore ought, in my humble Opinion, instead of a Whipping, to have a Statue erected in my Memory." According to Franklin, Polly's speech so moved her judges that they dispensed with her punishment; it even "induced one of her Judges to marry her the next Day."

Although Franklin may have been merely poking fun at the double standard for women, the story seems to have been widely taken as an authentic account of an event. It was kept alive by many subsequent reprintings in both America and Britain. No one was more bamboozled by "The Speech of Miss Polly Baker" than Abbé Raynal. Raynal picked it up from an English publication and, believing it to be a true story, inserted it in his immensely popular *Histoire philosophique et politique des établissements et du commerce des Européens dans les deux Indes* (1770). The ever earnest abbé thought the story was meant to show the puritanical severity of New England's laws, which made it enormously appealing to all those enlightened French intellectuals eager to show their sympathy for the oppressed of the world. Only during Franklin's mission in France did Raynal discover that the story was made up. Franklin told Raynal that as a young printer he had had the habit of creating "anecdotes and fables and fancies," and that Polly Baker's speech was one of those. Surprised, the abbé quickly recovered. "Oh, very well, Doctor, I had rather relate your stories than other men's truths."[59]

To the infatuated French all Franklin's writings seemed praiseworthy. In 1777 his *The Way to Wealth* was translated as *La Science du Bonhomme Richard, ou moyen facile de payer les impôts.* It became the most widely read American work in France, going through four editions in two years and five others over the next two decades.[60] Although Franklin viewed his work as a hodgepodge of borrowed proverbial wisdom, and sometimes satirized his own prudential advice, the French in their passion for Franklin described his Bonhomme Richard maxims as sublime philosophy worthy of Voltaire and Montaigne. Timeworn adages such as "One Today is worth two Tomorrows" and "Laziness travels so slowly, that Poverty soon overtakes him" were extolled as serious moral philosophy.[61]

Indeed, French excitement over the proverbs of Bonhomme Richard reveals some of what we might call the early beginnings of modern French structuralism and deconstruction. In his eulogy on Franklin's death, the Marquis de Condorcet, the French *philosophe* and Masonic friend of Franklin, expressed a peculiar form of Gallic logic. Bonhomme Richard, said Condorcet, was a "unique work in which one cannot help recognizing the superior man without it being possible to cite a single passage where he allows his superiority to be perceived." Condorcet, who died in prison during the French Revolution while writing about the perfectibility of mankind, declared that there was nothing in the thought or style of Franklin's work that showed anything above "the least developed intelligence." But, said Condorcet, in an argument worthy of Jacques Derrida, "a philosophic mind" could discover the "noble aims and profound intentions" behind the maxims and proverbs.[62]

Although *The Way to Wealth* may have been his best-selling work in France, Franklin was anything but a bourgeois businessman to the French. He understood the French aristocrats' love of honor and liberality and, despite being a former artisan from the lowest rungs of the social ladder, he knew how to deal with them. He tried to tell the American foreign secretary Robert R. Livingston the way to approach the French. "This is really a generous Nation, fond of Glory and particularly that of protecting the Oppress'd." The French nobility, "who always govern here," was not really concerned with trade. To tell these French aristocrats that "their *Commerce* will be advantag'd by our Success, and that it is their *Interest* to help us, seems as much to say, Help us and we shall not be obliged to you."[63] Franklin knew better. The French foreign minister, the Comte de Vergennes, noted that all the Americans had "a terrible mania for commerce." But not Franklin: "I believe," said Vergennes, "his hands and heart are equally pure."[64]

Although Franklin never liked snobbery, was always eager to defend obscure but honest men, and often ridiculed the idea of aristocracy and claims of blood, he was eager to share the French aristocracy's contempt for commerce, which he generally equated with *"Cheating."* Of course, by commerce he meant the kind of international trade that great wholesale merchants and nations engaged in; he did not generally mean the kind of buying and selling that he had done as a tradesman in Philadelphia. But he was no defender of rapacious moneymaking. His severest criticism of a nation was to say, as he did of Holland in 1781, that it had "no other Principles or Sentiments but those of a Shopkeeper."[65]

Precisely because he had begun his career as a tradesman, he seems to have had a much greater need than the other Founders to show the world that he was truly genteel and "free from Avarice." All these condemnations of commerce and shopkeepers suggest something of the emotional price Franklin paid for his remarkable rise. But they also reveal the peculiar way this former tradesman who had become the representative American endeared himself to the French.[66]

THE PROBLEMS OF THE MISSION

Symbol or no symbol, Franklin faced extraordinary difficulties and very unpromising circumstances in Paris, difficulties and circumstances that make the achievements of his mission all the more remarkable. In 1776 he seemingly had everything against him. The British immediately expressed dismay at his presence in France, and Louis XVI was not at all happy to have his monarchy encouraging republican rebels against another king. Queen Marie-Antoinette was especially opposed to aiding the Americans, and some members of the ministry agreed with her. Franklin and his fellow commissioners knew that their task was to bring France into the war on America's side. But the French government did not believe itself ready yet for open war with England. As the commissioners reported in the spring of 1777, France wanted to avoid offering "an open Reception and Acknowledgement of us, or entering into any formal Negotiation with us, as Ministers from the Congress."[67] Indeed, out of fear of precipitating a premature war with Britain, France initially put all sorts of restrictions on American behavior, including preventing Americans from enlisting French officers and forbidding American privateers to sell captured prizes in French ports. The French were willing to open their ports to American commerce and to supply arms and money, however, as long as no one talked about it.

France's hesitation was quite understandable. Ever since independence the Continental army had been in pell-mell retreat from the British forces, and the prospect of sustaining the Revolution seemed doubtful. Even in these difficult circumstances the United States was prepared to offer the French very little. The most the new republic would promise was that if French aid to the United States led France into war with Great Britain, America would not assist Britain in such a war.

Congress offered little guidance; indeed, Franklin and his colleagues essentially had to teach themselves diplomacy. With no word from Congress for months, the commissioners had no knowledge of what was going on in America. "Our total Ignorance of the truth or Falsehood of Facts, when Questions are asked of us concerning them," they complained, "makes us appear small in the Eyes of the People here, and is prejudicial to our Negotiations."[68] Added to this confusion was the extraordinary number of solicitors the commissioners, especially Franklin, had to deal with. The esteemed doctor was overwhelmed with correspondents and visitors at the very time he was trying to win over the French while struggling with a foreign language and different social customs. His grasp of French was never strong. Once, at a public gathering where there were many speeches, Franklin had a hard time understanding what was being said; but he followed the lead of one of his lady friends and applauded when she did. Later his grandson told him that he had been applauding praises of himself, and more vigorously than anyone.[69]

Everybody interested in America, it seemed, wanted him for something or other—merchants and traders looking to make money from an American deal, inventors and savants seeking his blessing, and especially French and other European officers eager to be recommended for commissions in the American army. "These Applications," he wrote to one of his French friends, "are my perpetual Torment. People will believe, notwithstanding my continually repeated Declarations to the Contrary, that I am sent hither to engage Officers. In Truth, I never had such Orders.... You can have no Conception how I am harass'd. All my Friends are sought out and teiz'd to teaze me; Great Officers of all Ranks in all Departments, Ladies great and small, besides profess'd Sollicitors, worry me from Morning to Night."[70]

All this pestering would have taxed the energies of a young man, but Franklin by eighteenth-century standards was an old man, suffering from a variety of maladies—gout, painful bladder or kidney stones, a chronic skin disease, and swollen joints. He had gained weight and walked with more and more difficulty. The sea voyage had been especially difficult and, as he later recalled, had "almost demolish'd" him.[71] Indeed, the French thought him much older than he was.

If these difficulties were not enough, the Paris in which Franklin was expected to operate was a hotbed of espionage and counterespionage. The most ingenious spy novelist could scarcely have invented the Parisian world of these years. Every nation had agents in Paris, even the Americans. In fact, at the outset the American commissioners themselves may well have been involved in secretly releasing information to the British. Before the French formally allied with the Americans, the situation was very complicated. The British were warning the French that they could not tolerate much longer France's supplying arms to the American rebels. The commissioners thus had a vested interest in manipulating the information to be revealed to the British in order to precipitate a British declaration of war against France or, after war broke out, to influence British opinion against continuing the war against the

Americans. It was all these attempts to manipulate information that led some people at the time and some subsequent historians to believe that Franklin was spying on behalf of the British.[72]

The British, however, had such an extensive network of spies in Paris keeping watch on Franklin, whom George III called "that insidious man," that they may not have needed Franklin's help as a spy.[73] Franklin never suspected that Paul Wentworth, a wealthy émigré from New Hampshire, ran the British network and had several other Americans working for him. Nor did Franklin realize that the secretary of the American legation, Massachusetts-born Edward Bancroft, was also a spy in the pay of the English government.

In fact, not only did Franklin not suspect Bancroft, but he had great affection for him. Franklin had successfully sponsored Bancroft for membership in the Royal Society and had introduced him to many of his friends in London. Bancroft had been present in the Cockpit during Wedderburn's diatribe against Franklin, and he had been one of the few defenders of Franklin in the London press during the affair of the Hutchinson letters—something that was bound to win Franklin's heart. Even though some Americans suspected that Bancroft might be a spy, Franklin trusted him completely.

Bancroft was actually a double agent who sometimes spied on behalf of the American cause, but most of his spying was done for the English. He supplied Wentworth with regular reports on the American negotiations with France and Spain, the commissioners' correspondence with Congress, the names of ships and captains employed by the commissioners, and news of sailings and prizes seized by privateers. Bancroft wrote his reports in invisible ink and dropped them off in a sealed bottle in the hollow of a tree on the south side of the Tuileries, where they were picked up every Tuesday evening at nine thirty.[74]

Despite being surrounded by spies, Franklin was not at all worried and, in fact, blithely dismissed the possibility of spies having any harmful effects on his mission. As long as he was involved "in no Affairs that I should blush to have made publick; and to do nothing but what Spies may see and welcome," he could not care less about spies. "If I was sure . . . that my Valet de Place was a Spy, as probably he is, I think I should not discharge him for that, if in other Respects I lik'd him."[75] These facetious remarks that confused his own moral behavior with state affairs involving American lives and property reveal once again how much Franklin tended to see the Revolution in personal terms.[76] He did have one fright, however, when he thought a spy had tried to poison him; he knew the Paris chief of police well enough to have the suspected culprit locked up in the Bastille.[77]

Not only did Franklin have to convince the French to support America, but he also had to persuade his countrymen to trust France, and that turned out to be much the harder task. As former Englishmen, Americans had always known France as England's traditional enemy. Indeed, by the eighteenth century the English had come to define much of their national identity by their differences from the French, from the extent of their liberties and their consumption of beef to their religious views—especially their religious views. France was Roman Catholic, and to be English was to be Protestant. Although Americans were now fighting England, it would not be easy for them to shed their inherited English dislike of France and fear of Catholicism. Besides, they had just fought a long and costly war against the French and their Indian allies, and the memory of that war lingered. For Franklin to get his fellow Americans to trust the French as much as he came to trust them remained his greatest challenge throughout his nearly eight-year-long mission—one he was never entirely successful in meeting.

THE BURDEN OF HIS FELLOW COMMISSIONERS

The character of his two fellow commissioners, Deane and Lee, did not help matters any. Deane had been in Paris since the spring of 1776 seeking aid secretly from the French government. He had joined up with Pierre-Augustin Caron de Beaumarchais, a man of many talents who had strong connections to the French court. Between writing *Le Barbier de Séville* and *Le Mariage de Figaro,* Beaumarchais organized a fictitious trading company to act as a front for the French government's supplying of arms to the Americans. Beaumarchais seems to have hoped to make money out of this gunrunning enterprise, but whether Deane hoped to is not clear;

Deane's accounts turned out to be such a mess that no one at the time or ever since has been able to untangle them. At any rate Beaumarchais lost a fortune in the business, and Deane was eventually accused of embezzlement and profiteering by his fellow commissioner Arthur Lee.

Lee was a very difficult man, a superpatriot mistrustful of everyone who did not think as he did, including his two fellow commissioners.[78] He was unable to relate to the Comte de Vergennes, the French foreign minister, with whom the commission had to deal. Lee distrusted France and missed no opportunity to let Vergennes know how fortunate the French were in being able to help the Americans. France, of course, wanted revenge against Britain for its defeat in the Seven Years War, but there were other things France might have done besides going to war with Britain in support of America, including trying to recover its lost territory in North America.[79] Lee never appreciated that, but Franklin did.

Because Franklin did get along with Vergennes and refrained from vigorously pressing him for an alliance, Lee assumed that Franklin had been taken in by the French or, worse, had shifted his allegiance to France. Lee, of course, had been suspicious of Franklin back in London in the early 1770s, and thus he had his eye on the old man from the moment they got together in Paris.

To complicate the situation further, Congress in July 1777 appointed Lee's brother William as minister to Berlin and Vienna and Ralph Izard, a wealthy South Carolina planter, as minister to Tuscany. Because none of these European states wished to recognize the new republic—in a monarchical world, governments that did away with kings were not very welcome, especially if their rebellion did not succeed—William Lee and Izard had their credentials as ministers refused. Instead, the two disgruntled ministers settled in Paris and convinced themselves that they too should be members of the commission to France. They sniped and quarreled and made life miserable for Franklin. They complained that they could not get Franklin to attend meetings or sign papers, saying that the only thing he was punctual for was his dinner. They charged him with withholding information and ignoring them and with collaborating with Deane in a system of "disorder, and dissipation in the conduct of public affairs." Finally, because Franklin was haughty and self-sufficient and "not guided by principles of virtue and honor," they charged him with being "an improper person to be trusted with the management of the affairs of America."[80]

Although Izard thought Franklin was more dangerous than Deane, because "he had more experience, Art, cunning and Hypocricy," Arthur Lee tended to mistrust Deane more.[81] He thought that Deane had creamed off profits for himself during the time he was supplying arms for the American cause. With the aid of Richard Henry Lee, his brother in the Continental Congress, he launched a campaign against Deane that eventually resulted in Congress's recalling the Connecticut merchant in November 1777 to answer the charges of embezzlement and other matters. The accusations against Deane divided the Congress between those zealous patriots like Richard Henry Lee and Samuel Adams, who saw wickedness and corruption everywhere, and those more worldly moderates like Robert Morris and John Jay, who realized that financing a revolution required that some people make money. Many of these kinds of important urbane people supported Deane, and Franklin was one of them.

Franklin liked Deane, and he endorsed him in a letter to the Congress. He told Henry Laurens, the president of the Congress, in March 1778 that there must be some mistake in the Congress's recalling of Deane, perhaps "the Effect of some Misrepresentation from an Enemy or two" in France. He had lived intimately with Deane for fifteen months, and he found him to be "a faithful, active and able Minister, who to my Knowledge has done in various ways great and important Services to his Country."[82]

Since Franklin got along so well with Deane, Lee assumed that Franklin had to be in cahoots with him. "I am more and more satisfied that the old doctor is concerned in the plunder," he wrote to his brother Richard Henry Lee in Congress that September, "and that in time we shall collect the proofs."[83] Deane's subsequent actions only deepened Lee's suspicion of Franklin. Deane eventually became so angry at the shabby way he was being treated that he publicly denounced the Congress, repudiated the Revolution, and settled in England. Since Franklin had defended Deane, the Lees and other zealous patriots such as Samuel Adams had grounds for questioning Franklin's patriotism.[84]

Despite the Lee faction's criticism, Franklin carried out his duties brilliantly. He bore his colleagues' malice and abuse with silence and restraint. He sloughed off the charges that he was lazy and spent too much time dining and seeing people. He knew that diplomacy was not simply a matter of writing letters and shuffling papers. He knew too that the French feared that the Anglo-Saxons might get back together, and he skillfully played on these fears. He encouraged concessions from the British government and simply allowed these to spur Vergennes, who was always worried about a British-American rapprochement, into increased activity on behalf of the Americans. All the while Franklin charmed the French and put the best face he could on the course of events as he waited for an American victory. When told in the summer of 1777 that General William Howe had taken Philadelphia, he replied: "You mean, Sir, Philadelphia has taken Sir Wm. Howe."[85] With the news of the defeat and surrender of British troops at Saratoga that October, he at last had a substantial American victory to convince the French that the American cause was worth supporting with an open military alliance. With the prospect of France's entering the war openly on behalf of the Americans, the alarmed British were now prepared to offer the colonists everything they had wanted short of independence.

THE FRENCH ALLIANCE

Although some Americans were suspicious of Franklin's devotion to the cause, in fact no one was more committed to American independence than Franklin. Whatever loyalty Franklin had earlier felt for the British Empire was gone. He was now completely dedicated to the success of what he called "a miracle in human affairs" and "the greatest revolution the world ever saw."[86] Consequently, he initially ignored all British efforts to talk about ending the war short of American independence. At several points he even destroyed or refused to pass on to America offers from the British government for reconciliation, out of fear that some wobbly Americans back home might have second thoughts about continuing the struggle for complete independence. Only when the French kept hesitating about openly allying with America did he, in January 1778, finally agree to meet with Paul Wentworth, ostensibly an emissary from the British government but actually the chief British spy in France. He knew that the French would learn of this meeting and would perhaps be goaded into an alliance.

Wentworth, according to his own account, opened the two-hour conversation with some compliments, to which, he said, Franklin was "very open." Wentworth reminded Franklin that the doctor had formerly favored imperial union rather than American independence. But Franklin said that was then; circumstances were different now. When Wentworth read him a letter from someone in England promising unqualified independence, Franklin replied: "Pity it did not come a little sooner." In the process of recalling the various negotiations he had been involved in during the early 1770s, Franklin, according to Wentworth, "worked Himself into passion and resentment." Wentworth tried to tell him "that His resentments should be lost in the Cause of his Country; that His [cause] was too great to mix private quarrells with." Although Franklin replied that "His warmth did not proceed from a feeling of personal Injuries" alone, Wentworth was not mistaken in observing the way the highly agitated Franklin lost his breath in describing "the burning of Towns, the neglect or Ill treatment of Prisoners," and the other "Barbarities inflicted on His Country." Wentworth had never known Franklin to be so discombobulated; normally Franklin was succinct and pointed, "but He was diffuse and unmethodical to day." As much as Wentworth tried, he could not get Franklin to calm down and stop talking about English savagery.[87]

But, angry as he was, Franklin was no fool. He knew that this meeting between himself and a British agent would arouse Vergennes to act. Vergennes and his king, the young Louis XVI, finally decided that they had better pin down the Americans in an alliance before they reached terms with the English. In February 1778 France signed two treaties with the United States—one a commercial agreement, the other a military alliance pledged to American independence.

Franklin had not originally wanted a formal alliance with any foreign state, but he now willingly participated in the greatest diplomatic triumph in American history. During the ceremonial signing of the treaties Franklin wore an old blue velvet coat. When Deane asked why he was wearing that particular coat, Franklin replied, "To give it a little revenge. I wore this Coat on the day Widderburn abused me at Whitehall."[88]

THE MISCHIEVOUS MADMAN, JOHN ADAMS

John Adams of Massachusetts, Deane's replacement, arrived that April, too late to participate in making the treaties with France. Compared with Franklin, Adams was a babe in the woods. Where Franklin was reserved and impenetrable, Adams was impulsive and open. He was awkward and anything but diplomatic. He knew nothing of European politics, he had never laid eyes on a king or queen or the foreign minister of a great power, and he had never been in a city larger than Philadelphia. Still, he had been one of the firmest advocates for American independence, and he had a strong sense of his own worth, which most called vanity.

He soon became irritated that Franklin, "the old Conjurer," was getting all the credit when he was doing all the work. In a 1779 letter to the chief justice of Pennsylvania, Thomas McKean, Adams conceded that Franklin was "a Wit and Humourist. . . . He may be a Philosopher, for what I know, but he is not a sufficient Statesman, he knows too little of American affairs or the Politicks of Europe, and takes too little Pains to inform himself of Either. He is too old, too infirm, too indolent and dissipated, to be sufficient for the Discharge of all the important Duties" he had to fulfill.[89] Franklin, Adams complained, seemed to spend all his time with women and never deigned to meet with him.

Adams was shocked at the way Franklin flirted with women, especially with his wealthy and beautiful neighbor, Anne-Louise de Harancourt Brillon de Jouy, who openly showed her affection for Franklin even in the presence of her elderly husband. Madame Brillon used to call Franklin "Cher Papa" while sitting on his lap. Adams was surprised to learn that a "very plain and clumzy" woman who was often present in the company was not the friend of Madame Brillon as he had assumed, but was actually the mistress of Monsieur Brillon. "I was astonished," recalled Adams, "that these People could live together in such apparent Friendship and indeed without cutting each others throats. But I did not know the World."

When Adams did get to know the French world that Franklin moved in, he did not at all like it. He particularly resented all the attention Franklin received from the French. Every day, as soon as Franklin finished his breakfast, Adams recounted sarcastically, he was surrounded by his many admirers who came "to have the honour to see the great Franklin, and to have the pleasure of telling Stories about his Simplicity, his bald head and scattering strait hairs, among their Acquaintances." Adams never appreciated Franklin's contribution to the American cause. Adams advised his cousin Samuel Adams that the mission ought to be in the hands of a single minister, namely himself.[90]

Franklin himself suggested to the Continental Congress that France had more ambassadors than it needed. Three were already too many, he told James Lovell, a member of its foreign affairs committee. Izard regarded himself as a fourth, said Franklin, "and is very angry that he was not consulted in making the Treaty which he could have mended in several Particulars." William Lee, who was returning from a trip, would soon make a fifth.[91] In September 1778 Congress finally recalled all the other commissioners and made Franklin sole minister plenipotentiary, largely because France insisted upon it. Adams was mortified and returned to America to participate in the writing of the Massachusetts Constitution; but Izard and the Lees stayed on for another year, making more trouble for Franklin.

Not only were the Lees and Ralph Izard sure that Franklin was too lazy, too partial to France, and unable or unwilling to do his job as representative of America, but they were also convinced that Franklin had been Deane's partner in corruption and was continuing to make money out of his position as minister. They even suggested that Franklin's loyalties might not really be with America. After all, his grandson, Temple Franklin, worked as his secretary, and wasn't his grandson the son of the notorious loyalist William Franklin, the former royal governor of New Jersey? In fact, one of Pennsylvania's congressional delegates charged that from these connections *"much evil might ensue to the United States."*[92]

These charges stirred up the Congress and resulted in days of debate in April 1779 over whether or not to recall Franklin, along with the other commissioners. The Congress even spent a day debating Franklin's character.[93] Largely because France insisted on Franklin's continued presence as minister and lobbied the Congress to that end, Virginia and North Carolina were ultimately the only states to support Franklin's recall. Nonetheless, many members of Congress continued to question whether the old man was up to being minister. Ralph Izard repeatedly told Congress that "the political salvation of America depends upon the recalling of Dr. Franklin."[94]

Much to Franklin's chagrin, the Congress even sent Henry Laurens's twenty-six-year-old son, John, to negotiate a new loan from the French. Franklin suppressed his anger at this insult, and in a letter to the president of the Congress in March 1781 he, in effect, asked for a vote of confidence. He suggested that his age had caught up with him, that the press of business was too heavy, and that perhaps the United States would like another person to replace him. He assured the Congress that he had no dissatisfaction with it or any doubts about the success of "the glorious Cause." But he did warn that, if replaced, he would remain in France at least until the peace and perhaps for the remainder of his life.[95]

Franklin was pleased when Congress reaffirmed his appointment as minister plenipotentiary—again largely because France had let Congress know in no uncertain terms that it wanted Franklin as minister. But Franklin sensed that Congress was full of doubts about him, and he was not at all happy with its lack of gratitude. Franklin reminded the wealthy merchant Robert Morris, who had just become superintendent of finance, what he might expect from serving the American public. First of all, he told Morris, the public office would take so much time and attention that his private interests would inevitably be injured. But worse: "the Publick is often niggardly even of its Thanks, while you are sure of being censured by malevolent Criticks and Bug Writers, who will abuse you while you are serving them and wound your Character in nameless Pamphlets." Such critics, he said with uncharacteristic bitterness, resembled "those little dirty stinking Insects, that attack us only in the dark, disturb our Repose, molesting & wounding us while our Sweat & Blood is contributing to their Subsistence."[96]

In the meantime John Adams had returned to Paris with the authority to negotiate peace with Britain. But since Britain was not ready to negotiate peace, Adams, "having nothing else here wherewith to employ himself," as Franklin ruefully told the Congress, had decided to try "supplying what he may suppose my Negociations defective in." Adams thought that Franklin was entirely wrong in the deferential way he approached the French. "He thinks as he tells me himself," reported Franklin in August 1780, "that America has been too free in Expressions of Gratitude to France; for that she is more obliged to us than we to her: and that we should shew Spirit in our Applications."[97]

Unfortunately, Adams in a series of undiplomatic letters said many of the same things directly to Vergennes, much to Franklin's embarrassment. Vergennes became so angry with Adams's bumptious manner that he ceased communicating with him and asked Franklin to send Adams's letters to Congress in order for it to decide whether Adams ought to be entrusted with any important mission. Ultimately, Congress in June 1781 decided to assign the peace negotiations to a commission composed of Adams, Thomas Jefferson, John Jay, Henry Laurens, and Franklin.[98] According to Arthur Lee, it was Franklin whom Congress almost left out. The only reason Franklin was included, said Lee, was "because France wills it."[99]

Although Jefferson declined the appointment and Laurens was captured at sea and imprisoned in the Tower of London, the other three commissioners were on hand in Paris by the fall of 1782. Jay and Adams were nearly as suspicious of their colleague's partiality to France as Arthur Lee had been. They also thought their French ally was not to be trusted. According to Franklin, Adams especially thought that Vergennes was "one of the greatest Enemies" of the United States. For Americans "to think of Gratitude to France," said Adams, "is the greatest of Follies," and "to be influenced by it, would ruin us." Franklin told the American foreign secretary, Robert R. Livingston, that Adams was beguiled by conspiratorial notions. Adams believed that Vergennes and Franklin were "continually plotting against him and employing the News writers of Europe to depreciate his Character, &ca." And worse: Adams said all this publicly, in "extravagant and violent Language," even in front of English officials. What could be done with such a man? Perhaps Franklin was too generous in his famous summary of the man from Massachusetts, when he said that Adams "means well for his Country, is always an honest Man, often a Wise One, but sometimes and in some things, absolutely out of his Senses."[100]

Franklin hoped that "the ravings of a certain mischievous Madman here against France and its Ministers, which I hear every Day will not be regarded in America."[101] But Adams was not alone in his views; many Americans at home shared Adams's suspicions that Franklin was too attached to France. Franklin's "Enemies" in Congress, his friend Robert Morris warned him, were spreading the word "that a sense of Obligation to France seals your Lips when you should ask their Aid."[102]

Franklin was sorry to hear such criticism of America's connection with France. He wanted his critics to know that they were doing America "irreparable harm" by destroying "the good understanding that has hitherto so happily subsisted between this court and ours." America's connection with France was what gave the United States weight with England and the respect of Europe. Therefore Franklin believed that "the true political interest of America consists in observing and fulfilling with the greatest exactitude the engagements of our alliance with France."[103] He was grateful to France for its aid in the Revolution, and he thought all of America ought to be too.

FRANKLIN'S DIPLOMATIC ACHIEVEMENT

All this American carping about overweening French influence could have eroded the Franco-American alliance. Indeed, without Franklin's presence it is hard to see how the alliance could have held together as it did, and without the alliance it is hard to see how the Americans could have sustained their revolution. By the early 1780s Vergennes had become virtual first minister of the French government and the chief supporter of aiding the Americans. He retained the confidence of Louis XVI, and Franklin alone among the American commissioners retained Vergennes's confidence.[104] Probably only Franklin could have persuaded Vergennes to keep on supporting the American cause, and probably only Franklin could have negotiated so many loans from an increasingly impoverished French government. Certainly no one else could have represented America abroad as Franklin did. He was the greatest diplomat America has ever had.

Not only did Franklin hold the Franco-American alliance together, but he also oversaw the initial stages of the successful peace negotiations with Britain. And he did all this with a multitude of demands placed on him. In addition to his duties as minister plenipotentiary, which included dealing with countless persons offering advice, seeking favors, and asking for information, he effectively acted as consul general, director of naval affairs, and judge of admiralty. He handled mercantile matters, commissioned privateers, and served as judge in the condemnation and sale of the prizes captured by the privateersmen; at one point he was even called upon to help plan a prospective French invasion of England.

All the while countless Europeans continually pestered him for letters of recommendation that they hoped would be passports to prosperity in America. Many of these would-be emigrants, said Franklin, had very little money but often had "such romantic Schemes and Expectations as must end in Disappointment and Poverty." He tried to dissuade all who had no "useful Trade or Art by which they may get a living." But many were fools and would not listen. They "hope for Offices and Public Employments" and "value themselves and expect to be valued by us for their Birth or Quality, though I tell them those things bear no Price in our Markets."[105] Finally, to keep from having to repeat himself over and over to these prospective settlers, Franklin in February 1784 published a short piece, *Information to Those Who Would Remove to America.*

In it he laid out a description of the New World that contributed mightily to the emerging myth of American exceptionalism. America, said Franklin, was "the Land of Labour" where land was cheap and labor was dear and where hard work could lead to a moderate prosperity. Birth counted for nothing in America. There "People do not enquire concerning a Stranger, *What IS he?* but *What can he DO?*" Those who hoped for some lucrative political office in America would be greatly disappointed, for there were few civil offices there and no superfluous ones, as in Europe. Indeed, he said, emphasizing a point of utmost importance to him, some of the states had established a rule "that no Office should be so profitable as to make it desirable."[106]

But these difficulties in France with supplicants and would-be emigrants were nothing compared with the problems Franklin faced having to raise and spend money for the United States abroad. He had to request loan after loan from France, and time after time Vergennes came through for him. At times it seemed as if it was Vergennes's trust in Franklin alone that made the many French loans and subsidies possible. By 1783 France had granted more than twenty-five million livres in loans and subsidies to the United States in a war that eventually cost France over one billion livres.[107] Without this French financial aid the Americans could scarcely have continued their fight.

Franklin was increasingly embarrassed to keep asking Vergennes for money. His fellow Americans back home seemed to think "that France has Money enough for all her Occasions and all ours besides; and that if she does not supply us, it is owing to her Want of Will, or to my Negligence." It was especially mortifying that the American states could not even agree on "a most reasonable proposition" of granting the Confederation the power to levy a 5 percent impost on imported goods. "Our People certainly ought to do more for themselves," he complained. "It is absurd the Pretending to be Lovers of Liberty while they grudge Paying for the Defence of it."[108]

Not only did Franklin have to apply continually to France for loans, but he also had to ensure that Congress did not overdraw on them. In fact, Congress had the habit of drawing on European loans that had not yet been negotiated, and it was up to Franklin to manage somehow to pay them. "The Storm of Bills which I found coming upon us both," he wrote to John Jay in Spain in October 1780, "has terrified and vexed me to such a Degree that I have been deprived of Sleep, and so much indisposed by continual Anxiety as to be render'd almost incapable of Writing."[109] Franklin lived in dread that congressional bills would arrive that could not be met, with the "Consequences of Ruin to our Public Credit both in America and Europe."[110]

Despite his feeling for France, Franklin did not object when the American delegation decided to go ahead, in violation of Congress's instructions, and make a separate peace with Britain. By hinting at the possibility of weakening the Franco-American alliance, the commissioners persuaded Britain in the provisional treaty signed on November 30, 1782, to recognize the independence of the United States and to agree to much more generous boundaries for the new country than anyone could have expected.

It was left to Franklin, however, to apologize to Vergennes for the Americans' negotiating a separate peace with Britain. He did so in a beautifully wrought diplomatic letter. He admitted to Vergennes that the American commissioners had neglected a point of propriety. He hoped, however, that this "single Indiscretion of ours" would be excused

Treaty of Paris, *unfinished, by Benjamin West, 1783.* Left to right: *John Jay, John Adams, Benjamin Franklin, Henry Laurens, Temple Franklin*

and would not endanger the great work that Louis XVI had accomplished. He stressed that he and his countrymen loved and honored the king as much as the French themselves. Then he added, in a brilliant stroke, that he had just learned that the English "flatter themselves they have already divided us." Which, of course, was true. But, said Franklin, he hoped that "this little Misunderstanding will be kept a perfect Secret," and that the English "will find themselves totally mistaken." When he read this, Vergennes must have smiled at the wiliness of the American diplomat.

At the same time, of course, Franklin made still another request for money. He pointed out to Vergennes that "the whole Edifice" of the alliance "falls to the ground immediately" if France should refuse "to give us any farther Assistance." A month later he was still asking for more money. "Considering the enormous Expence this extensive War must occasion to his Majesty," he had hoped to avoid coming back to Vergennes. He had tried to procure money elsewhere, but nothing had worked out. "As Peace will diminish both the King's Expence and ours," he told the French minister with a straight face, "I hope this Request may be granted, and that it may be sufficient for our Occasions."[111]

Franklin was able to get away with these kinds of diplomatic shenanigans because he always maintained the overwhelming support of Vergennes and the French public, or at least the aristocratic part of that public that counted. And that support, indeed that adulation by the French public, enabled him to weather every storm and every difficulty during these turbulent years. His reputation with the French was the greatest source of his political support in the Continental Congress. Without the repeated insistence of the French government that it preferred to deal with Franklin and Franklin alone, it is quite possible that the Congress would have recalled him; certainly his enemies thought so. But his extraordinary reputation in France, in fact in all of Europe, not only helped to maintain his political support back home; it was also a principal source of whatever strength America had in international politics. When Franklin told Congress that America's connection with France was what gave the United States weight with England and the respect of Europe, he might well have added that he, Franklin, was the person who stood for America, and it was his personal connection to France that really counted in the Franco-American relationship. If Washington was indispensable to the success of the Revolution in America, Franklin was indispensable to the success of the Revolution abroad.

FIVE

BECOMING AN AMERICAN

THE *AUTOBIOGRAPHY*, ONCE AGAIN

The nearly eight years that Franklin spent in France were the happiest of his life. He did what he had long yearned to do—shape events on a world stage. The French alliance and the peace treaty with Great Britain recognizing American independence were vindications of all that he had believed about the ability of a few men of reason and common sense—indeed, perhaps, as he said, "even one Man of tolerable Abilities"—to make a difference in world affairs.[1] He had always hoped that he could manipulate world events in the way he manipulated chessmen on a board. "Life," he wrote sometime during his mission in France, "is a kind of chess, in which we have often points to gain, & competitors or adversaries to contend with, and in which there is a vast variety of good and ill events, that are, in some degree, the effects of prudence or the want of it."[2] The British Empire had come apart because the British officials had not approached the political situation in the 1760s and 1770s with the prudence, foresight, circumspection, caution, and patience that good chess players have. But he and the other American diplomats had known how to approach their tasks as good chess players. As the principal American diplomat abroad he especially had realized that there were points to gain and adversaries to contend with, and he had discreetly brought about good effects by approaching his negotiations with the French and British with his chess-instilled habits in mind. He had demonstrated that reason and prudence could indeed "work great Changes, and accomplish great Affairs among Mankind."[3]

That success and that confidence in reason were expressed in the second part of his *Autobiography,* which he resumed writing in 1784. With the peace treaty signed and the press of business eased, Franklin, still residing in Passy, had more leisure to take up his pen. But he probably would not have resumed writing his *Autobiography* without some prodding from friends.

Before leaving America for France in the fall of 1776, Franklin had turned over all his papers, including the only copy of the first part of the *Autobiography,* for safekeeping to Joseph Galloway, his former close friend, whom he made one of his executors. Instead of remaining neutral as Franklin expected, Galloway had fled to the British army in New York in December 1776, at the same time that Franklin arrived in France. Two years later Galloway sailed for England, leaving behind his wife and his estate, neither of which he ever saw again. When Galloway's wife died in America in 1782, Franklin's papers, including the *Autobiography,* apparently came into the hands of Abel James, who was one of her executors.

Sometime late that year or early in 1783, Franklin received a letter from James, who was an old Quaker friend. James had read the fragment of the *Autobiography* that Franklin had written in 1771, and he now urged Franklin to resume his memoir. This work, James said, "would be useful & entertaining not only to a few, but to millions." It would have an especially strong influence on America's youth. Indeed, James told Franklin that he knew of "no Character living nor many of them put together, who has so much in his Power as Thyself to promote a greater Spirit of Industry and early Attention to Business, frugality and Temperance with the American Youth." Not that the work would not have other uses, but James believed its potential influence on young people was "of such vast Importance" that he knew "nothing that can equal it." Despite all his enthusiasm, James could scarcely have foreseen just how influential Franklin's *Autobiography* would become for young people.

Franklin's English friend Benjamin Vaughan read and wholeheartedly endorsed James's letter—even though he had not read a page of the *Auto-*

biography, but knew "only the character who lived it." Franklin had to tell the story of his life for a number of reasons, Vaughan told his friend in a letter written at the end of January 1783. First of all, he wrote, "your life is so remarkable, that if you do not give it, somebody else will certainly give it; and perhaps so as nearly to do as much harm, as your own management of the thing might do good." Moreover, Franklin's life would present such a view of America as to invite "settlers of virtuous and manly minds" to migrate there. All that had happened to Franklin, Vaughan said, "is also connected with the detail of the manner and situation of *a rising people.*" Even the writings of Caesar and Tacitus could not be more revealing of human nature and society. But even more important, said Vaughan, was the opportunity that "your life will give for the forming of future great men; and in conjunction with your *Art of Virtue,* (which you design to publish) of improving the features of private character, and consequently of aiding all happiness both public and domestic."

These works will "give a noble rule and example of self-education," especially for youth, in whom "the private and public character is determined." "But," said Vaughan, "your Biography will not merely teach self-education, but the education of *a wise man.*" Human beings have been blundering on in the dark from the beginning of time. "Shew then, Sir, how much is to be done, *both to sons and fathers;* and invite all wise men to become like yourself; and other men to become wise." Franklin could show people how it is possible "to be both great and domestic; enviable and good-humoured." He could especially teach people the "rules of prudence in ordinary affairs." Franklin's life, Vaughan told the American, would show people that he was not ashamed of his humble beginnings. He would "prove how little necessary all origin is to happiness, virtue, or greatness." He could also teach people patience and timing, so "that man should arrange his conduct so as to suit the *whole* of a life." James's letter, said Vaughan, was fine in praising "your frugality, diligence, and temperance," but James forgot to mention "your modesty, and your disinterestedness."

Because people will be interested in the sources of the "immense revolution of the present period," said Vaughan, they will want to know the motivations of the revolutionaries and whether they were virtuous. "As your own character will be the principal one to receive a scrutiny, it is proper (even for its effects upon your vast and rising country, as well as upon England and Europe), that it should stand respectable and eternal." Franklin's life could establish the central point of this enlightened age—that men were not born to obscurity and viciousness but through their own efforts could rise and do good work. Vaughan ended his letter by appealing to Franklin to write his life in order to get Americans and Englishmen thinking well of each other again. But not just Americans and Englishmen needed to learn about his life. "Extend your views even further: do not stop at those who speak the English tongue, but after having settled so many points in nature and politics, think of bettering the whole race of men."[4]

Franklin could hardly have resisted these exhortations to become an exemplar for a rising people. In 1784 he thus resumed writing his *Autobiography*—the second part of it, which, like a game of chess, presumes man's control over his life. Obviously influenced by Vaughan's letter, Franklin laid out in this section of his memoir his method for achieving happiness. All of the intellectuals in the age of Enlightenment—from Francis Hutcheson to Claude-Adrien Helvétius—were preoccupied with discovering the moral forces in the human world that were comparable to the physical forces in the natural world uncovered by Newton and other scientists. Franklin was no different. In the 1750s he had revealed the workings of electricity in the natural world, but he had longed to make an equally important contribution to the moral or social sciences. He had been thinking about writing a book on the "Art of Virtue" for decades.[5] But now he realized that he might not have time to write it. So instead he decided to describe in his *Autobiography* his "bold and arduous Project of arriving at moral Perfection."[6]

THE PROJECT FOR ACHIEVING MORAL PERFECTION

In his *Autobiography* Franklin set forth a series of moral injunctions for living a good life, including reading, practicing modesty, and avoiding "Taverns, Games, and Frolicks of any kind." He praised religion for whatever moral effects it had, but for little else. He believed that simply exhorting people to be good would not be enough; he wanted to present them with the means and manner of obtaining virtue—without relying on organized religion, which Franklin found often tended to divide people from one another rather than inspiring and promoting morality.

He listed thirteen virtues (temperance, silence, order, resolution, frugality, industry, sincerity, justice, moderation, cleanliness, tranquillity, chastity, and humility) with descriptions of each; for example, frugality—"Waste not"; industry—"Lose no time"; chastity—"Rarely use Venery but for Health or Offspring"; and humility—"Imitate Jesus and Socrates." These were not utopian virtues, requiring a complete change of heart; instead, they were realistic, down-to-earth virtues, capable of being managed by ordinary people and not just a saintly few.[7] By creating an elaborate "Plan for Self-Examination"—a daily checklist for each virtue—Franklin tells us how he worked diligently to eliminate faults and promote his thirteen virtues—all with the aim not only of pleasing God but, more important, of getting along in life. This is the project that D. H. Lawrence and other imaginative writers have so much detested.[8]

Franklin took his project to achieve moral perfection quite seriously, more seriously perhaps than many commentators have admitted. The Enlightenment promise of being able to make oneself over culturally seemed to be exemplified in Franklin's life. The seriousness with which he took his project to become morally perfect is revealed in the wonderful but complicated anecdote of the speckled ax. He had told the story many times to French friends, and now he incorporated it into this second section of his *Autobiography*.

In attempting to carry out the elaborate moral injunctions he had set for himself, he said, he had difficulty in ordering his time. In fact, he tells us, he made so little progress and had so many relapses in ordering his life that he was "almost ready to give up the Attempt" and content himself "with a faulty Character in that respect." At this point he injected the story of the speckled ax.

A man had bought a new ax and now wanted to have the whole surface of his ax as bright as the edge. The smith who had sold him the ax consented to grind it bright for him if the man would turn the wheel. The smith pressed the broad face of the ax hard and heavy against the stone, which made turning it very fatiguing. The man, becoming more and more tired, kept leaving the wheel to see how the grinding was coming. Finally, the exhausted man declared he would take his ax as it was without further grinding. No, said the smith, keep turning and sooner or later we'll have it bright; as yet, it was still only speckled. "Yes, says the Man; but—*I think I like a speckled Ax best.*"

This, said Franklin, was the way many people rationalized abandoning their efforts to break bad habits and establish good ones. They gave up the struggle "and concluded that *a speckled Ax was best.*"

It is stories like these that make interpreting Franklin and his *Autobiography* so difficult. Some otherwise sensitive readers have concluded from this anecdote that Franklin had learned his lesson—that seeking the sort of moral perfection that did violence to human nature was foolish. Indeed, Franklin himself suggests as much when he notes that every now and then he thought his entire project "might be a kind of Foppery in Morals," which, if it became known, would make him "ridiculous." He goes on to observe "that a perfect Character might be attended with the Inconvenience of being envied and hated," and therefore "a benevolent Man should allow a few Faults in himself, to keep his Friends in Countenance."

On the face of it such suggestions make Franklin appear to be a reasonable man, someone who counsels good sense and moderation instead of maintaining utopian fantasies of moral perfection. But for Franklin such thinking was only "something that pretended to be Reason," and not reason itself. With his seemingly sensible suggestions he was not really trying to justify giving up the effort to be morally perfect. The real message of his story is that one has to keep grinding away and not remain satisfied with a speckled ax.

Although Franklin admits that he had not attained moral perfection in his lifetime but had fallen far short of it, "yet I was by the Endeavour a better and a happier Man than I otherwise should have been, if I had not attempted it." In other words, Franklin tells us the delightful story of the speckled ax only to deny its lesson at the end. Any reader, however, is bound to be overwhelmed by the charm of the anecdote and the power of the rationalizations that excuse a less than perfect moral character. Hence, Franklin leaves us with a very morally ambiguous message. Which is why so many different readers can draw so many different lessons from the *Autobiography,* and indeed, from all of his writings.[9]

Franklin wanted his posterity to know, he says, that even at the age of seventy-eight this "little Artifice" of self-examination was the source of the health and felicity of his life. Above all, he owed "to the joint Influence of the whole Mass of the Virtues, even in their imperfect State he was able to acquire them, all that Evenness of Temper, & that Chearfulness in Conversation which makes his Company still sought for, & agreeable even to his younger Acquaintance."[10]

As this boast indicates and as Franklin disarmingly admitted, he never had much success "in acquiring the *Reality*" of the virtue of humility, but he "had a good deal with regard to the *Appearance* of it." Humility, he said, had not been on his original list of virtues; he had added it only because a friend had told him that he was too proud. Franklin was well aware of his pride and its near relation, vanity. He had begun his *Autobiography* by admitting the overwhelming power of vanity. "Most People," he had written in 1771, "dislike Vanity in others whatever Share they have of it themselves." But Franklin knew better. "I give it fair Quarter whenever I meet with it, being persuaded that it is often productive of Good to the Possessor and to others that are within his Sphere of Action." Now in 1784 at the end of the second part of his *Autobiography* he was still struggling with the vanity and pride in himself that he could not help feeling and that he knew were the real sources of his benevolence and success in life. Pride, he conceded, was the hardest passion to subdue. "Disguise it, struggle with it, beat it down, stifle it, mortify it as much as one pleases, it is still alive, and will every now and then peep out and show itself." Even if he could completely overcome his pride, he would probably then be proud of his humility.[11]

A STRANGER IN MY OWN COUNTRY

After the peace treaty was signed, Franklin reluctantly realized that he ought to end his days in America. But he had come to love France. It was "the civilest Nation upon Earth," he believed, and the French were "a delightful People to live with."[12] On at least two occasions he expressed a strong desire to settle there for good.[13] The first time was when he tried to arrange a marriage between his grandson Temple and the daughter of

Monsieur and Madame Brillon. To convince the Brillons that their daughter would not be taken away with Temple, Franklin promised not only to secure a diplomatic post in Europe for his grandson but also to remain in France for the rest of his life. The Brillons found reasons to put Franklin off, and the matter was dropped.

The second time Franklin declared he would remain in France was when he proposed marriage to Anne-Catherine Helvétius, the widow of the philosopher. Madame Helvétius was over sixty but still lively and attractive. But, more important, she maintained a spirited salon in Auteuil, next to Passy, that was celebrated for its wit and irreverence. Franklin, like many others, was smitten with her. "I see that statesmen, philosophers, historians, poets, and men of learning of all sort are drawn around you, and seem as willing to attach themselves to as straws about a fine piece of amber," he once told her. "We find in your sweet society, that charming benevolence, that amiable attention to oblige, that disposition to please and be pleased, which we do not always find in the society of one another. It springs from you; it has its influence on us all; and in your company we are not only pleased with you, but better pleased with one another and with ourselves."[14] It may have been Madame Helvétius who inspired Franklin's famous compliment, the kind of bon mot that any eighteenth-century French aristocratic woman would have prized. When one of these French ladies reproached the doctor for putting off a visit she had expected, Franklin, taken aback, supposedly replied, "Madame, I am waiting until the nights are longer."[15]

Franklin was so admiring of Madame Helvétius that he wanted everyone to meet her. When he introduced John Adams's wife, Abigail, to her, however, the puritanical lady from Massachusetts was not at all impressed; in fact, she was disgusted, as she was with Paris in general. Madame Helvétius was much too bold and loose for Mrs. Adams's taste, bawling out her greetings, throwing her arms about her dinner partners' chairs, sprawling on a settee, "where she shew more than her feet."[16] John Adams agreed with his wife about the dissolute behavior he observed in the Helvétius household. "Oh Mores," he said. "What Absurdities, Inconsistencies, Distractions and Horrors would these Manners introduce into our Republican Governments in America: No kind of Republican Government can ever exist with such national manners as these. Cavete Americani."[17]

Franklin shared none of this kind of straitlaced American reaction to French manners. He understood the French and was charmed by them, and especially by Madame Helvétius and the warm and bantering cheekiness of her household. He repeatedly proposed to her, but always with a certain playful detachment so their pride would not be endangered. His French friends, however, thought he was quite serious and blamed Madame Helvétius for letting him go. If Madame Helvétius had accepted him, the most expert authority on Franklin's female relations believes, the good doctor would never have returned to America.[18]

One can hardly blame him for wanting to stay in Europe. He was an old man, and, as John Adams noted, Frenchwomen had "an unaccountable passion for old age."[19] Franklin had spent all but three and a half years out of the previous twenty-seven years abroad, the last eight years in France. "I am here among a People that love and respect me, a most amiable Nation to live with," he wrote in 1784, "and perhaps I may conclude to die among them; for my Friends in America are dying off one after another, and I have been so long abroad that I should now be almost a Stranger in my own Country"—a phrase that he had used repeatedly over the previous decade or so when he thought about returning to America.[20] Indeed, all his most cherished friends were in Europe, not America; and his former close American confidants—Joseph Galloway and his own son William—had become loyalists, and he would have nothing to do with them. But even more important, his intimate connection with France and the symbolic importance he had had for France as an American—the very things that had helped make possible French aid to America—were now being turned against him by his fellow Americans.

By 1783 some of his countrymen had come to believe that he was more loyal to France than to America. He seemed entirely too close to the French, hobnobbing with members of the French aristocracy and spending much too much time with Frenchwomen in their salons. He even received from Louis XVI the gift of a small box containing the king's portrait. Edmund Randolph later declared that Franklin's accepting this gift was what led the Constitutional Convention of 1787 to insert in the Constitution the clause prohibiting officials of the United States from accepting presents or emoluments from foreign princes or states. The members of the Convention, said Randolph at the Virginia ratifying convention, had wanted to avoid in the future any possibility of foreign princes' corrupting America's ambassadors, in the manner in which some Americans in the early 1780s thought Franklin had been corrupted.[21]

In May 1783, Samuel Cooper, a clergyman friend in Boston, wrote Franklin that a party in America, based on information coming from John Adams, was casting doubt on his patriotism. Word was spreading, said Cooper, that Franklin was not to be trusted and that "it was entirely owing to the Firmness, Sagacity and Disinterestedness of M. Adams, with whom Mr. Jay united," that prevented American interests from being sacrificed to those of France.[22] These reports hurt Franklin deeply. After the final peace treaty was signed in September 1783, he sent a letter to all his fellow commissioners poignantly denying such charges. He knew he did not have long to live, he said, but he did not want to go to his grave with the world thinking that he had less "Zeal and Faithfulness" to America than any of his colleagues. He was not willing to "suffer an accusation, which falls little short of Treason to my Country, to pass without Notice."[23] He asked each of his fellow commissioners to certify his contribution to the peace negotiations in order, he said, to destroy the effects of these accusations. That the aged diplomat should have been reduced to such a humiliating request says a great deal about how differently France and America had come to view the great Dr. Franklin.

Still, with the letters from James and Vaughan and the writing of the second part of his *Autobiography*, he now knew that his destiny was linked to America. He had come to realize that the "Revolution" that he had "hardly expected I should live to see" and that he had done so much to bring to success had become "an important Event for the Advantage of Mankind in general."[24]

But the Continental Congress still had not answered his request to be recalled, leaving him uncertain about what to do. "During my long Absence from America," he told the secretary of the Congress Charles Thomson in May 1784, "my Friends are continually diminishing by Death, and my Inducement to return in Proportion."[25] Not only were his close friends in America dying off, but he also knew he had acquired many enemies in their place. With the signing of the Treaty of Paris, Franklin wanted his grandson Temple, who had been the secretary of the peace commission, to deliver the treaty to Congress. Instead, that honor went to a protégé of Adams who had not been involved in the peace negotiations at all. Since Franklin thought of Temple "as a Son who makes up to me my Loss by the Estrangement of his Father," he next asked Congress to name his twenty-four-year-old grandson secretary of the new commission designed to sign commercial treaties with the European nations. He even hoped that Temple might be named his successor to France. Or perhaps his grandson could be appointed American minister to Sweden. But Congress was now in the hands of his enemies and the outlook was not promising. Richard Henry Lee had become president of Congress. As Franklin's son-in-law, Richard Bache, dryly noted of Lee, "He is no friend to us, or our connections."[26]

Franklin's enemies in Congress now saw that they could get at Franklin through his grandson. Not only did Temple have "no Prospect of promotion," but, wrote a gloating Elbridge Gerry to John Adams, Franklin's grandson "has been actually superseded" by the appointment of Colonel David Humphreys, a protégé of Washington, as secretary of the new commission. Once he saw these congressional actions, said Gerry, Franklin "will have no Reason to Suppose that his Conduct is much approved." Indeed, said Gerry, Congress had ceased being "reserved . . . with respect to the Doctor." Franklin had become so useless that "it has become a matter of Indifference to Us, whether We employ him or the Count de Vergennes to negotiate our Concerns at the Court of Versailles."[27]

Rumors now abounded in both America and Britain that Franklin and his loyalist son William had been in collusion all along—each taking a side in order to protect the family regardless of who won the war. In November 1784 a New Yorker friend of William Franklin warned Temple not to get too close to his grandfather, for the old man's "Influence" in America was "very small." Even the reputation of the Marquis de Lafayette had been injured by his attempts to keep Franklin in France during the peace negotiations. These efforts by Lafayette "led People to suspect that he meant only to retain a Man that was perfectly subservient to his Court." Although this friend of William Franklin certainly exaggerated the weakness of Franklin's influence among his countrymen, he was not entirely wrong. Franklin in 1784 was not the important Founder he would later become. This cynical New Yorker knew what the Revolution meant and had some parting words of advice for Temple: "Make friends of every American, for in Republican Governments, you have many to please."[28]

Finally, in May 1785, Franklin received word from Congress that his mission was over and that he could return to America. Thomas Jefferson had arrived and was named American minister to France. Unlike Adams, Jefferson got along splendidly with Franklin. For Jefferson, Franklin was "the ornament of our country, and I may say, of the world."[29] He liked to tell the French that he could never be Franklin's replacement as minister. He might succeed Dr. Franklin, but nobody could replace him.

Franklin's reputation in Europe was extraordinary. A professor in Prague called him the Solon, the Socrates, and the Seneca of the present day. Jacques-Pierre Brissot de Warville called him "the ornament of the New World" and "a leader of modern philosophy." Another European dubbed him "the Cato of his age." From England, Erasmus Darwin (another great inventor and polymath and the grandfather of Charles Darwin) addressed him as "the greatest Statesman of the present, or perhaps of any century," who single-handedly had spread liberty among his countrymen and "deliver'd them from the house of bondage, and the scourge of oppression." From Florence, from Switzerland, from France, from all over Europe he was hailed as a great politician and scientist and the first man of the universe.[30]

Franklin knew that he was respected abroad, but he remained uncertain about his reputation in his own country. Jefferson too was uncertain of how his fellow Americans would regard the returning Franklin. Writing from Paris in 1785, Jefferson knew that Franklin was "infinitely esteemed" in Europe. But he was very anxious that his fellow Americans might not know just how much Europeans esteemed Franklin and thus might not treat him properly. Jefferson, who was always acutely sensitive to what liberal Europeans thought of America, more than once warned James Monroe, an influential member of the Congress, that "Europe fixes an attentive eye on your reception of Doctr. Franklin." The way Americans receive Franklin, Jefferson told his fellow Virginian, "will weigh in Europe as an evidence of the satisfaction or dissatisfaction of America with their revolution."[31]

THE RETURN TO PHILADELPHIA

Franklin arrived home in Philadelphia on September 14, 1785, and was met by cheering crowds and ringing bells—an "affectionate Welcome" that he claimed "was far beyond my Expectations."[32] With a population of fewer than forty thousand people, Philadelphia was no Paris or London, but it was booming and had become not only the largest city in America but its commercial and cultural center as well. Philadelphia had the only bank and the only library in the country that was open to the public—the Library Company, which Franklin had helped to found. The city also was the center of medical education in the nation and contained the most well-known scientific society in the country, the American Philosophical Society, which Franklin had also founded. Franklin's spirit was still present, for the city had just formed a society for the promotion of agriculture, and it was taking the lead in humanitarian reforms of various sorts. The city's artisans were organizing as never before and were demonstrating more political strength than they had had in Franklin's day.

Franklin no sooner landed than Charles Willson Peale, a Philadelphia artist of many talents, painted his portrait (see page 214), which Peale displayed in a gallery of Revolutionary heroes. It was one of the most accurate portrayals done of Franklin as an old man, complete with the new bifocal spectacles he had invented. Peale issued mezzotint prints based on his portrait, and Franklin's face was soon spread about the city. Peale attempted another portrait in 1789; but Franklin was too ill to sit, and Peale had to base his new picture on his original of 1785.

Philadelphia may have become the cultural and commercial center of the new nation, but it was still plagued by factional politics. Franklin, in fact, arrived in the middle of an election campaign between the two rudimentary parties that had emerged in Pennsylvania since 1776. On one side were the Constitutionalists, dominated by artisans and Scotch-Irish western farmers who supported the radical Pennsylvania Constitution of 1776, which Franklin had helped to draft. On the other side were the Republicans, dominated by Anglicans and wealthy merchants and professionals who wanted to change the state's constitution by introducing a governor

Franklin, by Charles Willson Peale, 1785

and an upper house and to bring the constitution more into line with those of the other states. In hopes of bringing unity to the state, both parties nominated Franklin for the executive council (a group of twelve that served as the executive in place of a governor). Franklin admitted that he "had not sufficient Firmness to refuse their Support."[33] Following his election, the council and assembly then elected him president of the council.

Thus, only a few weeks after his arrival he had become the head of the Commonwealth of Pennsylvania. It all had happened so fast that he scarcely had time to think about what he had done. At seventy-nine he was old, tired, and suffering from gout as well as bladder or kidney stones, and yet he had gotten himself into a "Business more troublesome than that I have lately quitted."[34] George Washington, who had conspicuously retired from all public business in 1783, thought Franklin was out of his mind to accept any political office. But Franklin had heard so many stories of how suspicious many Americans had been of him that the enthusiastic reception in Pennsylvania had gone to his head. He knew he ought to quit public life and enjoy some of the well-earned rest that he had yearned for in France, but his desire to be thought well of was too strong. Accepting the office of president of Pennsylvania seemed to vindicate his virtue.

He accepted reelection to the office twice more, in 1786 and 1787 (with no dissenting vote except his own); and he perhaps avoided a fourth term only because the Pennsylvania Constitution prohibited it. Whatever his status might have been with some of the rest of the American people, most of the citizens of Pennsylvania, except for a fashionable few, revered him.[35] "This universal and unbounded confidence of a whole People," he told his sister after his third election to the presidency, "flatters my Vanity much more than a Peerage could do."[36]

This emotional need to be elected to office in order to boost his morale was sad. Franklin had devoted much of his life to serving the American public, and yet some members of that public still seemed to doubt him. Despite praise from individual Americans and the naming of a renegade state in western North Carolina after him (later part of Tennessee), he was still uncertain about his reputation in his own country. Indeed, he found himself in the embarrassing position of having to write friends to find out what his fellow Americans really thought of him. He knew there were "Calumnies propagated" against him, "which appeared all to emanate from the Brantry Focus," that is, the Adamses of Braintree, Massachusetts. Nevertheless, he also knew that at his age, and considering who he was and what he had done, he should not be so concerned with what people thought of him. "You see," he admitted, "that old as I am, I am not yet grown insensible, with respect to Reputation."[37]

THE CONSTITUTIONAL CONVENTION

In March 1787 the Pennsylvania Assembly appointed Franklin to the state's delegation to the Convention that was to meet in Philadelphia in May to revise the Articles of Confederation. Although Franklin was confident that America was growing and prospering even under the Confederation, he realized that America's experiment in republicanism was on trial and that the Convention was designed to prove that free government could sustain itself. Even before the Convention met, Franklin organized the Society for Political Enquiries, which met weekly in Franklin's home seeking to study political science as the American Philosophical Society studied natural science.

On May 16, 1787, Franklin, as he explained to an English correspondent, hosted a dinner for "what the French call *une assemblée des notables*, a convention composed of some of the principal people from the several states of our confederation."[38] On May 25 this Constitutional Convention, this assembly of notables, finally had a quorum and began meeting officially. Franklin, described by one observer at the time as "a short, fat, trunched old man, in a plain Quaker dress, bald pate, and short white locks," was the oldest member in attendance. As the oldest he was supposed to nominate George Washington as president of the Convention, but heavy rain kept him home.[39] Instead, the Pennsylvania delegation as a whole nominated Washington, which, James Madison noted, was an act of "particular grace, as Doctor Franklin alone could have been thought of as a competitor."[40]

Although most of the delegates did not know Franklin personally, they did know him by reputation—as, in the words of William Pierce of Georgia, "the greatest philosopher of the age." Whatever Franklin's reputation as a philosopher, his claim to be a politician, Pierce thought, would have to wait for posterity to judge. Franklin was certainly unimpressive in public council. "He is no Speaker, nor does he seem to let politics engage his attention." Nevertheless, said Pierce, he was "a most extraordinary Man," who "tells a story in a style more engaging than anything I ever heard."[41]

Franklin did not often speak in the Convention, and when he did have more than a few words to say, he wrote out his speeches and had them read for him, since it was painful for him to stand. Most of his efforts were designed to conciliate and bring the delegates together, but he did make one important proposal concerning an issue that was dear to his heart. On June 2, he moved that all members of the executive branch in the new government should serve without pay.

He had long believed that there were "two Passions which have a powerful Influence in the Affairs of Men . . . *Ambition* and *Avarice*; the Love of Power and the Love of Money." Each separately was a forceful spur to action, but when united in the minds of some men they had the most violent effects. "Place before the Eyes of such Men a Post of *Honour,* that shall at the same time be a place of *Profit,* and they will move Heaven and Earth to obtain it."[42] The result had always been continual struggles between factions and the eventual destruction of all virtue. Franklin's evidence for his views was England. For many years he had believed, as he never tired of telling his English friends or anyone else who would listen, that "the Root of the Evil" in England's politics lay "in the enormous Salaries, Emoluments, and Patronage" of its "Great Offices."[43] Although Americans may now start out with moderate salaries for their rulers, pressures would arise to increase them, and eventually, he feared, America would end up as a monarchy. There was, he said, "a natural Inclination in Mankind to kingly Government."

If some thought his idea that all executive officials serve without salary was too utopian, he offered the examples of sheriffs, judges, and the arbiters in Quaker meetings who served without pay. "In all Cases of public Service, the less the Profit the greater the Honour." His final example was Washington, who as commander in chief had served eight years without salary. He was sure there were enough men of public spirit in America who would do the same in civil offices. (During his mission to France, Franklin had been on salary, although he had a hard time extracting it from the Congress.) Although his motion was seconded, it was tabled and never taken up again. "It was treated with great respect," Madison noted, "but rather for the author of it than from any conviction of its expediency or practicability."[44]

Franklin's proposal was classically republican, presuming, as it did, that civic life demanded virtue and self-sacrifice from its citizens. But this classically republican proposal was inevitably aristocratic and patrician in implication—one that would have confined the executive branch of the national government to wealthy gentlemen like Washington and himself who were rich enough to be able to devote themselves to public service. The proposal had grown out of his own experience, his own life, his own understanding of himself. Four decades earlier he as a wealthy tradesman had retired from business to dedicate his leisured life to philosophy and public service. In the future, could not others do the same? Only through such virtue and self-sacrifice could the pride, vanity, and desire for self-aggrandizement of ambitious individuals be prevented from destroying the state. He knew the power of his own pride and ambition and he knew how he had diverted that power into benevolence and good works. He had long believed in this aristocratic and classical notion of public service and had written it into the otherwise democratic Pennsylvania Constitution in 1776. It was as central to his life as anything he believed in. In a codicil to his will written a year before his death he once again stated his deeply held conviction that "in a democratical state there ought to be no offices of profit."[45]

But Franklin was no defender of a traditional aristocracy; indeed, he had a deep dislike of aristocratic pretensions, sharpened by the ways some Philadelphians had snubbed him since his return to America in 1785. Given his background, Franklin could have little interest in aristocratic claims of blood. His criticism of the Society of the Cincinnati, a hereditary organization of retired Continental army officers created in 1783, was as strong as anyone's in America. He believed in honors and distinctions, but not in their being passed on to heirs. "For Honour worthily obtain'd, as that for Example of our Officers," he told his daughter in 1784, "is in its Nature a personal Thing, and incommunicable to any but those who had some Share in obtaining it. . . . Let the Distinction die with those who have merited it."[46]

In 1789 plans were being laid for the meeting of a Pennsylvania state constitutional convention to revise the much criticized radical constitution of 1776. All sorts of proposals for reform, including creating a single independent governor and a two-house legislature, were flying about the press, and Franklin responded to one of these. In his remarks, which were never published, he laid out his political thinking with remarkable clarity, demonstrating once and for all that in the context of traditional eighteenth-century assumptions of politics he was an enthusiastic democrat.

In his ardent defense of the 1776 document, which he had helped create, he opposed a single executive magistrate and any lengthening of the executive's one-year term. Anything longer would put Pennsylvanians on the slippery slope toward monarchy, or at least a monarchy for life, like that of Poland. But it was the constitutional reformers' desire to replace the unicameral legislature with a bicameral one, including an upper house or senate, that really provoked him and led to a series of angry and sprawling queries and protests. Wouldn't the two houses fight with each other and cause expensive delays and promote factions among the people? Didn't we Pennsylvanians learn a lesson from the mischief caused by the aristocratic proprietary council that acted as an upper house in the colony? he asked. Why couldn't the wisdom that was supposed to exist in the upper house exist just as well in a single body? Haven't we seen neighboring states torn apart by contention, their governments paralyzed by splits between the two houses of their legislatures? Has our single-house legislature committed any major errors that it hasn't remedied by itself? A two-house legislature was like a two-headed snake trying to reach a brook for a drink, he said; it had to pass through a hedge but was blocked by a twig. One head wanted to go right, the other left, and consequently "before the Decision was completed, the poor Snake died of thirst."

What really angered Franklin was the suggestion in the press that the proposed senate should represent property, with separate property qualifications both for the senators and for those who would vote for them; part of this suggestion resembled the highly regarded constitution of Massachusetts, whose senate was also designed to represent property. Although Franklin did not mention it, he well knew that his 1776 Pennsylvania Constitution contrasted in almost every particular with the conservative Massachusetts Constitution of 1780, which had been largely written by none other than his nemesis John Adams. Franklin could not imagine having a legislative body representing a minority in the state attempting to balance and control the other legislative body chosen by the majority. "Why is this Power of Control, contrary to the Spirit of all Democracies, to be vested in a Minority, instead of a Majority?" Why is property to be represented at all? he asked.

"Private property," he declared, in a rousing expression of the most radical republican thinking of the day, "is a Creature of Society and is subject to the Calls of that Society whenever its Necessities shall require it, even to its last Farthing." Civil society was not a mercantile company composed of richer and poorer stockholders; it was a community in which every member had an equal right to life and liberty. Franklin had no desire to give the wealthy any special legal privileges. Suggestions for an upper house for Pennsylvania that would represent the property of the state, he wrote, expressed "a Disposition among some of our People to commence an Aristocracy, by giving the Rich a Predominancy in Government, a Choice peculiar to themselves in one half of the Legislature." To have wealthy officials serving in the executive branch without pay did not mean that such rich men should dominate the popular representative legislature.[47]

Given Franklin's passionate commitment to a unicameral legislature, it is remarkable that in the Philadelphia Convention of 1787 he contributed as he did to the making of the so-called Connecticut compromise, which allowed for equal representation of the states in an upper house of the national legislature. But Franklin's role in the Convention was generally limited by his age and health. Much of the time he seemed bewildered by the rapidity of the exchanges and the contentiousness of the debates. He was surprised by the extent of division in the Convention and continued to look for ways to bring people together. He had come to realize that "when you assemble a number of men, to have the advantage of their joint wisdom, you inevitably assemble with those men all their prejudices, their passions, their errors of opinion, their local interests, and their selfish views." This appreciation of diversity and clashing self-interestedness in America was new; he had not talked like this in 1776.

At the end of June 1787, he made the extraordinary proposal that the Convention from then on open its sessions with prayer. He had concluded that the confusion and divisions that he had witnessed in the Convention were "a melancholy Proof of the Imperfection of the Human Understanding. We indeed seem to *feel* our own want of political Wisdom, since we have been running all about in Search of it." Since the delegates were "groping, as it were, in the dark to find Political Truth," Franklin asked, why not apply "to the Father of Lights to illuminate our Understandings?" Such prayers had helped Americans during the struggle leading up to independence. Everyone engaged in the Revolution, he said, "must have observed frequent Instances of a superintending Providence in our Favour."

After some discussion, this proposal, like his earlier one concerning salaries, was allowed to die. Someone later claimed that Alexander Hamilton had declared that the delegates did not need the aid of any foreign powers.

Franklin had never fully believed that reason was all that was needed to accomplish great deeds in public life; but as a result of his experience in the Convention, he now seemed less confident than ever in reason. He had come to believe, he told the Convention, that "God governs in the Affairs of Men" and that an empire could not be built out of "little, partial, local Interests" without God's aid.

At any rate, a year later, in June 1788, he had abandoned his earlier view that all life resembled a game of chess. The Convention's forming of a new government had been anything but a game of chess. "The players of our game are so many," he told a French correspondent,

> their ideas so different, their prejudices so strong and so various, and their particular interests independent of the general, seeming so opposite, that not a move can be made that is not contested; the numerous objections confound the understanding; the wisest must agree to some unreasonable things, that reasonable ones of more consequence may be obtained; and thus chance has its share in many of the determinations so that the play is more like *tric-trac* with a box of dice.[48]

FRANKLIN'S STRUGGLE WITH CONGRESS

Perhaps his heightened sense that events had spun out of his control and were in the hands of God or Providence flowed from his nasty experience with the Confederation Congress, which still contained many of his enemies. Indeed, the Congress's extraordinary treatment of him at the end of his life revealed just how ambiguous a figure he was to his fellow Americans. Other than being told by Jefferson and others that Franklin was "infinitely esteemed" in Europe, many of his countrymen did not know what to make of him.[49] Temple realized that his grandfather's "Reputation is great throughout Europe," but, as he ruefully noted, this "Circumstance" was "possibly of no Consequence" in America.[50]

What exactly had Franklin done for the country? He had not spearheaded the Revolutionary movement like John Adams. He had not led armies like Washington. He had not written a great document like Jefferson. His great diplomatic achievements as minister to France were actually denounced by his enemies and unappreciated by most of his countrymen. Compared with the fates of the other Founders his was singular. None of the other great men of the Revolution ever had to endure the kind of mortification Franklin experienced at the hands of the national government.

After he had returned to America, he asked Congress to settle what it owed him and sent his grandson Temple to New York to meet with Congress. Franklin still hoped that Congress might offer a diplomatic post to the young man. Since Congress had refused to supply him with a secretary in France, he explained, he had been forced to employ his grandson as secretary; and the young man had thereby sacrificed an opportunity to study law. Franklin said that he was not alone in his opinion of Temple's talents. "Three of my Colleagues, without the smallest Solicitation from me, chose him Secretary of the Commission for Treaties." But Congress took no notice of his grandson. "This was the only Favour I ask'd of them," Franklin said with as much resentment as he ever expressed; "and the only Answer I receiv'd was a Resolution superseding him and appointing Col. Humphreys in his place," a man, he complained, who had no diplomatic experience and did not even speak French.[51]

Not only did Congress ignore his grandson, but it also said that it could not settle his accounts until it received more information from France. As Franklin in 1788 complained with barely suppressed anger in a letter meant for Cyrus Griffin, the president of the Congress, the Congress had had his accounts for the past three years and had done nothing with them. But this had not stopped members of Congress from spreading rumors about him. Indeed, "reports have for some time past been circulated here, and propagated in the News-Papers, that I am greatly indebted to the United States for large Sums that had been put into my Hands, and that I avoid a Settlement." This, said Franklin, made "it necessary for me to request earnestly" that Congress examine the accounts "without farther Delay" and let him know if something was not right so that he could explain the matter and bring these accounts to a close.[52]

He asked his friend Charles Thomson to present this letter to Griffin, "as you must be better acquainted with Persons and Circumstances than I am."[53] Such a request itself suggests Franklin's problematic standing in the United States in 1788. Would Washington, who was Franklin's only rival for international renown in the 1780s, or would any of the Revolutionary leaders, for that matter, ever have had to ask someone else to approach the president of Congress on their behalf? Because of the way Congress had treated his request to appoint his grandson to a diplomatic post, Franklin was now well aware of where he stood with that body. He had, he said, "flatter'd myself vainly that the Congress would be pleas'd with the Opportunity I gave them of showing that Mark of their Approbation of my Services. But," he added pathetically, "I suppose that present Members hardly know me or that I have perform'd any."[54]

In the letter that he finally wrote to Thomson, Franklin released all of the anger he had suppressed in his letter to President Griffin. Indeed, although he assured Thomson that he would not have lessened his "Zeal for the Cause" even if he had foreseen "such unkind Treatment from Congress, as their refusing me their Thanks," he must have come close to wondering whether he had chosen the right side in 1776.

He knew that republics were notoriously ungrateful, but he had not expected the United States to treat him so meanly. It was "customary in Europe," he told Thomson, "to make some liberal Provision for Ministers when they return home from foreign Service, during which their Absence is necessarily injurious to their private Affairs." He had hoped that the members of Congress might have done something for him. "At least" they might "have been kind enough to have shewn their Approbation of my Conduct by a Grant of some Tract of Land in their Western Country, which might have been of some Use and some Honour to my Posterity."

In case Congress had forgotten, he included with his letter a "Sketch of the Services of B. Franklin to the United States." In this sketch he described in the third person all he had done for the country—from his opposition to the Stamp Act to his encouragement of the Revolution and his missions abroad. He emphasized how many offices along with their salaries he had lost in service to the country and how much he had contributed to the cause out of his own pocket. He also stressed how difficult his service had been. When he was sent to Canada in 1776 he was "upwards of 70 Years of Age." It was winter and the weather was cold; he passed the Lakes "while they were yet not free from Ice," and "He suffer'd in his Health by the Hardships of this Journey, lodging in the

Woods, &c, in so inclement a Season." When Congress sent him to France, it gave him no advance on his expenses in the way the colony of Pennsylvania had done earlier. He "was badly accommodated in a miserable Vessel, improper for those northern Seas which was nearly founder'd in going and actually founder'd in her Return. In this Voyage he was so badly fed, that on his Arrival he had scarce Strength to stand." During his mission to France he took on "extra Services" that Congress may not have been aware of, and he listed them—consul, judge of admiralty, merchant, and treasurer for the United States abroad. All this time "Mr. F. could make no Journey for Exercise and Health as had been annually his Custom, and the Confinement brought on a Malady that is likely to afflict him while he lives." In short, he said, he never worked so hard in his life as he did during those eight years in France. And now he was at an age when "a Man has some Right to expect Repose."[55]

It was humiliating—that he should have been reduced to listing his services to the country in this self-pitying way. Once his services were known he could not believe that Congress would not do something for him. After all, it had paid Arthur Lee and John Jay for their service abroad. But then again, he reflected, as his anger began to mount, the rewards given to the American ministers were "trifling" compared with the compensation that Louis XVI had granted to France's minister in America upon his return from abroad.

"How different is what has happened to me!" he exclaimed, his anger palpable. When he returned from England in 1775 he had been given the office of postmaster general—understandably, for he had "some kind of Right" to the office, having transformed the colonial post office into a revenue-producing business. When he was sent to France in 1776 he had left the office in the hands of his son-in-law, Richard Bache, who was to act as his deputy. "But soon after my Departure it was taken from me and given to Mr. Hazard."

But his anger over losing the patronage of the post office reminded him of other irritations with the Congress concerning postal matters. Even the much hated British had not treated him as shabbily as the Congress had. When the British had taken away his position as deputy postmaster of North America in 1774, they had at least left him the privilege of not having to pay postage for his letters. That was the custom when a postmaster was displaced for any reason except malfeasance in office. By contrast, what did Congress do? "In America I have ever since had the Postage demanded of me, which since my Return from France has amounted to above £50 much of it occasion'd by having acted as Minister there."[56]

Franklin made these complaints privately to Thomson as a friend. Although he wanted Thomson to present his letter to the president of the Congress, along with some sense of Franklin's services to the United States, he declared he would never complain publicly about Congress's behavior.[57] For he knew "something of the Nature of such changeable Assemblies." With the constant turnover of membership, these assemblies could never keep track of the services provided by their agents abroad; not only did they never feel obliged for these services, they even forgot that their agents had rendered them. He knew too from bitter experience the effect "artful and reiterated malevolent Insinuations of one or two envious and malicious Persons may have on the Mind of Members, even of the most equitable, candid, and honourable dispositions." He was deeply hurt and angry. He realized his "Reproach thrown at Republicks, that they are apt to be ungrateful," may have gone too far. If so, then he "would pass these reflections into oblivion."[58]

In the end the American republic showed no gratitude whatsoever. All of Franklin's appeals to Congress to help his grandson or to straighten out his accounts came to nothing. Congress did not bother to acknowledge any of his requests or even to read his description of his services.[59]

In this mood in 1788 he resumed the writing of his *Autobiography.* He began this third part with a statement that he would have to rely largely on his memory, since many of his papers had been lost in the war. But he did have one document, "accidentally preserved," that he claimed he had written in 1731. This document stressed the inevitability of parties and the prevalence of self-interest in public affairs. He had thought his "united Party for Virtue" might be the best answer to the confusion and selfishness of the world. This party for virtue ought to have some sort of creed containing the essentials of all religions. These essentials included the belief that there was "one God" who "governs the World by his Providence"; that the way to serve God was to do good to man; that "the Soul is immortal"; and "that God would certainly reward Virtue and punish Vice either here or hereafter."[60]

In the rest of the *Autobiography* Franklin continued with a recital of his accomplishments in philanthropic and public affairs. The third section carried the narrative of his life up to his arrival in England in July 1757. The brief fourth section, which stops in 1758, was probably written in the winter of 1789–1790 and described only his negotiations with the proprietors as the agent of the Pennsylvania Assembly. These final two sections deal largely with the external events of Franklin's life; he revealed little of his inner life—his anger and his disappointments. At the end he was determined to show his readers only the extent of his good work on behalf of America and the number of his civic accomplishments. If Congress did not appreciate them, then maybe posterity would.

FRANKLIN AND SLAVERY

Although his body was failing, his mind and his curiosity and his benevolence were as active as ever. He thought about various reforms, including insuring farmers against natural disasters, lessening the brutality of criminal punishments, and the possibilities of eliminating privateering in wartime. But the humanitarian issue that preoccupied him most was slavery.

While we today can scarcely conceive of one person holding another in bondage, most early-eighteenth-century white Americans, living in a hierarchical society composed of ranks of dependency and unfreedom, accepted black slavery as a matter of course. Franklin was no exception. He had run advertisements for slaves in his newspaper, and he himself owned slaves for more than thirty years. His early questioning of slavery in 1751 was based solely on its effects on white society: with slaves "the white Children become proud, disgusted with Labour, and being educated in Idleness, are rendered unfit to get a living by Industry."[61] During his post office tours in the 1760s he saw a number of schools for blacks and developed "a higher Opinion of the natural Capacities of the black Race, than I had ever before entertained. Their Apprehension seems as quick, their Memory as strong, and their Docility in every Respect equal to that of White Children."[62]

But, like many other Americans, he did not begin seriously to question the existence of slavery until the early 1770s. Through the influence of his Quaker friend Alexander Benezet and the writings of British abolitionists, he began to hope that "the Friends to Liberty and Humanity will get the better of a Practice that has so long disgrac'd our Nation and Religion."[63] In France these early antislavery views were further stimulated by enlightened *philosophes,* especially the Marquis de Condorcet.[64] By the 1780s he was willing to lend his name to the abolitionist movement in Pennsylvania. In 1775 the Philadelphia Quakers had founded the first abolitionist group in North America, which came to be called the Society for Promoting the Abolition of Slavery and the Relief of Negroes Unlawfully Held in Bondage. Under the influence of this society, Pennsylvania became the first state to pass legislation providing for the gradual elimination of slavery. But more had to be done, as Franklin realized when he became the society's president in 1787.

In a statement in November 1789 signed by Franklin, the society declared that slavery was "such an atrocious debasement of human nature, that its very extirpation, if not performed with solicitous care, may sometimes open a source of serious evils." It was foolish, the statement said, to expect the freed slave, "who has long been treated as a brute animal," to behave as an ordinary citizen. Emancipated black people needed help in assimilating into free society. Therefore, it was the responsibility of the abolitionist organization not merely to work for the eradication of slavery but also "to instruct, to advise, to qualify those, who have been restored to freedom, for the exercise and enjoyment of civil liberty, to promote in them habits of industry, to furnish them with employments suited to their age, sex, talents, and other circumstances, and to procure their children an education calculated for their future situation in life."[65] Though tired and in considerable pain from his kidney or bladder stones, the eighty-four-year-old Franklin had lost none of his zest for improving the lives of his fellow Pennsylvanians.

A few months later, in February 1790, Franklin signed a memorial to the new federal Congress requesting the abolition of slavery in the United States. This was a very different Franklin from the earlier pragmatic Franklin. No longer was he the tactful conciliator looking for the practical compromise between very diverse opinions. With his antislavery petition he was eager to provoke. Surely knowing what Congress's response would be, he must have enjoyed sticking the issue to the heir of a body that had so long ignored and humiliated him, especially since Senators Richard Henry Lee and Ralph Izard, who had been his special tormentors, were Southern slaveholders. Since the new Congress had been created to secure "the blessings of Liberty to the People of the United States," these blessings, the petition read, ought to be administered "without distinction of colour to all descriptions of people." After all, said the petition, "Mankind are all formed by the same Almighty Being, alike the objects of his care, and equally designed for the enjoyment of happiness."[66]

As much as these views seem commonsensical to us today, they were not so in Franklin's day. The petition predictably outraged many in the Congress and the country, and Franklin and the Quakers were viciously attacked. Congressman James Jackson of Georgia was especially vociferous in defending slavery in the House of Representatives. The Bible and nature justified slavery, said Jackson. If the slaves were freed, who would tend the fields of the South? Who else could do the work in a hot climate? Who would indemnify the masters? Abolitionists like Franklin, declared Jackson, were threats to the social order and ought to be ignored. The congressional committee to which the petition had been sent reported on March 5 that Congress had no authority to interfere in the internal affairs of the states.[67]

Franklin saw his opportunity when he read Jackson's speech, and he made the most of it with the literary technique he knew best—a hoax. This, his final hoax, appeared in the *Federal Gazette* on March 25, 1790, under the signature of "Historicus." It purported to reprint a speech of Sidi Mehemet Ibrahim to the Divan, or council, of Algiers defending the time-honored custom of enslaving white Christians captured by Barbary pirates. Franklin took Jackson's arguments and placed them in the mouth of this Muslim apologist for enslaving Christians. The Koran justified slavery, the Muslim leader said, and by every calculation it is necessary. "If we cease our Cruises against the Christians, how shall we be furnished with the Commodities their Countries produce, and which are so necessary for us? If we forbear to make Slaves of their People, who in this hot climate are to cultivate our Lands?" Besides, these white infidels were "brought into a Land where the Sun of Islamism gives forth its Light and shines in full Splendor," and thus these poor benighted slaves had an opportunity of becoming "acquainted with the true Doctrine and thereby saving their immortal Souls." After many such arguments, the conclusion was the same one that Jackson had made to Franklin's petition to free the African slaves: "Let us hear no more of this detestable Proposition, the Manumission of Christian Slaves." Just as Congress had decided, after some huffing and puffing about the injustice of slavery, so too did Franklin have his Muslim Divan behave: "The Divan came to this Resolution," he wrote, that "'The Doctrine, that Plundering and Enslaving the Christians is unjust, is at best *problematical;* but that it is the Interest of this State to continue the Practice, is clear; therefore let the Petition be rejected.'"[68]

FRANKLIN'S DEATH

During that same month of March 1790, Ezra Stiles, president of Yale, wrote Franklin to ask about his religious views. Franklin said that it was the first time anyone had questioned him about the subject. He did not want to take Stiles's curiosity amiss, and he tried to answer him as succinctly as possible. He said that he believed "in one God, Creator of the Universe. That He governs it by his Providence. That he ought to be worshipped. That the most acceptable Service we can render to him, is doing Good to his other Children. That the Soul of Man is immortal, and will be treated with Justice in another Life respecting its Conduct in this." Franklin went on to say that he (like Jefferson) believed Jesus's "System of Morals and his Religion as he left them to us, the best the World ever saw, or is likely to see." He also expressed his doubts of Jesus's divinity, but did not want to argue the matter. Practical to the end, he saw no harm in people's believing in Christ's divinity since that belief would likely make his doctrines more respected and observed. Knowing that his own views might not be well received by his countrymen, he asked Stiles to keep them confidential.

Early in April, Franklin developed a fever and some sort of lung ailment that made breathing difficult. He had been in pain for some time and was taking opium for relief. With him at the end were his daughter, Sally, her husband, and Franklin's two grandsons, together with Mrs.

Stevenson's daughter Polly, who had succumbed to Franklin's appeals and had immigrated to Philadelphia with her family. At one point Sally told her father that she hoped he would recover and live many more years. He replied, "I hope not." He died on April 17, 1790. He was eighty-four.

His will, drawn up in 1788, was odd. Instead of leaving the bulk of his four-thousand-book library to the Library Company, as the directors expected, Franklin left only a single multivolume work. Most of the rest of his books he left to his grandsons and a cousin. To the Philadelphia Hospital he left over £5000 in old debts that he had been unable to collect—a bequest that the hospital's gentry patrons eventually turned down.[69] Perhaps tired of the social snubbing he was getting from some genteel Philadelphians, he became in the end increasingly interested in young artisans. In a lengthy codicil drawn up in 1789 he left £1000 each to the cities of Boston and Philadelphia in hopes of having other young men emulate his life. The cities were to use these funds as the source of loans for young journeyman mechanics setting themselves up in business. (At the present time these funds amount to millions of dollars.) By making these grants Franklin seemed to foresee something of the role he was to play in America following his death.[70]

THE REACTION TO FRANKLIN'S DEATH

Inevitably, the French reacted to Franklin's death with greater emotion than did his fellow Americans—no doubt in part because the French were in the beginning stages of their own revolution and needed Franklin more than ever as a symbol of the new order. On June 11, 1790, amid a discussion in the French National Assembly of whether titles of nobility ought to be abolished, the great orator the Comte de Mirabeau rose to announce that *"Franklin est mort."* He called upon the assembly to honor "this mighty genius" who was most responsible for spreading the rights of man throughout the world. Franklin, he said, was a philosopher "who was able to conquer both thunderbolts and tyrants." The assembly, electrified by Mirabeau's speech, decreed three days of national mourning for Franklin.

The French at once recognized the extraordinary significance of this gesture, the first of its kind by the National Assembly. By speaking for the entire nation and usurping a right that hitherto had belonged to the king, the assembly had become, said one French journal, "the representative assembly of the human race, the Areopagus of the universe." Bursting with enlightened enthusiasm, Brissot de Warville declared that the National Assembly's declaration of national mourning for Franklin was an act of utter sublimity unmatched by any political body in Europe.

That summer the National Assembly sent a message to the President and Congress of the United States expressing France's gratitude to Franklin, "the Nestor of America," for his contributions to liberty and the rights of man. Although Franklin was a foreigner, the National Assembly declared, the French people regarded him, as they regarded all great men, as one of the "fathers of universal humanity." His name "will be immortal in the records of Freedom and Philosophy," and his loss will be felt by all parts of humanity, but especially by the French, who were taking their "first steps towards liberty." The National Assembly hoped that it and the American Congress would march together in affection and understanding down the road toward freedom and happiness.

For months French aristocrats and *philosophes* delivered eulogy after eulogy in praise of the simple philosopher of humanity who had taught them so much about liberty and the foolishness of vain titles and hereditary distinctions. As late as 1792 the French linked the names and busts of Franklin, Rousseau, Voltaire, and Mirabeau as promoters of liberty and equality.[71] No other foreigner ever received such tributes from France as did Franklin. French mourning amounted to what one historian has called "a republican apotheosis of Franklin."[72]

This expression of French affection and adulation for Franklin contrasted sharply with what happened in America. To be sure, Franklin's death aroused crowds of ordinary mourners in Philadelphia, and under James Madison's leadership the House of Representatives adopted a moving tribute to Franklin on April 22, 1790, and urged its members to wear badges of mourning for a month. But the next day, when Senator Charles Carroll proposed that the Senate adopt a similar tribute to Franklin, several senators leaped to their feet in opposition even before the proposal could be seconded. Senator Oliver Ellsworth of Connecticut urged that the proposal be withdrawn since it was sure to be defeated. Consequently, the Senate did nothing.

The Senate's behavior was extraordinary but explicable. The president of the Senate, Vice President John Adams, had long been jealous of Franklin, and of Washington too for that matter. On April 4, two weeks before Franklin's death, Adams spilled out to Benjamin Rush his accumulated resentment of the ill-deserved adulation that other Revolutionary leaders were receiving, seemingly at his expense. "The history of our Revolution," he told Rush with biting sarcasm, "will be one continued Lye from one end to the other. The essence of the whole will be *that Dr. Franklin's electrical Rod, smote the Earth and out sprung General Washington. That Franklin electrified him with his rod—and thence forward these two conducted all the Policy, Negotiations, Legislatures and War.*"[73]

Inevitably then, Adams, as president of the Senate, was in no mood to honor Franklin. Several senators, namely Richard Henry Lee and Ralph Izard, inveterate enemies of Franklin, shared Adams's hostility. But other senators, such as Rufus King and William Samuel Johnson, who were not longtime enemies of Franklin, nonetheless also opposed endorsing the House's tribute. Their opposition to honoring Franklin had more to do with their dislike of the disorder of the emerging French Revolution, with which they now identified Franklin.

For a decade French *philosophes* had vigorously criticized the American constitutions for slavishly imitating the English constitution in their bicameral legislatures and separation of powers. Since Franklin himself had favored a unicameral legislature and a weak executive, he came to represent in the eyes of the Federalist opponents of the French Revolution all of the democratic turbulence that they feared for America. So that when the Senate early in 1791 received several communications from France honoring Franklin, including the tribute from the National Assembly, it treated these French tributes with what Senator William Maclay of Pennsylvania called astonishing "coldness and apathy." What will the French think, Maclay wrote in his diary, when they find out that "we cold as Clay, care not a fig about them, Franklin or Freedom"?[74]

For months Americans paid not a word of public tribute to Franklin. Although the American Philosophical Society decided two days after

Franklin's funeral to eulogize its founder and former president, it delayed its eulogy for almost a year. The two vice presidents of the society, the scientist David Rittenhouse and the Anglican priest William Smith, received an equal number of the members' votes to deliver the eulogy; and consequently for months nothing was done. When the French tributes arrived and were opened early in 1791, however, the delay became embarrassing. Smith was finally selected as the eulogist, and the occasion became far more important and public than had originally been intended; in fact, it became as close to an official eulogy of Franklin as the nation ever managed.

Smith had long been one of Franklin's enemies. In fact, back in 1764 he had accused Franklin of being an "inflammatory and virulent man," with a "foul" mouth and "crafty" and "wicked" spirit.[75] Thus, it is not surprising that his eulogy, delivered in Philadelphia on March 1, 1791, before an audience of dignitaries from the city, state, and nation, was what one literary historian has called "a half-hearted, colorless piece ... an artificial, uninspired, rhetorical exercise."[76]

Smith began by confessing that he was perhaps not the best person to be presenting the eulogy, the truth of which statement he proceeded to demonstrate. He first linked Franklin with two other patriots who had recently died, William Livingston, governor of New Jersey, and James Bowdoin, governor of Massachusetts—as if Franklin's stature was no different from theirs. He next apologized for Franklin's "low beginnings" and quickly passed over them. Smith admitted that he had a hard time describing Franklin's participation in Pennsylvania politics since he himself was "too much an actor in the scene to be fit for the discussion of it." Smith then summed up Franklin's contributions to the Revolution in a single short paragraph, declaring they were "too well known to need further mention."

Throughout the eulogy Smith emphasized that Franklin was "ignorant of his own *strength*," implying at times that Franklin did not know what he was doing. Smith did spend some time praising Franklin's electrical experiments, emphasizing Franklin's "caution and modesty" in communicating his findings in the form of guesses. "But," said Smith, "no man ever made bolder or happier guesses, either in *philosophy* or *politics*." It was true, Smith conceded, that Franklin never troubled himself with using mathematics to prove his speculations, but most of the time he guessed right. Smith quoted a letter of Jefferson's describing the fame Franklin enjoyed abroad, which he used to sum up Franklin's role as diplomat during the Revolution. Aside from listing a half dozen of Franklin's inventions and experiments, Smith did not have very much to say about what Franklin actually had contributed to America and the world. Even what little backhanded praise Smith could manage may have been a strain. When Smith's daughter asked him whether he believed one tenth of what he had said about "old Ben Lightning Rod," he only roared with laughter.[77]

In contrast to this single homage paid Franklin, Washington received hundreds of eulogies at his death a decade later. Even someone like James Bowdoin received at least a dozen funeral tributes. The relatively weak American response to Franklin's death was remarkable, and it shocked the French minister in America, Louis Otto. He reported home that "the memory of Dr. Franklin has been infinitely more honored in France than in America."[78]

Indeed, the more France honored Franklin, the more Franklin's image suffered, at least in the eyes of those Americans opposed to the French Revolution. The Federalists in the 1790s, believing that the Republican party's opposition to their leadership was fomented by the French Revolution, saw in Franklin a symbol of much of what they feared and hated. The fact that the Federalists' principal vilifier in the press was Franklin's grandson Benjamin Franklin Bache, the intemperate editor of the Philadelphia *General Advertiser* (later called the *Aurora*), only added to their dislike of Franklin.

Bache, called "Lightning-Rod Junior" by the Federalists, was notorious for his scurrilous attacks on President Washington and the Federalists. And inevitably the Federalists replied to this scurrility by assaulting Bache's grandfather for being, in the words of William Cobbett, the fiery immigrant from England, "a whore-master, a hypocrite, and an infidel."[79] Joseph Dennie, the arch-Federalist editor of the Anglophilic *Port Folio,* dismissed Franklin as "one of our first Jacobins, the first to lay his head in the lap of French harlotry; and prostrate the christianity and honour of his country to the deism and democracies of Paris."[80] It became conventional

Federalist wisdom that Franklin had been "a dishonest, tricking, hypocritical character" who had championed French infidelity and fanaticism.[81]

THE CELEBRATION OF WORK

At the same time, however, the publication of Franklin's *Autobiography* and some of his other writings in the 1790s began to create a quite different image of Franklin, at least among those who did not share the Federalists' view of the world. With the emergence of all sorts of middling people into unprecedented prominence in the northern Republican party, the image of Franklin became a political football, to be kicked about and used and abused in the decade's turbulent politics.[82]

In his will Franklin had bequeathed all his papers to Temple Franklin, who planned to publish the complete life along with his grandfather's other works. Temple was surprised, however, to learn of the publication in 1791 of a French translation of the first part of his grandfather's memoir.[83] Although Temple tried to prevent an English version of the French edition, two English translations appeared in London in 1793. One of these translations was combined with a short life of Franklin written by Henry Stuber, which had originally appeared serially in Philadelphia in the *Universal Asylum, and Columbia Magazine* beginning with the May 1790 issue. Between 1794 and 1800 this collection was reprinted at least fourteen times in the United States.[84] Franklin's *Way to Wealth* also began to be frequently reprinted. Although Temple did not bring out his own edition of Franklin's papers until 1817-1818, many Americans were already very familiar with the early life of Franklin.

Although the aristocratic Federalists described Franklin as a French-loving radical whose writings had sought "to degrade literature to the level of vulgar capacities . . . by the vile alloy of provincial idioms and colloquial barbarism," many middling Americans—tradesmen, artisans, farmers, proto-businessmen of all sorts—found in these popular writings a middling hero they could relate to.[85] As early as Independence Day 1795, the General Society of Mechanics and Tradesmen of New York, composed of both masters and journeymen, toasted "the memory of our late brother mechanic, Benjamin Franklin: May his bright example convince mankind that in this land of freedom and equality, talents joined to frugality and virtue, may justly aspire to the first offices of government."[86] Everywhere master mechanics and journeymen alike began naming their associations and societies after Franklin and turning the former craftsman into a symbol of their cause. Printers especially were eager to use Franklin to justify their enhanced status as something other than mechanics. They wanted the world to know that they were a "profession" whose higher branches were "not mechanical, nor bounded by rules, but . . . soar to improvements . . . valuable to science and humanity."[87]

The cause of these artisans was the cause of working and middling people throughout America. For too long, they said, "tradesmen, mechanics, and the industrious classes of society" had considered "themselves of TOO LITTLE CONSEQUENCE to the body politic."[88] But now, in the aftermath of a Revolution dedicated to liberty and equality, they said, things were to be different. These laboring people began organizing themselves in Democratic-Republican societies, and eventually they came to make up the body and soul of the northern part of the Republican party. Throughout their extraordinary speeches and writings of these years, these middling sorts vented their pent-up egalitarian anger at all those leisured aristocratic gentry who had scorned them because they had had to work for a living. For a half century following the Revolution these ordinary men stripped the northern Federalist gentry of their aristocratic pretensions, charged them at every turn with being idle drones, and relentlessly undermined their traditional role as rulers. In their celebration of productive labor, these middling working people came to dominate nineteenth-century northern American culture and society to a degree not duplicated elsewhere in the Atlantic world.

In the 1790s, when Jeffersonian Republicans such as Abraham Clark, Matthew Lyon, and William Manning described themselves as members of "the industrious part of the community," they meant all those, wage earners and employers alike, who lived by their labor. In other words, Franklin, as a wealthy printer and entrepreneur before he retired from business in 1748 and became a gentleman, would have been regarded as one of these laborers. Against them, artisans and farmers charged, were all those Federalist gentry who were "not . . . under the necessity of getting their bread by industry," which included "the merchant, phisition, lawyer & divine, the philosipher and school master, the Juditial & Executive Officers, & many others." Such gentlemen, they said, lived off "the labour of the honest farmers and mechanics"; their "idleness" rested on "other men's toil."[89]

So successful was this assault on the Federalist gentry, so overwhelming was the victory of these middling sorts in their celebration of labor, that by the early nineteenth century, in the northern parts of America at least, almost everyone had to claim to be a laborer. Even the aristocratic slaveholding planter George Washington now had to be described as a productive worker. Washington's popular biographer Parson Mason Weems (the inventor of the cherry tree myth) knew instinctively that he had to celebrate the great man as someone who worked as diligently as an ordinary mechanic. Of course, in a classical sense Washington had never worked a day in his life; he had been a farmer like Cicero who exercised authority over his plantation but had not actually labored on it. But for Weems and other spokesmen for the middling workers, exercising authority now became identified with labor and was praised as labor. Indeed, Weems wrote, "of all the virtues that adorned the life of this great man, there is none more worthy of our imitation than his admirable INDUSTRY." Washington "displayed the power of industry more signally" than any man in history. Rising early and working hard all day were the sources of his wealth and success. He was "on horseback by the time the sun was up," and he never let up; "of all that ever lived, Washington was the most rigidly observant of those hours of business which were necessary to the successful management of his vast concerns. . . . Neither himself nor any about him were allowed to eat the bread of idleness," idleness being for Weems "the worst of crimes."

Speaking to the new rising generation of entrepreneurs, businessmen, and others eager to get ahead, Weems was anxious to destroy the "notion, from the land of lies," which had "taken too deep root among some, that 'labour is a low-lived thing, fit for none but poor people and slaves! and that dress and pleasure are the only accomplishments for a gentleman!'" He urged all the young men who might be reading his book, "though humble thy birth, low thy fortune, and few thy friends, still think of Washington, and HOPE."[90]

Yet for these middling people who were eager to celebrate the dignity of working for a living, it was Franklin, the onetime printer, who became the Founding Father most easily transformed into a workingman's symbol.[91] Indeed, no one became more of a hero to all those laboring people than Franklin. High-toned Federalists could only shake their heads in disgust at all those vulgar sorts who had come to believe "that there was no other road to the temple of Riches, except that which run through—Dr. Franklin's works."[92] Everywhere, but in the northern states especially, speakers, writers, and publicists sought to encourage young men of lowly backgrounds to work hard and raise themselves up as Franklin had. They reached out beyond the cities to ordinary people in country towns and villages and followed Franklin's example in creating libraries, schools, almanacs, and printed matter of all sorts for broader and deeper levels of the working population. In 1802 teacher and small-time entrepreneur Silas Felton joined with thirteen other men in Marlborough, Massachusetts, to found a Society of Social Enquirers and urged others to follow this example. "Doct. Franklin relates, in his life," Felton pointed out, "that he received a considerable part of his information in this way."[93]

BECOMING THE SELF-MADE BUSINESSMAN

It was this image of the hardworking and bookish Franklin that captivated most middling folk. Everywhere village publicists encouraged ordinary people to read all the books within their reach, as Franklin had. Almanac-maker Robert Thomas of Sterling, Massachusetts, thought that winter was a good time for farmers to catch up on their reading. "The life of Dr. Franklin," he said, "I would recommend for the amusement of winter evenings."[94] Northern working people found in Franklin a means of both releasing their resentments and fulfilling their aspirations. In Boston and Philadelphia hundreds of artisans from dozens of different crafts took advantage of Franklin's bequest to better themselves.[95] They sponsored Franklin Lectures, issued numerous broadsides containing Franklin's "Maxims and Precepts for Conduct in Life and the Just Attainment of Success in Business," and published and republished account after account of Franklin's life.[96] It was not Franklin the scientist and diplomat they emulated but the young man who through industry and frugality had risen from obscurity to fame and fortune. "Who can tell," asked the president of the Mechanics Society of New York in 1820 of an audience of young artisans, "how many Franklins may be among you?"[97]

Between 1794 and 1828, twenty-two editions of Franklin's *Autobiography* were published. After 1798 editors began adding the Poor Richard essays, and especially *The Way to Wealth,* to editions of the *Autobiography.* Since it was young men who needed the inspiration of Franklin, writers and editors began aiming their works specifically at young readers.

Parson Weems, who had made so much money with his fanciful life of Washington in 1800, was bound to do something with Franklin. He began by publishing extracts from Franklin's *The Way to Wealth* and his *Autobiography.* And then in 1818 he created his own fictitious life of Franklin, which may have become more popular in the early nineteenth century than Franklin's actual *Autobiography.* Weems was eager to use Franklin as a moral example for wayward youth.

> O you time-wasting, brain-starving young men, who can never be at ease unless you have a cigar or a plug of tobacco in your mouths, go on with your puffing and champing—go on with your filthy smoking, and your still more filthy spitting, keeping the cleanly house-wives in constant terror for their nicely waxed floors, and their shining carpets—go on I say; but remember, it was not in this way that our little Ben became the GREAT DR. FRANKLIN.[98]

Franklin's life, wrote Weems, had essential lessons for the young. Sometimes, he said, young men were laughed at for their "oddities"—their poverty, their awkwardness, or their habit of reading. "Yet if, like Franklin, they will but stick to the *main chance,* i.e. BUSINESS AND EDUCATION, they will assuredly, like him, overcome at last, and render themselves the admiration of those who once despised them."

But it was not enough that Weems's Franklin was a model of entrepreneurial ambition and hard work. Since Weems was writing for ordinary people, and ordinary people in the early republic were deeply religious, he had to turn Franklin into a "true" Christian who "not only had religion, but had it in an eminent degree." Although Franklin might have neglected religion when he was young and did not attend church very often, he was, said Weems, always sincerely devoted to the teachings of Christ. Indeed, all his "extraordinary benevolence and useful life were imbibed, even *unconsciously* from the Gospel." According to Weems, Franklin gained comfort during his final illness by gazing at a picture of Christ on the cross. If Franklin was to be a hero to middling nineteenth-century Americans, he had to become a good Christian.[99]

Since Franklin's life, whether in bits and pieces of the *Autobiography* or in versions like that of Weems, was available everywhere, it could not help but inspire the dreams of countless individuals in the early republic. Indeed, some ambitious men actually attributed their rise to reading Franklin. In 1811 sixteen-year-old James Harper left his father's farm on Long Island for New York City after reading Franklin's life. Eventually he founded one of the most successful publishing firms in the country and became mayor of New York. When he had his portrait painted, he had the artist insert a profile of Franklin in it.

The experience of Thomas Mellon, the founder of the great banking fortune, was similar. In 1828 fourteen-year-old Mellon had thought he would remain a farmer like his father on their modest farm outside of Pittsburgh. But reading Franklin's *Autobiography* and Poor Richard's sayings became "the turning point" of his life. "For so poor and friendless a boy to be able to become a merchant or a professional man had before seemed an impossibility; but here was Franklin, poorer than myself, who by industry, thrift and frugality had become learned and wise, and elevated to wealth and fame." He "wondered if I might do something in the same line by similar means." He read Franklin's words over and over and began to apply himself in school as he never had before. When Mellon finally founded his bank, he placed Franklin's statue in front of it as a tribute to his inspiration. Near the end of his life he bought a thousand copies of Franklin's *Autobiography* and distributed them to young men who came seeking his advice. Franklin had come to epitomize the new and radical notion of the "self-made man."[100]

Prior to the early nineteenth century, social mobility generally had not been something to be proud of, as indicated by the pejorative terms—"upstarts," "arrivistes," "parvenus"—used to disparage those participants unable to hide the lowliness of their origins. But now mobile individuals began boasting of their humble beginnings. They had made it, they said, on their own, without family influence, without patronage, and without having gone to Harvard or Princeton or any college at all. A man was now praised for having "no relations or friends, but what his money made for him"; he was "the architect of his own fortune."[101]

Sensitive to the charge of vanity, Franklin in his *Autobiography* had played down the suggestion that he was the architect of his own fortune. He had written simply that he had "emerged from the Poverty and Obscurity in which I was born and bred, to a State of Affluence and some Degree of Reputation in the World." His grandson Temple, however, in his edition of Franklin's *Memoirs*, first published in 1817–1818, wanted to emphasize the great man's self-made character. So his edition read: "From the poverty and obscurity in which I was born, . . . I have raised myself to a state of affluence and some degree of celebrity in the world." *"Raised myself"!* That was quite a difference. As Temple's edition of the *Autobiography* was regarded as the standard text for the next half century, it was not surprising that Franklin should have emerged for businessmen everywhere as the perfect model of the self-made man.[102]

By the early nineteenth century many of these successful businessmen no longer felt the need, as Franklin had, to shed their leather aprons in order to acquire respectability. They were proud of being self-made men, and sometimes they even flaunted their lowly origins. Philadelphia manufacturer Patrick Lyon (1779–1829) began his career as a humble blacksmith and had actually been falsely imprisoned in the Walnut Street jail for three months for bank robbery. But after being released from prison and winning a civil compensation suit, he eventually became a successful businessman who in 1826, like Franklin three quarters of a century earlier, wanted his portrait painted. But unlike Franklin, who had wanted to display the ruffled silk of his new status as a gentleman, Lyon told the artist, John Neagle, that he had no desire to be "represented in the picture as a gentleman." He wanted to be painted as he once was, "at work at my anvil, with my sleeves rolled up and a leather apron on," with the Walnut Street Gaol in the background.

Pat Lyon at the Forge was an immediate popular success. When hung in the academies of New York and Philadelphia, Lyon's portrait, "looking

Pat Lyon at the Forge, *by John Neagle, 1826*

delightfully cheek by jowl" with the conventional genteel portraits, instantly reminded people, as one reviewer pointed out, "of the equality of mankind in everything but mind."[103] The difference between Lyon's portrait in 1826 and that of Franklin in 1748 (see page 58) is a measure of how radically the American Revolution had changed American society and culture. Aristotle must have turned in his grave—thousands of years of aristocratic contempt for trading and working for money shattered in just a few decades.[104]

In the generation following the Revolution thousands upon thousands of young men responded to the many appeals to make their own way in the world and took advantage of the multitudes of commercial opportunities opening up, especially in the northern states of America. Indeed, this first generation to come of age after the Revolution may have been the most important single cohort in American history. For not only did this generation create American capitalism but it also created a powerful conception of American identity—the America of enterprising, innovative, and equality-loving people—a conception so powerful in fact that it has lasted even into our own time.[105]

Many of these northern entrepreneurs—and nearly all of them were from the North—sought to imitate Franklin not only by making money and prospering but also by setting down in hundreds upon hundreds of memoirs the stories of their struggles and their achievements. Some of the memoirists were explicit in invoking Franklin's life as their model, but others simply portrayed events in ways that were remarkably similar to Franklin's depictions in his *Autobiography*. When John Ball, the tenth of ten children, found that his older brother, like Franklin's older brother, "claimed the right to direct the work [on their Vermont farm] in a way that to me was not always satisfactory," he became "determined to leave home" just as Franklin had. Ball eventually became a state legislator in Michigan and the architect of the state's public school system. In his memoir Chauncey Jerome described his arrival in New Haven in 1812 as a nineteen-year-old: "I wandered about the streets early one morning with a bundle of clothes and some bread and cheese in my hands." He recalled scarcely imagining then that he would become a prosperous clockmaker in the city, "or that I should ever be its Mayor." It was as if these successful men had to have begun their lives just as Franklin had, even to the point of duplicating his particular experiences.[106]

THE MYTH OF AMERICAN NATIONHOOD

The men who wrote these memoirs were successful businessmen who were proud of pulling themselves up by their own bootstraps. And cumulatively the stories they told, along with the numerous editions of Franklin's *Autobiography*, had an inordinate influence on America's understanding of itself. Out of these repeated messages of striving and success not only did ordinary northern white men acquire a heightened appreciation of their work and their worth; they were also able to construct an enduring sense of American nationhood—a sense of America as the land of enterprise and opportunity, as the place where anybody who works hard can make it, as the nation of free and scrambling money-making individuals pursuing happiness. This myth of American identity created during the several decades following the Revolution became so powerful that succeeding generations were scarcely able to question it.[107]

Among the peoples of the world only Americans of the early republic, as their great observer Alexis de Tocqueville pointed out, celebrated work as "the necessary, natural, and honest condition of all men." What most astonished Tocqueville was that Americans thought not only that work itself was "honorable," but that "work specifically to gain money" was "honorable." By contrast, European society not only possessed proportionally fewer middling people than America, but was still dominated by aristocrats who scorned working for profit. When they served the state, said Tocqueville, these European aristocrats claimed to do so without interested motives. "Their salary is a detail to which sometimes they give a little thought and to which they pretend to give none." But in democratic America serving the public without salary, as Washington and Franklin had, was no longer possible. "As the desire for prosperity is universal, fortunes are middling and ephemeral, and everyone needs to increase his resources or create fresh ones for his children," said Tocqueville; "all see quite clearly that it is profit which, if not wholly then at least partially, prompts them to work."

With everyone working for pay, everyone became alike. Even "servants do not feel degraded because they work," Tocqueville wrote, "for everyone around them is working. There is nothing humiliating about the idea of receiving a salary, for the President of the United States works for a salary." And Franklin, the Founder who wanted all members of the federal executive to serve without pay, nevertheless now became the special hero of all these middling men who prized the fact that everyone worked for a living.[108]

Of course, as Tocqueville explained, the "Americans" he described were those "who live in the parts of the country where there is no slavery. It is they alone who provide a complete picture of a democratic society."[109] It was the northern working people of 1830 who created America's dominant sense of nationhood, not the cavalier South.

At the time of the Revolution in 1776, Virginia had thought itself to be the undisputed leader of the nation, with good reason. It was by far the most populous state, with a population of well over 600,000 people, 40 percent of whom were black slaves. It was over twice the size of its nearest competitor, Pennsylvania. It supplied much of the Revolutionary leadership and dominated the Constitutional Convention with its Virginia plan. In 1776 it had the strongest claim to the bulk of the western territory comprising most of the present-day Midwest. It is not surprising that four of the first five presidents and the longest-serving chief justice of the United States should have been Virginians. But by 1830 Virginia's day in the sun had passed, its population outstripped by both New York and Pennsylvania. Its economy had become largely engaged in the export of slaves to the burgeoning regions of the Deep South.

Virginia and the South always claimed that they had remained closer to the eighteenth-century beginnings of the nation, and they were right. It was the North that had changed and changed dramatically. Because northern Americans came to celebrate work so emphatically—with Franklin as their most representative figure—the leisured slaveholding aristocracy of Virginia and the rest of the South became a bewildered and beleaguered minority out of touch with the enterprise and egalitarianism that had come to dominate the country. As long as work had been held in contempt, as it had for millennia, slavery could never have been wholeheartedly condemned. But to a society that came to honor work as fully as the North did, a leisured aristocracy and the institution of slavery that supported it had to become abominations.

This dynamic, democratic, and enterprising world that Tocqueville described created the modern image of Franklin as the bourgeois moralist obsessed with the making of money and getting ahead. Although this image was the one that D. H. Lawrence and other imaginative writers have so much scorned, Franklin might not have been unhappy to learn that this powerful entrepreneurial symbol would be the way most people in the world would come to know him.

In some ways his career had come full circle. Near the end of his life he glimpsed that some people were coming to see him once again as the tradesman printer who had made it, and he seemed to welcome this view of himself. After seeing his grandson Temple rebuffed by Congress, he decided that his other grandson, Benjamin Franklin Bache (called Benny by Franklin), would not suffer the same fate. He told his son-in-law, Benny's father, that he was "determined to give him a Trade [as a printer] that he may have something to depend on, and not to be oblig'd to ask Favours or Offices of any body."[110]

As he had always done when he wanted to boost himself in moments of lagging self-esteem, he took pride in the fact that he had been a successful tradesman and printer who had pulled himself up by his own bootstraps. In fact, he liked to startle French aristocrats by showing them how he could set type, and he bragged about his decision to leave money to two American cities for the encouragement of "young beginners in business."[111] In 1786 he backed the Philadelphia journeymen printers in their strike over wage cuts, and the journeymen responded by drinking toasts in celebration of his eighty-first birthday.[112] In 1788 he participated in the founding of the Franklin Society in Philadelphia, an organization designed to support printers with credit and insurance. The year before his death, he lamented that he was "too old to follow printing again my self, but loving the business," he had thrown all his energies into training his grandson in the trade. He now looked forward to his *Autobiography*'s being read by future generations, realizing that the early parts of it would have the most significance for young readers—"as exemplifying strongly the Effects of prudent and imprudent Conduct in the Commencement of a life of business."[113]

It is the image of the hardworking self-made businessman that has most endured. Franklin was one of the greatest of the Founders; indeed, his crucial diplomacy in the Revolution makes him second only to Washington in importance. But that importance is not what we most remember about Franklin. It is instead the symbolic Franklin of the bumptious capitalism of the early republic—the man who personifies the American dream—who stays with us. And as long as America is seen as the land of opportunity, where you can get ahead if you work hard, this image of Franklin will likely be the one that continues to dominate American culture.

NOTES

The following abbreviations are used in the notes.

Adams, *Diary and Autobiography*	Lyman H. Butterfield et al., eds., *Diary and Autobiography of John Adams* (Cambridge, Mass.: Harvard University Press, 1961)
Papers of Adams	Robert J. Taylor et al., eds., *The Papers of John Adams* (Cambridge, Mass.: Harvard University Press, 1977–)
BF	Benjamin Franklin
BF, *Autobiography*	Leonard Labaree et al., eds., *The Autobiography of Benjamin Franklin* (New Haven: Yale University Press, 1964)
Papers of Franklin	Leonard Labaree et al., eds., *The Papers of Benjamin Franklin* (New Haven: Yale University Press, 1959–)
Lemay and Zall, eds., *Franklin's Autobiography*	J. A. Leo Lemay and P. M. Zall, eds., *Benjamin Franklin's Autobiography: An Authoritative Text, Backgrounds, Criticism* (New York: Norton, 1986)
Franklin: Writings	J. A. Leo Lemay, ed., *Benjamin Franklin: Writings* (New York: Library of America, 1987)
PMHB	*Pennsylvania Magazine of History and Biography*
WMQ	*William and Mary Quarterly*, 3d series

INTRODUCTION

1. Lodge, in Nian-Sheng Huang, *Benjamin Franklin in American Thought and Culture, 1790–1990* (Philadelphia: American Philosophical Society, 1994), 136; Garry Wills, *James Madison* (New York: Times Books, 2002), 164.
2. John Adams to William Tudor, 5 June 1817, in *American Historical Review* 47 (1941–42): 806–7.
3. Brian M. Barbour, ed., *Benjamin Franklin: A Collection of Critical Essays* (Englewood Cliffs, N.J.: Prentice-Hall, 1979), introduction.
4. Howells, quoted in Lemay and Zall, eds., *Franklin's Autobiography,* 276.
5. Louis B. Wright, "Franklin's Legacy to the Gilded Age," *Virginia Quarterly Review* 22 (1946): 268.
6. Henry D. Gilpin, *The Character of Franklin: An Address Delivered Before the Franklin Institute of Pennsylvania* (Philadelphia, 1857), 15, 21. (I owe this reference to Barry Schwartz.)
7. Turner, quoted in Lemay and Zall, eds., *Franklin's Autobiography,* 274–75.
8. Richard D. Miles, "The American Image of Benjamin Franklin," *American Quarterly* 9 (1957): 124–25; *Atlantic Monthly,* Nov. 1889, 713; Carla Mulford, "Figuring Benjamin Franklin in American Memory," *New England Quarterly* 72 (1999): 424.
9. BF, Poor Richard, 1735, in *Papers of Franklin,* 2:9.
10. Irene Brouillard of Woonsocket, Rhode Island, quoted in *Providence Journal,* 15 Aug. 2002.
11. Mulford, "Figuring Benjamin Franklin in American Memory," 426; P. M. Zall, *Franklin's Autobiography: A Model Life* (Boston: Twayne Publishers, 1989), 16. At the end of the nineteenth century, Paul Leicester Ford, the great bibliographer of Franklin's works, confronted with massive numbers of editions of *The Way to Wealth,* gave up after listing 155 titles, saying that it was "simply impossible to find and note all the editions." Paul Leicester Ford, *Franklin Bibliography: A List of Books Written by, or Relating to Benjamin Franklin* (Brooklyn, 1889), 55. For a more recent annotated bibliography of works about Franklin between 1721 and 1906, see Melvin H. Buxbaum, *Benjamin Franklin, 1721–1906: A Reference Guide* (Boston: G. K. Hall, 1983).
12. Twain, "The Late Benjamin Franklin" (1870), in Louis J. Budd, ed., *Mark Twain: Collected Tales, Sketches, Speeches, and Essays* (New York: Library of America, 1992), 425–26.
13. Howells, quoted in Lemay and Zall, eds., *Franklin's Autobiography,* 275–76.
14 Keats, quoted in Lemay and Zall, eds., *Franklin's Autobiography,* 257–58.
15. Joseph Dennie, quoted in Lewis Leary, "Joseph Dennie on Benjamin Franklin: A Note on Early American Literary Criticism," *PMHB* 72 (1948): 244.
16. *North American Review* 21 (Sept. 1818): 289–90.
17. Poe, "The Businessman," in *The Works of Edgar Allan Poe* (New York, 1903), 4:260, 265–66, 268. The story is conveniently available in Lemay and Zall, eds., *Franklin's*

Autobiography, 258–66. See also J. A. Leo Lemay, "Poe's 'The Businessman': Its Contexts and Satire of Franklin's Autobiography," *Poe Studies* 15 (1982): 29–37.

18. Melville, *Israel Potter,* in Harrison Hayford, ed., *Herman Melville* (New York: Library of America, 1984), 479, 486.
19. Hawthorne, "Biographical Stories," in *The Works of Nathaniel Hawthorne,* introduction by George Parsons Lathrop (Boston, 1888), 12:202.
20. Wright, "Franklin's Legacy to the Gilded Age," *Virginia Quarterly Review* 22 (1946): 268–79.
21. Max Weber, *The Protestant Ethic and the Spirit of Capitalism,* trans. Talcott Parsons (New York: Scribner, 1958), 52–54.
22. D. H. Lawrence, *Studies in Classic American Literature* (1923; reprint, New York: T. Seltzer, 1953), 19–31.
23. Floyd C. Watkins, "Fitzgerald's Jay Gatz and Young Benjamin Franklin," *New England Quarterly* 27 (1954): 249–52.
24. Fitzgerald, *The Great Gatsby* (New York: Scribner, 1925), 174–75, 182. See also J. A. Leo Lemay, "Franklin's Autobiography and the American Dream," in Lemay and Zall, eds., *Franklin's Autobiography,* 349–60.
25. BF to William Strahan, 2 June 1750, and BF to Abiah Franklin, 12 April 1750, in *Papers of Franklin,* 3:479, 475.
26. Carl Becker, "Benjamin Franklin," *Dictionary of American Biography,* ed. Allen Johnson and Dumas Malone (New York: Scribner, 1931), 6:596.
27. *The Federalist,* No. 72. See also Douglass Adair, "Fame and the Founding Fathers," in Trevor Colbourn, ed., *Fame and the Founding Fathers: Essays by Douglass Adair* (New York: Norton, 1974), 3–26.
28. On Franklin's strategy of humility, see Paul W. Conner, *Poor Richard's Politicks: Benjamin Franklin and His New American Order* (New York: Oxford University Press, 1965), 149–69.
29. J. Philip Gleason, "A Scurrilous Colonial Election and Franklin's Reputation," *WMQ* 18 (1961): 76.
30. Jennifer T. Kennedy, "Death Effects: Revisiting the Conceit of Franklin's *Memoir,*" *Early American Literature* 36 (2001): 204. J. A. Leo Lemay and P. M. Zall have a conveniently selected annotated bibliography of twentieth-century criticism of the *Autobiography* in their *Franklin's Autobiography,* 365–74. Among the many fine studies of the *Autobiography,* see David Levin, "The Autobiography of Benjamin Franklin: The Puritan Experiment in Life and Art," *Yale Review* 53 (1964): 258–75; John William Ward, "Benjamin Franklin: The Making of an American Character," in his *Red, White, and Blue: Men, Books, and Ideas in American Culture* (New York: Oxford University Press, 1969); Robert F. Sayre, *The Examined Self: Benjamin Franklin, Henry Adams, Henry James* (New Haven: Yale University Press, 1964); R. Jackson Wilson, *Figures of Speech: American Writers and the Literary Marketplace from Benjamin Franklin to Emily Dickinson* (Baltimore: Johns Hopkins

University Press, 1989), 21–65; William H. Shurr, "'Now, Gods, Stand Up for Bastards': Reinterpreting Benjamin Franklin's *Autobiography*," *American Literature* 64 (1992): 437–51; and Ormond Seavey, *Becoming Benjamin Franklin: The Autobiography and the Life* (University Park: Pennsylvania State University Press, 1988). For additional studies of the *Autobiography* see Seavey's list, ibid., 244–45.

31. BF, *Autobiography,* 75–76.
32. J. A. Leo Lemay, "The Theme of Vanity in Franklin's Autobiography," in Lemay, ed., *Reappraising Benjamin Franklin: A Bicentennial Perspective* (Newark: University of Delaware Press, 1993), 372–87.
33. Stanley Brodwin, "Strategies of Humor: The Case of Benjamin Franklin," *Prospects* 4 (1979): 121–67.
34. Verner W. Crane, ed., *Letters to the Press, 1758–1775* (Chapel Hill: University of North Carolina Press, 1950), xxx.
35. J. A. Leo Lemay, *The Canon of Benjamin Franklin: New Attributions and Reconsiderations* (Newark: University of Delaware Press, 1986), 135; Bruce Ingham Granger, *Benjamin Franklin: An American Man of Letters* (Ithaca, N.Y.: Cornell University Press, 1964).
36. BF, On Censure and Backbiting, in *Franklin: Writings,* 192–95.
37. BF, *Autobiography,* 87–88; J. A. Leo Lemay, "Franklin's Autobiography and the American Dream," in Lemay and Zall, eds., *Franklin's Autobiography,* 349–60.
38. BF, On Simplicity, 1732, in *Franklin: Writings,* 183; BF, Poor Richard, 1743, in *Papers of Franklin,* 2:370.
39. Lionel Trilling, *Sincerity and Authenticity* (Cambridge, Mass.: Harvard University Press, 1972), 17–18.
40. BF, Poor Richard, 1735, in *Papers of Franklin,* 2:8.

CHAPTER 1: BECOMING A GENTLEMAN

1. BF, *Autobiography,* 43.
2. BF, "Will and Codicil," 23 June 1789. (Franklin documents that are not yet published in the letterpress edition of his papers will be cited with their date.)
3. BF, *Autobiography,* 53.
4. BF, *Autobiography,* 58.
5. Jeffrey L. Pasley, *"The Tyranny of Printers": Newspaper Politics in the Early American Republic* (Charlottesville: University of Virginia Press, 2001), 27; Stephen Botein, "'Meer Mechanics' and an Open Press: The Business and Political Strategies of Colonial American Printers," *Perspectives in American History* 9 (1975): 136.
6. BF, *Autobiography,* 62.
7. Kenneth A. Lockridge, *Literacy in Colonial New England: An Enquiry into the Social Context of Literacy in the Early Modern West* (New York: Norton, 1974), 18–29. New England's literacy rate was among the highest in the Western world.

8. BF, *Autobiography,* 58.
9. BF, *Autobiography,* 59.
10. BF, *Autobiography,* 60. On Franklin's writing see Bruce Ingham Granger, *Benjamin Franklin: An American Man of Letters* (Ithaca, N.Y.: Cornell University Press, 1964). John Jay recounted a story Franklin had told him about the New Jersey Assembly in 1740. The assembly was engaged in a dispute with the governor and wanted to write a reply to the governor's message. But the committee assigned the task, "tho they were Men of good understanding and respectable, yet there was not one among them capable of writing a proper answer to the Message." They asked Franklin, whom one of the committee knew, and when he satisfied them with his writing, they made him their printer. J. A. Leo Lemay, *The Canon of Benjamin Franklin, 1722–1776: New Attributions and Reconsiderations* (Newark: University of Delaware Press, 1986), 95.
11. Frank Luther Mott, *American Journalism: A History of Newspapers in the United States Through 250 Years, 1690 to 1940* (New York: Macmillan, 1941), 9.
12. Botein, "'Meer Mechanics' and an Open Press," 193–96. Botein's articles are by far the most sophisticated work on colonial printers. It is a tragedy that he died prematurely before he could complete his study.
13. BF, *Autobiography,* 67.
14. [BF], "Silence Dogood, No. 4," in *Papers of Franklin,* 1:14. Franklin learned early the advantages of using pseudonyms. "When the Writer conceals himself, he has the Advantage of hearing the Censure both of Friends and Enemies, express'd with more Impartiality." On Literary Style, 2 Aug. 1733, in *Papers of Franklin,* 1:328.
15. BF, *Autobiography,* 68.
16. BF, *Autobiography,* 68–69.
17. BF, *Autobiography,* 68–71, 43.
18. BF, *Autobiography,* 75–76.
19. Susan E. Klepp, "Demography in Early Philadelphia, 1690–1860," in Susan E. Klepp, ed., *The Demographic History of the Philadelphia Region, 1600–1860,* American Philosophical Society, *Proceedings* 133 (June 1989), 103–4.
20. On Keimer, see Stephen Bloore, "Samuel Keimer: A Footnote to the Life of Franklin," *PMHB* 54 (1930): 255–87.
21. BF, *Autobiography,* 65.
22. Linda Rees Heaton, "'This Excellent Man': Littleton Waller Tazewell's Sketch of Benjamin Waller," *Virginia Magazine of History and Biography* 89 (1981): 147–50.
23. Hamilton to Edward Stevens, 11 Nov. 1769, in Harold C. Syrett et al., eds., *The Papers of Alexander Hamilton* (New York: Columbia University Press, 1961), 1:4.
24. BF, *Autobiography,* 80.
25. William Smith charged in 1764 that without the patronage of Allen and his friends Franklin probably would have remained in his original obscurity.

Steven C. Bullock, *Revolutionary Brotherhood: Freemasonry and the Transformation of the American Social Order, 1730–1840* (Chapel Hill: University of North Carolina Press, 1996), 74–75.

26. BF, *Autobiography*, 113.
27. BF, *Autobiography*, 121.
28. Bernard Bailyn, *The Peopling of North America: An Introduction* (New York: Knopf, 1985), 24–25; M. Dorothy George, *London Life in the Eighteenth Century* (New York: Capricorn Books, 1965), 21–25.
29. Liza Picard, *Dr. Johnson's London: Life in London, 1740–1770* (London: Weidenfeld & Nicolson, 2000); George Rudé, *Hanoverian London, 1714–1808* (Berkeley: University of California Press, 1971), 47.
30. BF, *Autobiography*, 87, 95.
31. BF, *Autobiography*, 96.
32. BF, *Autobiography*, 128.
33. BF, *Autobiography*, 99.
34. BF, *Autobiography*, 101.
35. BF, *Autobiography*, 114–15, 145–46.
36. BF to Benjamin Vaughn, 9 Nov. 1779, in *Papers of Franklin*, 31:59; BF, Poor Richard, 1739, and BF, Dialogue Between Two Presbyterians, 1735, ibid., 2:224, 33. On Franklin's religious views, see Elizabeth E. Dunn, "From a Bold Youth to a Reflective Sage: A Reevaluation of Benjamin Franklin's Religion," *PMHB* 111 (1987): 501–24; Douglas Anderson, *The Radical Enlightenment of Benjamin Franklin* (Baltimore: Johns Hopkins University Press, 1997), 54–89; and Kerry S. Walters, *Benjamin Franklin and His Gods* (Urbana: University of Illinois Press, 1999).
37. BF, *Autobiography*, 96.
38. Botein, "'Meer Mechanics' and an Open Press," 130–211; Stephen Botein, "Printers and the American Revolution," in Bernard Bailyn and John Hench, eds., *The Press and the American Revolution* (Worcester, Mass.: American Antiquarian Society, 1980), 14.
39. BF, *Autobiography*, 110.
40. BF, *Autobiography*, 112–13.
41. BF, *Autobiography*, 119.
42. BF, *Autobiography*, 128.
43. Claude-Anne Lopez and Eugenia W. Herbert, *The Private Franklin: The Man and His Family* (New York: Norton, 1975), 23.
44. BF, *Autobiography*, 129.
45. Carl Van Doren, *Benjamin Franklin* (New York: Viking, 1938), 125. For Franklin's view that if a tradesman's wife "does not *bring* a fortune" to the marriage, at least she "will help to *make* one," see BF to Jane Mecom, 21 May 1757, in *Papers of Franklin*, 7:216.

46. [BF], "Anthony Afterwit," "Celia Single," *Pennsylvania Gazette,* 10 and 24 July 1732, in *Franklin: Writings,* 185–87, 188–90.
47. [BF], "Rules and Maxims for Promoting Matrimonial Happiness," 8 Oct. 1730, and "Old Mistresses Apologue," 25 June 1745, in *Franklin: Writings,* 154, 302.
48. George Roberts to Robert Crafton, 8 Oct. 1763, in *Papers of Franklin,* 11:370–71n.
49. "Extracts from the Diary of Daniel Fisher, 1755," *PMHB* 17 (1893): 276; Lopez and Herbert, *Private Franklin,* 60; Sheila Skemp, "Family Partnerships: The Working Wife, Honoring Deborah Franklin," in Larry Tise, ed., *Benjamin Franklin and Women* (University Park: Pennsylvania State University Press, 1998), 23.
50. William Speck, *Stability and Strife: England, 1714–1760* (Cambridge, Mass.: Harvard University Press, 1970), 37; Steele, quoted in John Barrell, *English Literature in History, 1730–1780: An Equal, Wide Survey* (London: St. Martin's Press, 1983), 37; Paul Langford, *A Polite and Commercial People: England, 1727–1783* (Oxford: Oxford University Press, 1989), 65–66.
51. Adams, *Diary and Autobiography,* 1:198; Douglass Adair, ed., "The Autobiography of the Reverend Devereux Jarratt, 1732–1763," *WMQ* 9 (1952): 361. In the eighteenth century, writes historian Stuart Blumin, "the important hierarchical distinction was the one that set off the several elites from everyone else." In comparison with the great difference between the gentry and ordinary people, says Blumin, "differences between artisans and laborers were of no real consequence. The effect, needless to say, was to identify middling people much more closely with the bottom of society than with the top." Stuart M. Blumin, *The Emergence of the Middle Class: Social Experience in the American City, 1760–1900* (Cambridge: Cambridge University Press, 1989), 33. John Adams grounded the political theory of his *Defence of the Constitutions of the United States,* written in 1787–1788, on this traditional distinction: "The people, in all nations," he wrote, "are naturally divided into two sorts, the gentlemen and the simplemen, a word which is here chosen to signify the common people." *Defence,* in Charles F. Adams, ed., *Works of John Adams* (Boston, 1854), 6:185. For a fuller discussion of this distinction between the gentry and commoners, from which this account is drawn, see Gordon S. Wood, *The Radicalism of the American Revolution* (New York: Knopf, 1992), 24–42.
52. Adair, ed., "Autobiography of Jarratt," 361.
53. Adams, *Diary and Autobiography,* 1:198.
54. James Reid, "The Religion of the Bible and Religion of K[ing] W[illiam] County Compared," in Richard Beale Davis, ed., *The Colonial Virginia Satirist: Mid–Eighteenth Century Commentaries on Politics, Religion, and Society,* American Philosophical Society, *Transactions,* New Ser., 57, Pt. 1 (1967), 56.
55. Adams, *Diary and Autobiography,* 1:198.
56. Samuel Mather, *The Fall of the Mighty Lamented* (Boston, 1738), 10; Courtland Canby, "Robert Munford's *The Patriots,*" *WMQ* 6 (1949): 499–500.

57. Jonathan Boucher, *A View of the Causes and Consequences of the American Revolution* (London, 1797), 233; T. H. Breen, *Tobacco Culture: The Mentality of the Great Tidewater Planters on the Eve of the Revolution* (Princeton, N.J.: Princeton University Press, 1985), 160.
58. Carl Bridenbaugh, ed., *Gentleman's Progress: The Itinerarium of Dr. Alexander Hamilton, 1744* (Chapel Hill: University of North Carolina Press, 1948), 163, 8; Pauline Maier, *The Old Revolutionaries: Political Lives in the Age of Samuel Adams* (New York: Knopf, 1980), 240; Richard L. Bushman, *King and People in Provincial Massachusetts* (Chapel Hill: University of North Carolina Press, 1985), 69–70; Jack P. Greene, "Society, Ideology, and Politics: An Analysis of the Political Culture of Mid-Eighteenth-Century Virginia," in Richard M. Jellison, ed., *Society, Freedom, and Conscience: The Coming of the Revolution in Virginia, Massachusetts, and New York* (New York: Norton, 1976), 18–19; Hunter Dickinson Farish, ed., *Journal and Letters of Philip Vickers Fithian* (Williamsburg, Va.: Colonial Williamsburg Foundation, 1945), 29; Carl Bridenbaugh, *The Colonial Craftsman* (Chicago: University of Chicago Press, 1950), 164; John K. Alexander, *Render Them Submissive: Responses to Poverty in Philadelphia, 1760–1800* (Amherst: University of Massachusetts Press, 1980), 18.
59. Richard L. Bushman, *The Refinement of America: Persons, Houses, Cities* (New York: Knopf, 1992), 3–203; Smith, quoted in Bullock, *Revolutionary Brotherhood, 66*; Bushman, *King and People*, 70.
60. Wood, *Radicalism of the American Revolution*, 41–42.
61. BF to Peter Collinson, 9 May 1753, in *Papers of Franklin*, 4:481. "The great aim [of the society]," writes historian Paul Langford, "was to become rich enough to be idle." Paul Langford, *Englishness Identified: Manners and Character, 1650–1850* (Oxford: Oxford University Press, 2000), 38.
62. Langford, *Englishness Identified*, 31.
63. Derek Jarrett, *England in the Age of Hogarth* (London: Hart-Davis, MacGibbon, 1974), 79–80; Boston *Evening Post*, 14 Dec. 1761; BF, "On the Labouring Poor" (1768), in *Franklin: Writings*, 622–23.
64. Aristotle, *Politics*, VII, ix, 1328b33, trans. T. A. Sinclair, rev. by Trevor J. Saunders (New York: Oxford University Press, 1981), 415.
65. Harrington, quoted in Lance Banning, *The Jeffersonian Persuasion: Evolution of a Party Ideology* (Ithaca, N.Y.: Cornell University Press, 1978), 28; Defoe, quoted in Speck, *Stability and Strife*, 32; Jackson to BF, 17 June 1755, in *Papers of Franklin*, 6:77.
66. Venetia Murray, *High Society in the Regency Period, 1788–1830* (London: Penguin, 1998), 22; H. D. Farish, ed., *Journal and Letters of Fithian*, 161. For an illuminating discussion of the ancient Roman aristocracy's attitudes toward work and leisure, see Paul Veyne, "The Roman Empire," in Paul Veyne, ed., *A History of Private Life*, vol. 1, *From Pagan Rome to Byzantium* (Cambridge, Mass.: Harvard University Press, 1987), 117–59. The idea that the aristocracy had leisure while the common people worked, writes Veyne, "persisted from archaic Greece and

India down to Benjamin Constant and Charles Maurras" (p. 123). Northern Americans swept away this ancient idea in the aftermath of their revolution.

67. Buffon, quoted in Antonello Gerbi, *The Dispute of the New World: The History of a Polemic, 1750–1900,* trans. Jeremy Moyle (Pittsburgh: University of Pittsburgh Press, 1973), 19–20; Murray, *High Society in the Regency Period,* 22.
68. Locke, quoted in Harold Nicolson, *Good Behaviour: Being a Study of Certain Types of Civility* (Garden City, N.Y.: Doubleday, 1956), 194; Samuel Johnson, *Dictionary of the English Language* (London, 1730); Gaines, quoted in Botein, "Printers and the American Revolution," 18n.
69. "Letters and Papers of John Singleton Copley and Henry Pelham, 1739–1776," Massachusetts Historical Society, *Collections* 71 (1914): 661–66. "By the common people," wrote John Adams in his *Defence of the Constitutions,* "we mean laborers, husbandmen, mechanics, and merchants in general, who pursue their occupations and industry without any knowledge in liberal arts or sciences, or in any thing but their own trades or pursuits." C. Adams, ed., *Works of John Adams,* 6:185.
70. Rudé, *Hanoverian London,* 37, 56–57.
71. Howard B. Rock, *Artisans of the New Republic: Tradesmen of New York City in the Age of Jefferson* (New York: New York University Press, 1979), 295–322.
72. BF, *Autobiography,* 117–18.
73. Standing Queries for the Junto, 1732, in *Papers of Franklin,* 1:255–59.
74. BF, *Autobiography,* 161–62.
75. Bullock, *Revolutionary Brotherhood,* 55–63, 76–77.
76. BF, Observations on Reading History, 9 May 1731, in *Papers of Franklin,* 1:192–93; BF, *Autobiography,* 161–63.
77. BF, *Autobiography,* 163.
78. BF, *Autobiography,* 143, 130–31.
79. BF, *A Modest Enquiry into the Nature and Necessity of a Paper Currency* (1729), in *Papers of Franklin,* 1:156, 144.
80. On the Death of his Son, 30 Dec. 1736, in *Papers of Franklin,* 2:154.
81. BF, *Autobiography,* 207.
82. BF, *Autobiography,* 131, 93.
83. BF, Poor Richard, 1741, in *Papers of Franklin,* 2:296; Botein, "Printers and the American Revolution," 18.
84. BF, "Obadiah Plainman," *Franklin: Writings,* 275–83.
85. Lemay, *Canon of Franklin,* 97–103.
86. BF, "Tract Relative to the English School in Philadelphia" [1789].
87. BF, "Idea of an English School," 1751, in *Papers of Franklin,* 4:108.
88. Robert Hare to BF, 14 July 1789.
89. BF, "A Proposal for Promoting Useful Knowledge," 1743, in *Franklin: Writings,* 295–96; BF to Cadwallader Colden, 15 Aug. 1745, in *Papers of Franklin,* 3:36. See

also H. W. Brands, *The First American: The Life and Times of Benjamin Franklin* (New York: Doubleday, 2000), 168; and Van Doren, *Franklin,* 139.

90. BF, *Plain Truth: Or, Serious Considerations on the Present State of the City of Philadelphia and Province of Pennsylvania* (1747), in *Papers of Franklin,* 3:201, and BF, "Anthony Afterwit," *Pennsylvania Gazette,* 10 July 1732, ibid., 1:237.
91. BF, "Blackamore, on Molatto Gentlemen," *Pennsylvania Gazette,* 30 Aug. 1733, in *Franklin: Writings,* 219–20.
92. Daniel Defoe, *The Compleat English Gentleman,* ed. Karl D. Bülbring (London, 1890), 13. For a study of Defoe's struggle with the question of gentility, see Michael Shinagel, *Daniel Defoe and Middle-Class Gentility* (Cambridge, Mass.: Harvard University Press, 1968).
93. BF, *Autobiography,* 126.
94. Charles Coleman Sellers, *Franklin in Portraiture* (New Haven: Yale University Press, 1962), 2–3; Van Doren, *Franklin,* 125–29. Franklin was devastated by the death of little Franky and had the boy's portrait painted following his death, with Franky's face probably modeled after Franklin's own, since the son was thought to resemble his father. Sellers, *Franklin in Portraiture,* 11.
95. BF, *Autobiography,* 171.
96. Botein, "Printers and the American Revolution," 16–17.
97. BF, "Apology for Printers" (1731), in *Franklin: Writings,* 172.
98. Botein, "'Meer Mechanics' and an Open Press," 177, 181–87, 190; Botein, "Printers and the American Revolution," 29–32.
99. BF, *Autobiography,* 164.
100. BF, Poor Richard, 1739, and Poor Richard Improved, 1750, in *Papers of Franklin,* 2:218, 7:326–50.
101. BF, *Autobiography,* 172.
102. BF to Strahan, 10 July 1743, 4 July 1744, in *Papers of Franklin,* 2:338–39, 409.
103. BF, *Autobiography,* 166, 181; Ralph Frasca, "From Apprentice to Journeyman to Partner: Benjamin Franklin's Workers and the Growth of the Early American Printing Trade," *PMHB* 114 (1990): 229–38.
104. Van Doren, *Franklin,* 123; Brands, *First American,* 189; Articles of Agreement with David Hall, 1 Jan. 1748, Account of Money Received from David Hall, 1748–1757, in *Papers of Franklin,* 3:263; Wood, *Radicalism of the American Revolution,* 112.
105. Botein, "'Meer Mechanics' and an Open Press," 167.
106. Lopez and Herbert, *Private Franklin,* 42; Van Doren, *Franklin,* 188–89, 193.
107. J.-P. Brissot de Warville, *New Travels in the United States of America, 1788,* trans. Mara Soceanu Vamos and Durand Echeverria (Cambridge, Mass.: Harvard University Press, 1964), 188n; Carl Bridenbaugh, *The Colonial Craftsman* (Chicago: University of Chicago Press, 1950), 61–62.
108. In 1775 Franklin told his friends that "Most of the little Property I have, consists of Houses in the Seaport Towns," which he assumed the British were going to

burn. BF to John Sargent, 27 June 1775, and BF to Jonathan Shipley, 7 July 1775, in *Papers of Franklin,* 22:72, 95.

109. Ronald W. Clark, *Benjamin Franklin: A Biography* (New York: Random House, 1983), 45.
110. BF, *Autobiography,* 192.
111. BF, *Plain Truth* (Phila., 1747), in *Papers of Franklin,* 3:188–204, quotation at 201.
112. Richard Peters to the Proprietors, 29 Nov. 1747, in *Papers of Franklin,* 3:214–16.
113. David S. Shields, *Civil Tongues and Polite Letters in British America* (Chapel Hill: University of North Carolina Press, 1997), 130.
114. BF, Observations on Reading History, 9 May 1731, in *Papers of Franklin,* 1:193; Adam Smith, *An Inquiry into the Nature and Causes of the Wealth of Nations,* ed. R. H. Campbell and A. S. Skinner (Oxford: Clarendon Press, 1976), 2:781–83.
115. From Robert Grace: Lease, 30 Dec. 1745, BF to Colden, 29 Sept. 1748, and Josiah Franklin to BF, 26 May 1739, all in *Papers of Franklin,* 3:51, 318; 2:29–30n; John F. Ross, "The Character of Poor Richard: Its Sources and Alterations," *Publications of the Modern Language Association* 55 (1940): 785–94.
116. BF, "Advice to a Young Tradesman, Written by an Old One" (1748), in *Franklin: Writings,* 320–22.
117. Sellers, *Franklin in Portraiture,* 4–5, 25–28. Although Sellers dates this portrait no later than 1746, Wayne Craven more recently dates it at 1748, when Feke made a professional visit to Philadelphia. Wayne Craven, "The American and British Portraits of Benjamin Franklin," in J. A. Leo Lemay, ed., *Reappraising Benjamin Franklin: A Bicentennial Perspective* (Newark: University of Delaware Press, 1993), 249.
118. BF, *Autobiography,* 125–26, 172.
119. Richard L. Bushman, *The Refinement of America: Persons, Houses, Cities* (New York: Knopf, 1992), 70.
120. BF, *Autobiography,* 183.
121. BF, *Autobiography,* 238. In 1748 Franklin had refused to be a candidate for the assembly, but in 1751 after his retirement from business he gladly accepted election to the assembly. See BF to Colden, 29 Sept. 1748, in *Papers of Franklin,* 3:318.

CHAPTER 2: BECOMING A BRITISH IMPERIALIST

1. When the Anglican clergyman Samuel Johnson received Franklin's plans for education reform in 1750 and learned that Franklin had only a tradesman's education, he was surprised. "Nobody would imagine that the draught you have made for an English education was done by a Tradesman," Johnson told Franklin in words that could only have warmed the former printer's heart. "But so it sometimes is, a True Genius will not content itself without entering more or less into almost everything." Samuel Johnson to BF, Nov. 1750. in *Papers of Franklin,* 4:74.

2. BF, *Autobiography,* 196; BF to Cadwallader Colden, 29 Sept. 1748, in *Papers of Franklin,* 3:318.
3. Edmund S. Morgan, *Benjamin Franklin* (New Haven: Yale University Press, 2002), 6.
4. BF to John Pringle, 1 Dec. 1762, in *Papers of Franklin,* 10:159–60; Morgan, *Franklin,* 6–9.
5. I. Bernard Cohen, *Benjamin Franklin's Experiments: A New Edition of Franklin's "Experiments and Observations on Electricity"* (Cambridge, Mass.: Harvard University Press, 1941), 48.
6. Claude-Anne Lopez and Eugenia W. Herbert, *The Private Franklin: The Man and His Family* (New York: Norton, 1975), 44–46.
7. BF, *Autobiography,* 240.
8. Carl Van Doren, *Benjamin Franklin* (New York: Viking, 1938), 157; Lopez and Herbert, *Private Franklin,* 44.
9. BF to Peter Collinson, 28 July 1747, in *Papers of Franklin,* 3:158.
10. BF to Collinson, 28 Mar. 1747, in *Papers of Franklin,* 3:118–19.
11. I. Bernard Cohen, *Benjamin Franklin: Scientist and Statesman* (New York: Scribner, 1975), 50; Cohen, *Franklin's Experiments,* 64–65, 72–73.
12. Lopez and Herbert, *Private Franklin,* 45; BF to Jacques Barbeu-Dubourg and Thomas-François Dalibard, c. 25 May 1773, in *Papers of Franklin,* 20:210–13.
13. For a recent book that claims that Franklin never performed his kite experiment but told the story as a hoax, see Tom Tucker, *Bolt of Fate: Benjamin Franklin and His Electric Kite Hoax* (New York: Public Affairs, 2003). Most historians probably would agree with Walter Isaacson that Tucker's argument is unpersuasive. Walter Isaacson, *Benjamin Franklin: An American Life* (New York: Simon & Schuster, 2003), 534.
14. Cohen very much doubts Franklin's account in his *Autobiography* that some of his findings were "laughed at by connoisseurs" in the Royal Society. But to believe that obviously fit Franklin's mood when he wrote his *Autobiography.* Cohen, *Franklin's Experiments,* 80.
15. Collinson to BF, 27 Sept. 1752, in *Papers of Franklin,* 4:358.
16. BF to Jared Eliot, 12 Apr. 1753, 12 Sept. 1751, in *Papers of Franklin,* 4:466–67, 194.
17. Cohen, *Franklin: Scientist and Statesman,* 65.
18. Lopez and Herbert, *Private Franklin,* 47.
19. BF, *Autobiography,* 209.
20. Van Doren, *Franklin,* 170; BF to Collinson, 5 Nov. 1756, in *Papers of Franklin,* 7:11.
21. Stiles to BF, 26 Feb. 1766, in *Papers of Franklin,* 13:175. In 1773 Franklin was appointed a foreign associate of the French Royal Academy of Sciences, a special honor. The next American appointment did not come until nearly a century later, with the selection of Louis Agassiz. Cohen, *Franklin's Experiments,* 117.
22. BF to John Lining, 18 Mar. 1755, in *Papers of Franklin,* 5:526–27.

23. BF to Colden, 11 Oct. 1750, in *Papers of Franklin,* 4:68.
24. BF, *Autobiography,* 196.
25. BF, *Autobiography,* 197.
26. For a tough-minded account of Franklin's involvement in Pennsylvania politics, see William S. Hanna, *Benjamin Franklin and Pennsylvania Politics* (Stanford, Calif.: Stanford University Press, 1964).
27. Thomas Penn to Richard Peters, 30 Mar., 9 June 1748, in *Papers of Franklin,* 3:186n.
28. BF, "Observations Concerning the Increase of Mankind," 1751, in *Franklin: Writings,* 367–74.
29. Conyers Read, "The English Elements in Benjamin Franklin," *PMHB* 64 (1940): 314.
30. BF, "Observations Concerning the Increase of Mankind," 374. When the pamphlet was reprinted in 1760 and 1761, these references to the Palatine Boors were omitted, but they were certainly remembered by Franklin's political enemies in 1764. *Papers of Franklin,* 4:234n.
31. BF to James Parker, 20 Mar. 1751, in *Papers of Franklin,* 4:117–20. It is this statement by Franklin that has led to the invoking of the so-called Indian influence thesis, which misled some Americans in the 1980s and 1990s. Since Franklin was present at the Albany Congress, the Second Continental Congress, and the Constitutional Convention of 1787, he was in a position, it was said, to present the model of the Iroquois union to his colleagues, and thus the Indians should be given their due in helping to create the Constitution. The theory is built on the assumption that the colonists had no previous experience with confederations and unions and needed the Iroquois to tell them about dividing political power. Yet the colonists' history from the beginning had been all about the parceling of power upward, from the counties and towns to the colonial governments, and from the colonial governments to confederations, such as the New England Confederation of 1643. For the debate over the Indians' presumed influence on the American Constitution and its refutation, see the succinct summary in Timothy J. Shannon, *Indians and Colonists at the Crossroads of Empire: The Albany Congress of 1754* (Ithaca, N.Y.: Cornell University Press, 2000), 6–8, and the articles cited there.
32. BF to Parker, 20 Mar. 1751, in *Papers of Franklin,* 4:117–20.
33. On the Albany Congress, see the excellent study by Shannon, *Indians and Colonists at the Crossroads of Empire.*
34. BF, *Autobiography,* 210.
35. BF to James Alexander and Colden, 8 June 1754, in *Papers of Franklin,* 5:335–38.
36. BF to Colden, 14 July 1754, in *Papers of Franklin,* 5:392.
37. BF, The Albany Plan of Union, 1754, in *Papers of Franklin,* 5:374–92, quotation at 390.
38. BF to Collinson, 29 Dec. 1754, in *Papers of Franklin,* 5:454.

39. Theodore Draper, *A Struggle for Power: The American Revolution* (New York: Times Books, 1996), 26–48.
40. Alison Gilbert Olson, "The British Government and Colonial Union," *WMQ* 17 (1960): 31.
41. BF, *Autobiography,* 210.
42. BF to Colden, 29 Sept. 1748, in *Papers of Franklin,* 3:319.
43. BF to William Franklin, 14 Oct. 1754, in *Papers of Franklin,* 5:438.
44. BF to William Shirley, 3 Dec. 1754, in *Papers of Franklin,* 5:443.
45. The letters to Shirley of 3 and 22 December have not survived in manuscript form; they are known solely from their publication in the *London Chronicle* in 1766. The letter of December 4 we have only in the hand of an unknown copyist but signed by Franklin and endorsed by him, "Copy of a Letter to Gov. Shirley." It also bears the notation "To P Collinson," which is in Collinson's own hand. The editors of volume 5 of the *Papers of Franklin* speculated that this was the version furnished to Strahan, who published this letter and the others in the *London Chronicle.* I owe this information to Ellen Cohn, current editor in chief of the *Papers of Franklin.*
46. BF to Shirley, 4 Dec. 1754, in *Papers of Franklin,* 5:443. William Blackstone, the great summarizer of eighteenth-century English law, did in fact consider the American colonies to be conquered countries. Because the English common law had no way of accounting for the acquisition of land except through descent or conquest, the legal status of the colonies remained problematic. William Blackstone, *Commentaries on the Laws of England* (Oxford, 1765), 1:104–5. (I owe this reference to Craig Yirush.)
47. BF to Shirley, 22 Dec. 1754, in *Papers of Franklin,* 5:449–50; BF, *Autobiography,* 253.
48. BF, *Autobiography,* 213.
49. BF, *Autobiography,* 240.
50. BF, *Autobiography,* 238–39.
51. Richard Peters to Penn, 29 Apr., 1 June 1756, in *Papers of Franklin,* 7:73.
52. William Peters to Penn, 4 Jan. 1756, in *Papers of Franklin,* 6:409; Lopez and Herbert, *Private Franklin,* 65.
53. Colden to Collinson, 5 Nov. 1756, in *Papers of Franklin,* 7:13n; BF to Collinson, 5 Nov. 1756, ibid., 7:13–15.
54. BF to George Whitefield, 2 July 1756, in *Papers of Franklin,* 6:468.
55. BF, A Plan for Settling Two Western Colonies, 1754, in *Papers of Franklin,* 5:459–60.
56. BF to Whitefield, 2 July 1756, in *Papers of Franklin,* 6:468–69.
57. BF to William Parsons, 22 Feb. 1757, in *Papers of Franklin,* 7:136.
58. On the colonial agents in London during the era of the American Revolution, see Michael G. Kammen, *A Rope of Sand: The Colonial Agents, British Politics, and the American Revolution* (Ithaca, N.Y.: Cornell University Press, 1968).

59. BF to Joseph Galloway, 11 April 1757, in *Papers of Franklin,* 7:179. On the relationship between Franklin and Galloway, see Benjamin H. Newcomb, *Franklin and Galloway: A Political Partnership* (New Haven: Yale University Press, 1972).
60. "Extracts from the Diary of Daniel Fisher, 1755," *PMHB* 17 (1893): 276; Lopez and Herbert, *Private Franklin,* 60, 61, 69, 165.
61. Poor Richard Improved, 1758, in *Papers of Franklin,* 7:326–50.
62. Patrick Sullivan, "Benjamin Franklin, the Inveterate (and Crafty) Public Instructor: Instruction on Two Levels in 'The Way to Wealth,'" *Early American Literature* 21 (1986–1987): 248–59.
63. George Rudé, *Hanoverian London, 1714–1808* (Berkeley: University of California Press, 1971), 55; John Brewer, *The Pleasures of the Imagination: English Culture in the Eighteenth Century* (New York: Farrar, Straus and Giroux, 1997), 31.
64. The tall narrow Georgian house at 36 Craven Street still stands in the heart of London and is being restored for tourists and others to visit in 2005. During the restoration more than twelve hundred pieces of human bones from the eighteenth century were discovered in a pit in the basement. The most plausible explanation for the bones is that William Hewson, who married Polly Stevenson in 1770, operated an anatomy school in the house during the early 1770s. Hewson was a student of John and William Hunter who were the great anatomists of the day. To make room for Hewson's school, Franklin and Mary Stevenson sought other lodging on Craven Street. After Hewson died of blood poisoning in 1774 at age thirty-four, leaving Polly with two young sons and an unborn daughter, Franklin and Polly's mother moved back to 36 Craven Street. *Manchester Guardian Weekly,* 27 Aug. 2003, p. 21. (I owe this citation to Brendon McConville.) See also www.rsa.org.uk/franklin/no36/bones.html.
65. BF to Deborah Franklin, Jan. 1758, in *Papers of Franklin,* 7:369; Sellers, *Franklin in Portraiture,* 56–57.
66. Adam Sisman, *Boswell's Presumptuous Task* (London: Penguin, 2000), 138.
67. BF to Deborah Franklin, 6 Sept. 1758, in *Papers of Franklin,* 8:134.
68. Sellers, *Franklin in Portraiture,* 55, 58–60.
69. BF to Joseph Galloway, 7 Apr. 1759, in *Papers of Franklin,* 8:310; Lopez and Herbert, *Private Franklin,* 89.
70. BF to Deborah Franklin, 21 Jan. 1758, in *Papers of Franklin,* 7:364.
71. BF to Deborah Franklin, 10 June 1758, in *Papers of Franklin,* 8:93; BF, *Autobiography,* 129; Lopez and Herbert, *Private Franklin,* 82–83; Paul W. Conner, *Poor Richard's Politicks: Benjamin Franklin and His New American Order* (New York: Oxford University Press, 1965), 215; *The Craven Street Gazette,* Sept. 1770, in *Papers of Franklin,* 17:220–26.
72. Strahan to Deborah Franklin, 13 Dec. 1757, in *Papers of Franklin,* 7:297.
73. Hugh Roberts to BF, 15 May 1760, in *Papers of Franklin,* 9:113.
74. Lopez and Herbert, *Private Franklin,* 89.

75. BF, *London Chronicle*, 9 May 1759, in *Papers of Franklin*, 8:342.
76. BF to Lord Kames, 3 Jan. 1760, in *Papers of Franklin*, 9:6–7.
77. BF, *The Interest of Great Britain Considered* (1760), in *Papers of Franklin*, 9:59–100, quotation at 90.
78. BF to William Franklin, 22 Mar. 1775, and Journal of Negotiations in London, in *Papers of Franklin*, 21:546–47.
79. BF to Isaac Norris, 14 Jan. 1758, in *Papers of Franklin*, 7:361–62.
80. BF to Norris, 16 Sept. 1758, 19 Jan. 1759, in *Papers of Franklin*, 8:157, 236. Later, in June 1760, the Board of Trade criticized the weakness of the proprietary governor in dealing with the Pennsylvania Assembly. Such weakness, the Board declared, was bound to exist "while the Prerogatives of Royalty are placed in the feeble hands of Individuals, and the Authority of the Crown is to be exercised, without the Powers of the Crown to support it." This could be read as a desire to make the colony royal, and Isaac Norris in Pennsylvania certainly read it that way. Board of Trade: Report on Pennsylvania Laws, 24 June 1760, ibid., 9:173. On these efforts to royalize Pennsylvania, see James H. Hutson, *Pennsylvania Politics, 1764–1770: The Movement for Royal Government and Its Consequences* (Princeton, N.J.: Princeton University Press, 1972).
81. Robert Middlekauff sees Franklin's attempt to turn Pennsylvania into a royal colony as the "surprising" action of an "irrational" man. Franklin was normally "a generous and calm spirit," writes Middlekauff, "but in this case his feeling about Penn overcame all his usual standards of conduct, skewed his vision, and set him on a course that he abandoned only after years of reckless behavior." Middlekauff, *Benjamin Franklin and His Enemies* (Berkeley: University of California Press, 1996), 55–114, quotation at 107. Edmund S. Morgan likewise finds Franklin's confidence that he could get the British government to cancel all the powers of the proprietors "a mystery." Morgan writes that in Franklin's two years at home, from November 1762 to November 1764, he was afflicted "with a prolonged fit of political blindness. . . . He made mistakes," says Morgan, "mistakes that make us wonder if *we* have made mistakes in our attempts to understand him." Morgan, *Franklin*, 120, 129. I think we have indeed made mistakes in our attempts to understand Franklin. Once we accept the fact that Franklin in these years was a fervent royalist who very much wanted to participate in the grandeur of the British Empire—which was, after all, a *royal* empire—much of the surprise, confusion, and mystery about his behavior in the early 1760s falls away. Pennsylvania was no longer as important to him as the empire.
82. William D. Liddle, "'A Patriot King, or None': Lord Bolingbroke and the American Renunciation of George III," *Journal of American History* 45 (1979): 951. In assessing Franklin's views of the imperial relationship, it is important that we do not mingle his statements of the early 1760s with those later in the decade or in the early 1770s.

83. BF to Deborah Franklin, 14 Sept. 1761, in *Papers of Franklin,* 9:356.
84. BF to Strahan, 8 Aug., 19 Dec. 1763, in *Papers of Franklin,* 10:320, 407–8.
85. Hutson, *Pennsylvania Politics,* 144–46; BF to Thomas Becket, 17 Dec. 1763, in *Papers of Franklin,* 10:395n; Shelia L. Skemp, *William Franklin: Son of a Patriot, Servant of a King* (New York: Oxford University Press, 1990), 40, 302. John Adams tells the story of Franklin's pride in his ability to influence the British government. When someone expressed some doubt about the extent of that influence, Franklin, according to Adams's autobiography, "broke out into a Passion and swore, contrary to his usual reserve, 'that he had an Influence with the Ministry and was intimate with Lord Bute.'" Adams, *Diary and Autobiography,* 4:150–51.
86. R. C. Simmons, "Colonial Patronage: Two Letters from William Franklin to the Earl of Bute, 1762," *WMQ* 59 (2002): 123–34.
87. Thomas Bridges to Jared Ingersoll, 30 Sept. 1762, in *Papers of Franklin,* 10:146–47n. John Adams always assumed that Franklin had to have had some considerable influence with Lord Bute in order for his son to be appointed governor of New Jersey. "Without the Supposition of some kind of Backstairs Intrigues," said Adams, "it is difficult to account of that mortification of the pride, affront to the dignity and Insult to the Morals of America, the Elevation to the Government of New Jersey of a base born Brat." Adams, *Diary and Autobiography,* 4:150–51.
88. BF to Strahan, 12 Feb. 1745, in *Papers of Franklin,* 3:13–14.
89. BF, *Proposals Relating to the Education of Youth in Pensilvania* (1749), in *Papers of Franklin,* 3:400.
90. Bernard Bailyn, *The Ideological Origins of the American Revolution* (Cambridge, Mass.: Harvard University Press, 1967), 89–92.
91. BF to Collinson, 9 May 1753, and BF to Galloway, 17 Feb. 1758, in *Papers of Franklin,* 4:486; 7:375.
92. BF to Mary Stevenson, 25 Mar. 1763, in *Papers of Franklin,* 10:232.
93. BF to Richard Jackson, 8 Mar. 1763, in *Papers of Franklin,* 10:210.
94. BF to Ingersoll, 11 Dec. 1762, in *Papers of Franklin,* 10:174–76.
95. BF to Galloway, 9 Jan. 1760, and BF to Strahan, 23 Aug. 1762, in *Papers of Franklin,* 9:17; 10:149.
96. BF to Jackson, 8 Mar. 1763, in *Papers of Franklin,* 10:210.
97. BF to Strahan, 8 Aug. 1763, and BF to Deborah Franklin, 18 June 1763, in *Papers of Franklin,* 10:320, 291.
98. BF to John Fothergill, 14 Mar. 1764, in *Papers of Franklin,* 11:101–5.
99. Hutson, *Pennsylvania Politics,* 125–27; BF, *Cool Thoughts on the Present Situation of Our Public Affairs* (1764), in *Papers of Franklin,* 11:154–57, 171.
100. David L. Jacobson, "John Dickinson's Fight Against Royal Government 1764," *WMQ* 19 (1962), 71–77.

101. Editorial note, *Papers of Franklin,* 11:195n.
102. Philip J. Gleason, "A Scurrilous Colonial Election and Franklin's Reputation," *WMQ* 18 (1961), 68–84.
103. Hutson, *Pennsylvania Politics,* 180–82.
104. BF to Strahan, 1 Sept. 1764, in *Papers of Franklin,* 11:332.
105. BF, Remarks on a Late Protest Against the Appointment of Mr. Franklin an Agent for This Province, 5 Nov. 1764, in *Papers of Franklin,* 11:431–33.
106. Bernard Bailyn, *The Origins of American Politics* (New York: Knopf, 1968); Hanna, *Benjamin Franklin and Pennsylvania Politics,* 171.
107. Martin Howard Jr. to BF, 16 Nov. 1764, and Samuel Johnson to BF, Nov. ? 1764, in *Papers of Franklin,* 11:459–60, 477–78.
108. Gleason, "A Scurrilous Colonial Election," 84.

CHAPTER 3: BECOMING A PATRIOT

1. BF to Richard Jackson, 11 Feb. 1764, in *Papers of Franklin,* 11:76.
2. BF to Jackson, 16 Jan. 1764, in *Papers of Franklin,* 11:19–20.
3. BF to Peter Collinson, 30 Apr. 1764, in *Papers of Franklin,* 11:182.
4. BF to David Hall, 14 Feb. 1765, in *Papers of Franklin,* 12:65–67.
5. BF, Scheme for Supplying the Colonies with a Paper Currency (1768), in *Papers of Franklin,* 12:55.
6. BF to Joseph Galloway, 11 Oct. 1766, in *Papers of Franklin,* 13:449.
7. BF to Charles Thomson, 11 July 1765, in *Papers of Franklin,* 12:208.
8. The best account of the Stamp Act crisis is Edmund S. Morgan and Helen M. Morgan, *The Stamp Act Crisis: Prologue to Revolution* (Chapel Hill: University of North Carolina Press, 1953).
9. James Macdonald, *A Free Nation Deep in Debt: The Financial Roots of Democracy* (New York: Farrar, Straus and Giroux, 2003), 140.
10. *New York Mercury,* 21 Oct. 1765, in Edmund S. Morgan, ed., *Prologue to Revolution: Sources and Documents on the Stamp Act Crisis, 1764–1766* (Chapel Hill: University of North Carolina Press, 1973), 94.
11. Adams, *Diary and Autobiography,* 1:260. In 1765, Hutchinson was fifty-four and Franklin was fifty-nine. For an elegant and sympathetic study of Hutchinson, see Bernard Bailyn, *The Ordeal of Thomas Hutchinson* (Cambridge, Mass.: Harvard University Press, 1974).
12. Thomas Hutchinson to BF, 27 Oct., 18 Nov. 1765, in *Papers of Franklin,* 12:339–40, 380–81.
13. Richard Penn Jr., quoted in Morgan and Morgan, *Stamp Act Crisis,* 206.
14. Bailyn, *Hutchinson,* 62.
15. John Hughes to BF, 8–17 Sept. 1765, in *Papers of Franklin,* 12:264–66.
16. Hall to BF, 6 Sept. 1765, in *Papers of Franklin,* 12:259.

17. Benjamin Rush to Ebenezeer Hazard, 5 Nov. 1765, in L. H. Butterfield, ed., *Letters of Benjamin Rush* (Princeton, N.J.: Princeton University Press, 1951), 1:18; Claude-Anne Lopez and Eugenia W. Herbert, *The Private Franklin: The Man and His Family* (New York: Norton, 1975), 129.
18. BF to Hughes, 9 Aug. 1765, Hall to BF, 6 Sept. 1765, James Parker to BF, 14 June 1765, and Peter Timothy to BF, 3 Sept. 1768, all in *Papers of Franklin,* 12:234–35, 255–59, 174–76; 15:200–201; Stephen Botein, "'Meer Mechanics' and an Open Press: The Business and Political Strategies of Colonial American Printers," *Perspectives in American History* 9 (1975): 212–14; Stephen Botein, "Printers and the American Revolution," in Bernard Bailyn and John Hench, eds., *The Press and the American Revolution* (Worcester, Mass.: American Antiquarian Society, 1980), 24–29.
19. BF to Hughes, 9 Aug. 1765, in *Papers of Franklin,* 12:234–35.
20. BF to Collinson, 28 May 1754, in *Papers of Franklin,* 5:330a.
21. As Stephen Conway has pointed out, Halifax's opinion was extreme. Although Grenville himself seems to have regarded the colonists as separate from the British nation, apologists for the Stamp Act necessarily had to assume that the Americans were part of the same British community under Parliament; otherwise, they would have no way of explaining why the colonists should contribute taxes to the realm. Stephen Conway, "From Fellow-Nationals to Foreigners: British Perceptions of the Americans, circa 1739–1783," *WMQ* 59 (2002): 83–84.
22. T. H. Breen, "Ideology and Nationalism on the Eve of the American Revolution: Revisions Once More in Need of Revising," *Journal of American History* 84 (1997): 29–32; Conway, "From Fellow-Nationals to Foreigners," 69. On the development of British and English identities in the eighteenth century, see Gerald Newman, *The Rise of English Nationalism: A Cultural History, 1740–1830* (New York: St. Martin's Press, 1997); Kathleen Wilson, *The Sense of the People: Politics, Culture, and Imperialism in England, 1715–1785* (Cambridge, England: Cambridge University Press, 1998; Linda Colley, *Britons: Forging the Nation, 1707–1837* (New Haven: Yale University Press, 1992); Colin Kidd, *British Identities Before Nationalism: Ethnicity and Nationhood in the Atlantic World, 1600–1800* (Cambridge, England: Cambridge University Press, 1999); Paul Langford, *Englishness Identified: Manners and Character, 1650–1850* (Oxford, England: Oxford University Press, 2000); Eliga H. Gould, *The Persistence of Empire: British Political Culture in the Age of the American Revolution* (Chapel Hill: University of North Carolina Press, 2000).
23. James Otis, *A Vindication of the British Colonies . . .*, in Bernard Bailyn, ed., *Pamphlets of the American Revolution, 1750–1776* (Cambridge, Mass.: Harvard University Press, 1965), 1:568; Hutchinson to BF, 1 Jan. 1766, in *Papers of Franklin,* 13:3.
24. Breen, "Ideology and Nationalism," 29–32.
25. BF, Invectives Against the Americans, 1765, in *Franklin: Writings,* 563.

26. Maynard Mack, "The Muse of Satire," in Richard C. Boys, ed., *Studies in the Literature of the Augustan Age: Essays Collected in Honor of Arthur Ellicott Case* (New York: Gordian Press, 1966), 218–31.
27. BF, "Pacifus," 23 Jan. 1766, in *Papers of Franklin,* 13:55–57.
28. Hutchinson to BF, 1 Jan. 1766, in *Papers of Franklin,* 13:3. Franklin's August 1765 letter is lost; we know of it and his question from Hutchinson's reply.
29. On the letters to Shirley, see note 45, p. 260; and *Papers of Franklin,* 5:441–47, 449–51, 455–56.
30. BF to unknown correspondent, 6 Jan. 1766, and BF to Lord Kames, 25 Feb. 1767, in *Papers of Franklin,* 13:23; 14:65.
31. Morgan and Morgan, *Stamp Act Crisis,* 14, 111.
32. BF to Kames, 25 Feb. 1767, in *Papers of Franklin,* 14:64.
33. BF to William Franklin, 9 Nov. 1765, in *Papers of Franklin,* 12:363–64.
34. Paul Langford, *Englishness Identified: Manners and Character, 1650–1850* (Oxford: Oxford University Press, 2000), 212, 319.
35. BF, Examination Before the Committee of the Whole of the House of Commons, 1766, in *Papers of Franklin,* 13:136, 137, 158, 137.
36. Thomson to BF, 20 May 1766, in *Papers of Franklin,* 13:279.
37. BF to Joseph Fox, 24 Feb. 1766, in *Papers of Franklin,* 13:168.
38. On the sovereignty of Parliament, see Bernard Bailyn, *The Ideological Origins of the American Revolution* (Cambridge, Mass.: Harvard University Press, 1968), 200–202, 216–17; and Gordon S. Wood, *The Creation of the American Republic, 1776–1787* (Chapel Hill: University of North Carolina Press, 1969), 347–49.
39. BF to Hall, 24 Feb. 1766, and BF to Fox, 24 Feb. 1766, in *Papers of Franklin,* 13:170, 168.
40. BF to Jane Mecom, 1 Mar. 1766, in *Papers of Franklin,* 13:188. This display of optimism is not to deny Franklin's often pessimistic view of human nature, which he especially expressed when he felt he had been wronged. See Ronald A. Bosco, "'He That Best Understands the World, Least Likes It': The Dark Side of Benjamin Franklin," *PMHB* 111 (1987): 525–54.
41. BF, Examination Before the House of Commons, in *Papers of Franklin,* 13:153.
42. BF, Marginalia in Protests of the Lords Against Repeal of the Stamp Act, 1766, in *Papers of Franklin,* 13:212–20.
43. BF to Kames, 25 Feb. 1767, in *Papers of Franklin,* 14:68.
44. On the colonists' anticipation of the commonwealth theory of the British Empire, see Randolph Adams, *Political Ideas of the American Revolution: Britannic-American Contributions to the Problem of Imperial Organization, 1765 to 1775* (Durham, N.C.: Trinity College Press, 1922). Apparently Wilson also reached his position in the late 1760s, even though he did not publish his views until 1774.
45. BF to William Franklin, 13 Mar. 1768, in *Papers of Franklin,* 15:75–76.
46. BF to Thomas Crowley, for the London *Public Advertiser,* 21 Oct. 1768, in *Papers of Franklin,* 15:241.

47. BF, Marginalia in Protests of the Lords, 1766, in *Papers of Franklin*, 13:225.
48. BF to Mary Stevenson, 14 Sept. 1767, in *Papers of Franklin*, 14:253.
49. BF to unknown correspondent, 28 Nov. 1768, in *Papers of Franklin*, 15:272–73.
50. Bailyn, *Hutchinson*, 233. See also David Morgan, *The Devious Dr. Franklin: Benjamin Franklin's Years in London* (Macon, Ga.: Mercer University Press, 1996).
51. BF, *Autobiography*, 60.
52. Charles Coleman Sellers, *Franklin in Portraiture* (New Haven: Yale University Press, 1962), 328–30.
53. Botein, "Printers and the American Revolution," 30–31.
54. BF to Hall, 14 Sept. 1765, and BF to William Franklin, 25 Nov., 29 Dec. 1767, all in *Papers of Franklin*, 12:268; 14:326, 349.
55. Bailyn, *Ideological Origins*, 94–159; Gordon S. Wood, "Conspiracy and the Paranoid Style: Causality and Deceit in the Eighteenth Century," *WMQ* 39 (1982): 401–41.
56. Bailyn, *Ideological Origins*, 151; Wood, "Conspiracy and the Paranoid Style," 417; Thomas Jefferson, "A Summary View of the Rights of British North America" (1774), in Julian P. Boyd et al., eds., *The Papers of Thomas Jefferson* (Princeton, N.J.: Princeton University Press, 1950), 1:125.
57. George Rudé, *The Crowd in History: A Study of Popular Disturbances in France and England, 1730–1848* (New York: Wiley, 1964), 55–57.
58. Pauline Maier, "John Wilkes and American Disillusionment with Britain," *WMQ* 20 (1963), 373–95; Pauline Maier, *From Resistance to Revolution: Colonial Radicals and the Development of American Opposition to Britain, 1765–1776* (New York: Knopf, 1972), 163–69.
59. BF to William Franklin, 16 Apr., 5 Oct. 1768, BF to Galloway, 14 May 1768, and BF, On the New Office of the Secretary of State for America, 21 Jan. 1768, all in *Papers of Franklin*, 15:98–99, 127–28, 224, 19.
60. BF, On the New Office of the Secretary of State, BF to Cadwallader Evans, 26 Feb. 1768, and BF, On Railing and Reviling, 6 Jan. 1768, all in *Papers of Franklin*, 15:19, 52, 14. On the pride and arrogance of the British government and the steady alienation of Franklin's affections toward the empire in the late 1760s and early 1770s, see Jack P. Greene, *Understanding the American Revolution: Issues and Actors* (Charlottesville: University of Virginia Press, 1995), 18–47, 247–84.
61. "Benevolus" (BF), On the Propriety of Taxing America, *London Chronicle*, 9–11 Apr. 1767, in *Papers of Franklin*, 14:114.
62. BF, "American Discontents," *London Chronicle*, 5–7 Jan. 1768, in *Papers of Franklin*, 15:12.
63. BF to Samuel Cooper, 8 June 1770, 27 Apr. 1769, in *Papers of Franklin*, 17:163; 16:118.
64. BF to Kames, 25 Feb. 1767, in *Papers of Franklin*, 14:69.
65. BF to William Franklin, 1 Oct. 1768, in *Papers of Franklin*, 15:224–27.
66. Deborah Franklin to BF, 3 Nov., 6 Oct. 1765, 21–22 Jan. 1768, and 20–25 Apr. 1767, all in *Papers of Franklin*, 12:354, 294; 15:23; 14:136.

67. Lopez and Herbert, *Private Franklin,* 155.
68. Deborah Franklin to BF, 3 July 1767, 21–22 Jan. 1768, 1 May 1771, 30 June 1772, and BF to Deborah Franklin, 14 July 1772, 1 Sept. 1773, all in *Papers of Franklin,* 14:207; 15:24; 18:91; 19:192, 207; 20:383; Lopez and Herbert, *Private Franklin,* 120–21, 134–36, 164–73. Lopez and Herbert's book, to which I am much indebted, is a fair and balanced account of Franklin's relationship with his family.
69. BF to William Franklin, 9 Jan. 1768, in *Papers of Franklin,* 15:16.
70. BF to Jane Mecom, 30 Dec. 1770, in *Papers of Franklin,* 17:314.
71. BF to William Franklin, 2 July 1768, in *Papers of Franklin,* 15:159, 162, 160.
72. BF to William Franklin, 2 July 1768, in *Papers of Franklin,* 15:161, 162, 164.
73. BF to William Franklin, 2 July 1768, in *Papers of Franklin,* 15:163.
74. See Peter Marshall, "Lord Hillsborough, Samuel Wharton and the Ohio Grant, 1769–1775," *English Historical Review* 80 (1965), 717–39.
75. Bernard Bailyn, *Voyagers to the West: A Passage in the Peopling of America on the Eve of the Revolution* (New York: Knopf, 1986), 29–36, 49–57, 64–65.
76. BF to Thomson, 18 Mar. 1770, and BF to Cooper, 8 June 1770, in *Papers of Franklin,* 17:112, 164.
77. BF, Account of His Audience with Hillsborough, 16 Jan. 1771, in *Papers of Franklin,* 18:12–16.
78. BF to Cooper, 5 Feb. 1771, in *Papers of Franklin,* 18:24–25.
79. William Strahan to William Franklin, 3 Apr. 1771, in *Papers of Franklin,* 18:65.
80. James Campbell, *Recovering Benjamin Franklin: An Exploration of a Life of Science and Service* (Chicago: Open Court, 1999), 178.
81. BF to Sarah Franklin Bache, 29 Jan. 1772, in *Papers of Franklin,* 19:46.
82. Notes, in *Franklin: Writings,* 1557; J. A. Leo Lemay, "Benjamin Franklin," in Everett Emerson, ed., *Major Writers of Early American Literature* (Madison: University of Wisconsin Press, 1972), 238–39; Melvin H. Buxbaum, *Benjamin Franklin and the Zealous Presbyterians* (University Park: Pennsylvania State University Press, 1975), 225; Ormond Seavey, *Becoming Benjamin Franklin: The Autobiography and the Life* (University Park: Pennsylvania State University Press, 1988), 17. Because literary scholars are anxious to show Franklin as an artist in complete control of his materials, many of them tend to see all four parts of the *Autobiography* as a unified whole, directed at the same general reader. I am more inclined to agree with William H. Shurr's argument that the first part addressed to Franklin's son is distinctive. Shurr, "'Now, Gods, Stand Up for Bastards': Reinterpreting Benjamin Franklin's *Autobiography,*" *American Literature* 64 (1992): 435–51. See also Hugh J. Dawson, "Franklin's Memoirs in 1784: The Design of the Autobiography, Parts I and II," *Early American Literature* 12 (1977–1978): 286–93; Hugh J. Dawson, "Fathers and Sons: Franklin's 'Memoirs' as Myth and Metaphor," *Early American Literature* 14 (1979–1980): 269–92; and Christopher Looby, "'The Affairs of the Revolution Occasion'd the Interrup-

tion': Writing, Revolution, Deferral, and Conciliation in Franklin's *Autobiography*," *American Quarterly* 38 (1986): 72–96.

83. BF to Abiah Franklin, 12 Apr. 1750, and BF to Strahan, 2 June 1750, in *Papers of Franklin*, 3:475, 479.
84. BF to William Franklin, 30 Jan. 1772, in *Papers of Franklin*, 19:50.
85. BF to William Franklin, 30 Jan. 1772, in *Papers of Franklin*, 19:48.
86. BF to Galloway, 22 Aug. 1772, in *Papers of Franklin*, 19:275.
87. BF to William Franklin, 19–22 Aug. 1772, in *Papers of Franklin*, 19:259.
88. The editors of Franklin's *Papers* say that in the Hutchinson affair Franklin "crossed, without recognizing it, a personal Rubicon. The days of his usefulness in London were numbered." *Papers of Franklin*, 19:xxxii.
89. The Hutchinson Letters, 1768–1769, in *Papers of Franklin*, 20:550; Bailyn, *Hutchinson*, 227.
90. Tract Relative to the Affair of Hutchinson's Letters, Feb. 1774?, *Papers of Franklin*, 21:419. Most people at the time thought that John Temple was the person who had passed Whately's correspondence on to Franklin. Bailyn believes that it was Thomas Pownall who gave Franklin the letters. But the editors of the *Papers* suggest John Temple and William Strahan, as well as Pownall, as possibilities. Bailyn, *Hutchinson*, 225, 231–35; *Papers of Franklin*, 19:403–7.
91. The editors of Franklin's *Papers* believe that his sending of these letters to the radicals in Massachusetts "was probably the most controversial act of his career." *Papers of Franklin*, 19:401.
92. BF to Thomas Cushing, 2 Dec. 1772, in *Papers of Franklin*, 19:411–13.
93. BF to Cushing, 2 Dec. 1772, in *Papers of Franklin*, 19:411–12. Bailyn thinks that these words "must be either the most naïve or the most cynical that Franklin ever uttered." Bailyn, *Hutchinson*, 237. Perhaps they are both. Since Franklin was still so emotionally committed to the empire that he had come to believe that almost anything, even the sacrifice of one's honor, justified trying to save it, his words may be more naïve than cynical. At the same time, he seems to have sincerely believed that his former friend Hutchinson had become so duplicitous and so detested by the people of Massachusetts that he deserved to have his reputation destroyed for the sake of the empire. See BF to William Franklin, 6 Oct. 1773, in *Papers of Franklin*, 20:437, 439.
94. BF to Cushing, 2 Dec. 1772, 3 Jan. 1773, in *Papers of Franklin*, 19:409–13; 20:7–10.
95. If fixing blame on local officials in order to absolve the English ministry was indeed Franklin's motivation, then the editors of his *Papers* believe that "his miscalculation was spectacular, and does small credit to his acumen." *Papers of Franklin*, 19:408.
96. BF to William Franklin, Mar. 1775, in *Papers of Franklin*, 21:552.
97. BF, Last Will and Testament, 22 June 1750, and BF to John Winthrop, 25 July 1773, in *Papers of Franklin*, 3:481; 20:330.

98. BF to Cushing, 2 Dec. 1772, in *Papers of Franklin,* 19:411; Bailyn, *Hutchinson,* 223. Bailyn has the fullest account of Franklin's involvement in the affair of the Hutchinson letters.
99. BF to Lord Dartmouth, 21 Aug. 1773, in *Papers of Franklin,* 20:373.
100. Bailyn, *Ideological Origins,* 121–22.
101. BF, "Rules by Which a Great Empire May Be Reduced to a Small One," 11 Sept. 1773, and BF, "An Edict by the King of Prussia," 22 Sept. 1773, in *Papers of Franklin,* 20:389–99, 413–18.
102. BF, "Rules by Which a Great Empire May Be Reduced to a Small One," BF to William Franklin, 6 Oct. 1773, and BF to Mecom, 1 Nov. 1773, all in *Papers of Franklin,* 20:393, 436–39, 457–58.
103. London *General Evening Post,* 11 Jan. 1774, in Verner W. Crane, ed., *Letters to the Press, 1758–1775* (Chapel Hill: University of North Carolina Press, 1950), 239.
104. BF, Extract of a Letter from London, 19 Feb. 1774, in *Papers of Franklin,* 21:112.
105. The Final Hearing Before the Privy Council, 29 Jan. 1774, in *Papers of Franklin,* 21:60, 47, 48–49.
106. The Final Hearing Before the Privy Council, 29 Jan. 1774, in *Papers of Franklin,* 21:70.
107. BF to Galloway, 18 Feb. 1774, in *Papers of Franklin,* 21:109–10.
108. *European Magazine* (London) 3 (March 1783), quoted in P. M. Zall, ed., *Ben Franklin Laughing: Anecdotes from Original Sources by and About Benjamin Franklin* (Berkeley: University of California Press, 1980), 77.
109. BF to Galloway, 12 Oct. 1774, in *Papers of Franklin,* 21:334.
110. BF to Galloway, 12 Oct. 1774, in *Papers of Franklin,* 21:334.
111. BF to Timothy, 7 Sept. 1774, BF to Mecom, 28 July, 26 Sept. 1774, BF to William Franklin, 1 Aug. 1774, and BF to Jonathan Shipley, 28 Sept. 1774, in *Papers of Franklin,* 21:291, 265, 317–18, 266, 321.
112. BF to Shipley, 28 Sept. 1774, BF to Jonathan Williams Sr., 28 Sept. 1774, and BF to Cushing, 3 Sept., 6 Oct. 1774, in *Papers of Franklin,* 21:280, 322, 323, 327.
113. BF to William Franklin: Journal of Negotiations in London, 22 March 1775, and BF to Thomson, 5 Feb. 1775, in *Papers of Franklin,* 21:579, 581, 478.
114. BF to William Franklin: Journal of Negotiations in London, 22 March 1775, in *Papers of Franklin,* 21:583.
115. BF to William Franklin: Journal of Negotiations in London, 22 March 1775, BF, Proposed Memorial to Lord Dartmouth, March 1775, and BF to Galloway, 25 Feb. 1775, in *Papers of Franklin,* 21:583, 526, 598, 509; BF to Strahan, 19 Aug. 1784. In May 1774 Franklin published a bitterly satiric account in the London press suggesting that the commander in chief of His Majesty's forces in America and five battalions march up and down the continent and castrate all American males. The essay was undoubtedly stimulated by the British general's remark, which he recalled in his 1784 letter to Strahan. Crane, *Letters to the Press,* 262–64.

116. BF to David Hartley, 3 Oct. 1775, in *Papers of Franklin,* 22:217.
117. Lopez and Herbert, *Private Franklin,* 196.
118. Samuel Johnson, *Tyranny No Taxation* (1775), in *Political Writings,* ed. Donald J. Greene, Yale Edition of the Works of Samuel Johnson, vol. 10 (New Haven: Yale University Press, 1977), 444.

CHAPTER 4: BECOMING A DIPLOMAT

1. H. W. Brands, *The First American: The Life and Times of Benjamin Franklin* (New York: Doubleday, 2000), 494.
2. In 1769 William had considered bringing his illegitimate son Temple to America under the guise of "the Son of a poor Relation, for whom I stood God Father and intended to bring up as my own." Apparently William's wife did not know about the existence of Temple until Franklin showed up with him in America in 1775. William Franklin to BF, 2 Jan. 1769, in *Papers of Franklin,* 16:5; Sheila L. Skemp, *William Franklin: Son of a Patriot, Servant of a King* (New York: Oxford University Press, 1990), 179.
3. Claude-Anne Lopez and Eugenia W. Herbert, *The Private Franklin: The Man and His Family* (New York: Norton, 1975), 197, 201.
4. John Adams to Mrs. Mercy Warren, 8 Aug. 1807, Massachusetts Historical Society, *Collections.,* 5th ser., 4 (1878): 431.
5. As Adams recalled in his *Autobiography,* Franklin "often and indeed always appeared to me to have a personal Animosity and very severe Resentment against the King. In all his conversations and in all his Writings, when he could naturally and sometimes when could not, he mentioned the King with great Asperity." Adams, *Diary and Autobiography,* 4:150.
6. John Adams to Abigail Adams, 23 July 1775, in L. H. Butterfield et al., eds., *Adams Family Correspondence* (Cambridge, Mass.: Harvard University Press, 1963), 1:253.
7. Joseph Hewes to Samuel Johnson, 13 Feb. 1776, in Paul H. Smith et al., eds., *Letters of Delegates to the Congress, 1774–1789* (Washington, D.C.: Library of Congress, 1976–), 3:247. Franklin even stopped wearing a wig when he arrived in America. Despite a scalp irritation, in London he would never have dared to go out in public without a wig; but in America this symbol of hierarchy was not the fashionable necessity it was in England. Charles Coleman Sellers, *Franklin in Portraiture* (New Haven: Yale University Press, 1962), 97.
8. Arthur Lee to Samuel Adams, 10 June 1771, in R. H. Lee, *Life of Arthur Lee* (Boston, 1829), 1:216–18.
9. William Goddard to Isaiah Thomas, 15 Apr. 1811, quoted in Ralph Frasca, "From Apprentice to Journeyman to Partner: Benjamin Franklin's Workers and the Growth of the Early American Printing Trade," *PMHB* 114 (1990): 245n.
10. William Bradford to James Madison, 2 June 1775, and Madison to Bradford, 19 June 1775, in William T. Hutchinson et al., eds., *The Papers of James Madison*

(Chicago: University of Chicago Press, 1962), 1:149, 151–52. That Franklin was a British spy may seem improbable to us, but at least one modern historian, Cecil B. Currey, in his *Code No. 72: Benjamin Franklin, Patriot or Spy* (Englewood Cliffs, N.J.: Prentice-Hall, 1972), has suggested the possibility of Franklin's being a British spy while serving as envoy to France.

11. BF to William Strahan, 3 Oct. 1775, in *Papers of Franklin,* 22:219. (I owe this citation to Konstantin Dierks.)
12. Proposals and Queries to Be Asked the Junto, 1732, in *Franklin: Writings,* 209.
13. BF to Strahan, 5 July 1775, in *Papers of Franklin,* 22:85. David Freeman Hawke, in *Franklin* (New York: Harper & Row, 1976), 353–54, says that Franklin's July 5 letter to Strahan was widely published in America and Europe, but there is no evidence for this. Yet it seems evident to me that Franklin wrote this letter for local effect and showed it to friends and members of Congress in Philadelphia. There was no other reason for his writing such an overwrought and impassioned letter to one of his oldest British friends, especially since his other letters to English friends at this time express none of this exaggerated personal enmity. Moreover, the fact that two days later, on July 7, Franklin wrote a letter to Strahan, now lost, that presumably was as friendly as ever reinforces the idea that Franklin designed the July 5 letter to thwart rumors of his being a spy.
14. Bradford to Madison, 18 July 1775, in Hutchinson, *Papers of Madison,* 1:158.
15. BF to Strahan, 3 Oct. 1775, and BF to Jan Ingenhouse, 12 Feb.–6 Mar. 1777, in *Papers of Franklin,* 22:219; 23:310.
16. BF to Strahan, 3 Oct. 1775, and BF to John Sargent, 27 June 1775, in *Papers of Franklin,* 22:218, 72.
17. BF to Sargent, 27 June 1775, BF to David Hartley, 12 Sept. 1775, BF to Jonathan Shipley, 13 Sept. 1775, and BF to Strahan, 3 Oct. 1775, all in *Papers of Franklin,* 22:72, 196, 199–201, 218.
18. BF to Hartley, 3 Oct. 1775, and BF to Lord Kames, 3 Jan. 1760, in *Papers of Franklin,* 22:217; 9:7.
19. BF to Shipley, 7 July 1775, in *Papers of Franklin,* 22:94.
20. BF to Shipley, 7 July 1775, in *Papers of Franklin,* 22:95–98.
21. BF to Charles Dumas, 2 May 1782.
22. BF to William Franklin, 2 Feb., 7 May 1774, in *Papers of Franklin,* 21:75, 211–12; Skemp, *William Franklin,* 181.
23. Strahan to BF, 14 July 1778, in *Papers of Franklin,* 27:97.
24. BF to William Franklin, 16 Aug. 1784.
25. BF, Will Codicil, 23 June 1789; Lopez and Herbert, *Private Franklin,* 278–79, 305.
26. Adams, *Diary and Autobiography,* 3:77; Lopez and Herbert, *Private Franklin,* 247.
27. Pennsylvania State Constitution (1776), Section 36, in Jack P. Greene, ed., *Colonies to Nation, 1763–1789: A Documentary History of the American Revolution* (New York: Norton, 1967), 343.

28. Gordon S. Wood, *The Creation of the American Republic, 1776–1787* (Chapel Hill: University of North Carolina Press, 1969), 233.
29. Adams, Notes for an Oration at Braintree, 1772, in Adams, *Diary and Autobiography*, 2:57–60.
30. Wood, *Creation of the American Republic*, 236, 568–87.
31. BF to Lord Howe, 20 July 1775, in *Papers of Franklin*, 22:519–21.
32. Adams, *Autobiography and Diary*, 3:418–19.
33. Lord Howe's Conference with the Committee of Congress, 11 Sept. 1776, in *Papers of Franklin*, 22:601–5.
34. BF, Sketch of Propositions for a Peace [after 26 Sept. and before 25 Oct. 1776], in *Papers of Franklin*, 22:630–32.
35. Currey, *Code No. 72*, 77–78; Walter Isaacson, *Benjamin Franklin: An American Life* (New York: Simon & Schuster, 2003), 321–22.
36. Rockingham, quoted in Carl Van Doren, *Benjamin Franklin* (New York: Viking, 1938), 573.
37. Thomas Penn to Richard Peters, 14 May 1757, in *Papers of Franklin*, 7:111.
38. BF to William Franklin, 19–22 Aug. 1772, in *Papers of Franklin*, 19:259.
39. Rockingham, quoted in Van Doren, *Franklin*, 573.
40. Alfred Owen Aldridge, *Franklin and His French Contemporaries* (New York: New York University Press, 1957), 26. Aldridge's book is the best work on the French adoration of Franklin, and my account is much indebted to it.
41. BF to Mary Stevenson, 14 Sept. 1767, in *Papers of Franklin*, 14:254–55.
42. Aldridge, *Franklin and His French Contemporaries*, 29.
43. Durand Echeverria, *Mirage in the West: A History of the French Image of American Society to 1815* (Princeton, N.J.: Princeton University Press, 1957), 27n.
44. Echeverria, *Mirage in the West*, 18.
45. For a full discussion of this debate over the New World as a human habitat, see Antonello Gerbi, *The Dispute of the New World: A History of a Polemic, 1750–1900*, trans. Jeremy Moyle (Pittsburgh: University of Pittsburgh Press, 1973).
46. Simon Schama, *Citizens: A Chronicle of the French Revolution* (New York: Knopf, 1989), 172; Paul Robinson, *Opera and Ideas: From Mozart to Strauss* (Ithaca, N.Y.: Cornell University Press, 1985), 8–57.
47. Aldridge, *Franklin and His French Contemporaries*, 61, 66.
48. Van Doren, *Franklin*, 576; Brands, *First American*, 528.
49. BF to Sarah Franklin Bache, 3 June 1779, in *Papers of Franklin*, 29:613.
50. Sellers, *Franklin in Portraiture*, 96–139; Ellen G. Miles, "The French Portraits of Benjamin Franklin," in J. A. Leo Lemay, ed., *Reappraising Benjamin Franklin: A Bicentennial Perspective* (Newark: University of Delaware Press, 1993), 272–89.
51. BF to Thomas Diggs, 25 June 1780, in *Papers of Franklin*, 32:590.
52. Van Doren, *Franklin*, 632. On the many images of Franklin in France, see Bernard Bailyn's illustrated essay, "Realism and Idealism in American

Diplomacy: Franklin in Paris, *Couronné par la Liberté*," in Bailyn, *To Begin the World Anew: The Genius and Ambiguities of the American Founders* (New York: Knopf, 2003), 60–99.

53. According to Darcy R. Fryer, one of the editors of the *Papers of Franklin*, the story of the chamber pot adorned with Franklin's face on the bottom probably originated with Madame Campan, *Memoirs of the Private Life of Marie Antoinette* (London, 1823), 1:230–31. Campan wrote that Louis XVI "had a vase de nuit made at Sevres manufactory at the bottom of which, was the medallion [of Franklin] with its fashionable legend, and he sent the utensil to the countess Diana as a new year's gift." H-Net/OIEAHC, 11 Dec. 2001.
54. Adams, *Diary and Autobiography*, 4:81.
55. Aldridge, *Franklin and His French Contemporaries*, 61.
56. BF to Emma Thompson, 8 Feb. 1777, in *Papers of Franklin*, 23:298. Franklin had long thought about the political implications of dress. "Simplicity is the homespun Dress of Honesty, and Chicanery and Craft are the Tinsel Habits and the false Elegance which are worn to cover the Deformity of Vice and Knavery," he had written in 1732. BF, On Simplicity, 1732, in *Writings of Franklin*, 181–84. On the political significance of clothing and dress, see Michael Zakim, "Sartorial Ideologies: From Home-Spun to Ready-Made," *American Historical Review* 106 (2001): 1553–86.
57. BF to William Carmichael, 29 July 1778, in *Papers of Franklin*, 27:176.
58. Ronald C. Clark, *Benjamin Franklin: A Biography* (New York: Random House, 1983), 341.
59. BF, "The Speech of Miss Polly Baker" (1747), in *Papers of Franklin*, 3:120–25; Van Doren, *Franklin*, 721–22; Max Hall, *Benjamin Franklin and Polly Baker: The History of a Literary Deception* (Chapel Hill: University of North Carolina Press, 1960).
60. The famous preface to *Poor Richard's Almanack* for 1758, known in different versions as "Father Abraham's Speech" and *The Way to Wealth*, was reprinted at least 145 times in seven different languages before the end of the eighteenth century and many times since. BF, *Autobiography*, 164n.
61. BF, Poor Richard Improved, 1758, *Papers of Franklin*, 7:342. Most of the Poor Richard sayings, as Franklin's persona admitted, were not of his own making. They were gleaned from a variety of sources, ranging from the works of George Herbert and James Howell to the writings of Thomas Fuller, Lord Halifax, and Samuel Richardson. He even borrowed some from Montaigne. He usually modified the borrowed sayings by making them more simple, more concrete, more euphonious, and often more bawdy. See Bruce Ingham Granger, *Benjamin Franklin: An American Man of Letters* (Ithaca, N.Y.: Cornell University Press, 1964), 65–75.
62. Aldridge, *Franklin and His French Contemporaries*, 50.
63. BF to Robert Livingston, 4 Mar. 1782 in *Papers of Franklin*, 36:646.

64. Comte de Vergennes to Marquis de Lafayette, 7 Aug. 1780, in Stanley J. Idzerda et al., eds., *Lafayette in the Age of the American Revolution: Selected Letters and Papers, 1776–1790* (Ithaca, N.Y.: Cornell University Press, 1977), 3:130. Actually French views have not much changed. In 2001 the wife of French president Jacques Chirac told her fellow citizens what made her husband a perfect public official. "He is not a money man," she said. "Money has never been any kind of motivation for him. Never." *International Herald Tribune,* 11 Apr. 2002.
65. BF, Positions to Be Examined, 4 Apr. 1769, BF to Jane Mecom, 30 Dec. 1770, BF, Last Will and Testament, 22 June 1750, and BF to Dumas, 6 Aug. 1781, all in *Papers of Franklin,* 16:109; 17:315; 3:481; 35:341.
66. See J. A. Leo Lemay, *The Canon of Benjamin Franklin: New Attributions and Reconsiderations* (Newark: University of Delaware Press, 1986), 53, for Franklin's harsh views on commercial dealings.
67. Commissioners to Committee of Secret Correspondence, 12 Mar.–7 Apr. 1777, in *Papers of Franklin,* 23:467.
68. Commissioners to Committee of Secret Correspondence, 12 Mar.–7 Apr. 1777, in *Papers of Franklin,* 23:467. On the lack of guidance from Congress, see Jonathan R. Dull, "Franklin the Diplomat: The French Mission," American Philosophical Society, *Transactions* 72 (1982), 68–69.
69. Van Doren, *Franklin,* 650.
70. BF to Jacques Barbeu-Dubourg?, after 2 Oct. 1777, in *Papers of Franklin,* 25:21.
71. BF to Richard and Sally Bache, 10 May, 1785.
72. Currey, *Code No. 72.* Elizabeth M. Nuxoll, one of the editors of the Robert Morris Papers, has suggested that the charges of Franklin's being a British spy come from these murky circumstances in which the commissioners were secretly trying to manipulate the release of information. H-Net/OIEAHC, 7 Apr. 1999.
73. George III, quoted in Van Doren, *Franklin,* 573.
74. Samuel F. Bemis, "British Secret Service and the French-American Alliance," *American Historical Review* 29 (1923–1924): 474–95; David Schoenbrun, *Triumph in Paris: The Exploits of Benjamin Franklin* (New York: Harper & Row, 1976); Dull, "Franklin the Diplomat," 33–42.
75. BF to Juliana Ritchie, 19 Jan. 1777, in *Papers of Franklin,* 23:211.
76. It is Franklin's casual, even sloppy, attitude toward spying and record keeping that convinced Cecil B. Currey that Franklin "—covertly perhaps, tacitly at least, possibly deliberately—cooperated with and protected" a British spy cell operating out of his home in France. Unfortunately, Currey seems to have forgotten what Franklin said about his inability to maintain order in his affairs. Currey, *Code No. 72,* 12.
77. Claude-Anne Lopez, *My Life with Benjamin Franklin* (New Haven: Yale University Press, 2000), 61–72.

78. For a balanced study of Lee, see Louis W. Potts, *Arthur Lee: A Virtuous Revolutionary* (Baton Rouge: Louisiana State University Press, 1981).
79. Morgan, *Franklin*, 259–60.
80. Arthur Lee to Committee of Foreign Affairs, 1 June 1778, and Ralph Izard to Henry Laurens, 29 June 1778, in Francis Wharton, ed., *The Revolutionary Diplomatic Correspondence of the United States* (Washington, D.C., 1889), 2:600–603, 629–31.
81. Adams, *Diary and Autobiography*, 4:87. In addition to telling John Adams that Franklin was more to be mistrusted than Deane, Izard told him that "Dr. Franklin was one of the most unprincipled Men upon Earth: that he was a Man of no Veracity, no honor, no Integrity, as great a Villain as ever breathed." Ibid.
82. BF to Laurens, 31 Mar. 1778, in *Papers of Franklin*, 26:203–4. See also BF to James Lovell, 21 Dec. 1777, in *Papers of Franklin*, 25:329–30.
83. A. Lee to Richard Henry Lee, 12 Sept. 1778, quoted in Lopez and Herbert, *Private Franklin*, 235.
84. John Adams thought that Deane's public denunciation of the Congress in December 1778 was "the most astonishing Measure, the most unexpected and unforeseen Event, that has ever happened, from the Year 1761 . . . to this Moment." It seemed to threaten the existence of the Confederation and French confidence in America. Since Adams continued to believe that Deane epitomized corruption and treachery, anyone who admired Deane had to be contemptible. To Mercy Otis Warren's accusation in her 1805 *History* that "Mr. Adams was not beloved by his Colleague Dr. Franklin," Adams had a simple retort that he believed to be devastating: "Mr. Deane was beloved by his Colleague Dr. Franklin." Adams, *Diary and Autobiography*, 2:348, 353; 4:118.
85. "Excerpts from the Papers of Dr. Benjamin Rush," *PMBH* 29 (1905): 27–28.
86. Arthur Lee, Journal, 25 Oct. 1778, in *Papers of Franklin*, 25:100, 102.
87. Paul Wentworth to William Eden, 7 Jan. 1778, in *Papers of Franklin*, 25:436–38.
88. "Excerpts from the Papers of Rush," 27–28.
89. J. Adams to Thomas McKean, 20 Sept. 1779, in *Papers of Adams*, 8:162.
90. Adams, *Diary and Autobiography*, 4:47, 118–19, 107–8.
91. BF to Lovell, 22 July 1778, in *Papers of Franklin*, 27:135.
92. Richard Bache to BF, 22 Oct. 1778, in *Papers of Franklin*, 27:599–601.
93. John Fells Diary, 21 April 1779, in Smith, *Letters of Delegates*, 12:362. On the congressional controversy over Franklin and the other commissioners, see H. James Henderson, "Congressional Factionalism and the Attempt to Recall Benjamin Franklin," *WMQ* 27 (1970): 246–67, and his *Party Politics in the Continental Congress* (New York: McGraw-Hill, 1974), 200–206.
94. Izard to R. H. Lee, 15 Oct. 1780, in Edmund C. Burnett, ed., *Letters of Members of the Continental Congress* (Washington, D.C.: Carnegie Institution, 1931), 5:362n.
95. BF to Samuel Huntington, 12 Mar.–12 Apr. 1781, in *Papers of Franklin*, 34:446.
96. BF to Robert Morris, 26 July 1781, in *Papers of Franklin*, 35:311–12.

97. BF to Huntington, 9 Aug. 1780, in *Papers of Franklin,* 33:162.
98. Adams's wife, Abigail, was even more disgusted with Franklin's behavior. She thought that Franklin and his grandson Temple, the "old Deceiver" and the "young Cockatrice," were "wicked unprincipled debauched wretches." Lopez and Herbert, *Private Franklin,* 273; Abigail to John Adams, 21 Oct. 1781, in Butterfield, *Adams Family Correspondence,* 4:230.
99. A. Lee to James Warren, 8 Apr. 1782, in Smith, *Letters of Delegates,* 18:441. See also Dull, "Franklin the Diplomat," 47.
100. BF to R. Livingston, 22 July 1783; and BF to Morris, 25 Dec. 1783. See also Lopez, *My Life with Franklin,* 176.
101. BF to Morris, 7 Mar. 1783.
102. Morris to BF, 28 Sept. 1782.
103. BF to Samuel Cooper, 26 Dec. 1782.
104. On Vergennes and his support for the American war, see Orville T. Murphy, *Charles Gravier, Comte de Vergennes: French Diplomacy in the Age of Revolution, 1719–1787* (Albany: State University of New York Press, 1982), 397–98; and Munro Price, *Preserving the Monarchy: The Comte de Vergennes, 1774–1787* (Cambridge: Cambridge University Press, 1995), 66, 236, 240. On Franklin's relationship with Vergennes, see Dull, "Franklin the Diplomat," 67–68.
105. BF to Richard and Sarah Bache, 27 July 1783.
106. BF, *Information to Those Who Would Remove to America* (1784), in *Franklin: Writings,* 975–83.
107. R. D. Harris, "French Finances and the American War, 1777–1783," *Journal of Modern History* 48 (1976): 236, 241. Jonathan R. Dull writes that French financial aid added up to some 40 million livres, which he says was equivalent to about $80 million in 1980s purchasing power. Dull, "Franklin the Diplomat," 11. Dull rightly concludes, "The French support for the Revolution was Franklin's work." Ibid., 50.
108. BF to R. Livingston, 5 Dec. 1782, and BF to Morris, 23 Dec. 1782.
109. BF to John Jay, 2 Oct. 1780, in *Papers of Franklin,* 33:356.
110. BF to Committee of Foreign Affairs, 26 May 1779, in *Papers of Franklin,* 29:555.
111. BF to Vergennes, 17 Dec. 1782, 25 Jan. 1783.

CHAPTER 5: BECOMING AN AMERICAN

1. BF, *Autobiography,* 163.
2. BF, "The Morals of Chess" (1779), in *Papers of Franklin,* 29:754.
3. BF, *Autobiography,* 163.
4. BF, *Autobiography,* 133–40.
5. See BF to Lord Kames, 3 May 1760, in *Papers of Franklin,* 9:104.
6. BF, *Autobiography,* 148.
7. Franklin's Art of Virtue was not at all based on the puritan tradition. Franklin, as Norman Fiering points out, had little or no interest in the inward states of

people, but instead had an essentially behaviorist approach to morality. See Fiering, "Benjamin Franklin and the Way to Virtue," *American Quarterly* 30 (1978): 199–223. On the down-to-earth character of Franklin's Art of Virtue, see also Ralph Lerner, *Revolutions Revisited: Two Faces of the Politics of the Enlightenment* (Chapel Hill: University of North Carolina Press, 1994), 3–18.

8. BF, *Autobiography*, 148–57.
9. BF, *Autobiography*, 155–57; R. Jackson Wilson, *Figures of Speech: American Writers and the Literary Marketplace, from Benjamin Franklin to Emily Dickinson* (Baltimore: Johns Hopkins University Press, 1989), 40–41.
10. BF, *Autobiography*, 148–57.
11. BF, *Autobiography*, 159, 44, 160.
12. BF to Elizabeth Partridge, 11 Oct. 1779, in *Papers of Franklin*, 30:514.
13. Claude-Anne Lopez, *My Life with Benjamin Franklin* (New Haven: Yale University Press, 2000), 174.
14. BF to Anne-Catherine de Ligniville Helvétius, Oct. 1778?, in *Papers of Franklin*, 27:670–71.
15. Claude-Anne Lopez, *Mon Cher Papa: Franklin and the Ladies of Paris* (New Haven: Yale University Press, 1966), 259; Carl Van Doren, *Benjamin Franklin* (New York: Viking, 1938), 647.
16. Abigail Adams to Lucy Cranch, 5 Sept. 1784, in Richard Alan Ryerson et al., eds., *Adams Family Correspondence* (Cambridge, Mass.: Harvard University Press, 1993), 5:436–37.
17. Adams, *Autobiography and Diary*, 4:59.
18. Lopez, *My Life with Franklin*, 174; Lopez, *Mon Cher Papa*, 264–71.
19. Richard B. Morris, *The Peacemakers: The Great Powers and American Independence* (New York: Harper & Row, 1965), 192.
20. BF to William Franklin, 16 Aug. 1784. See also BF to Deborah Franklin, 6 Apr., 1 Sept. 1773, and BF to Samuel Cooper, 27 Oct. 1779, all in *Papers of Franklin*, 20:145, 383; 30:598.
21. Debate in the Virginia Convention, 17 June 1788, in Max Farrand, ed., *The Records of the Federal Convention of 1787* (New Haven: Yale University Press, 1937), 3:327.
22. Cooper to BF, 5 May 1783.
23. BF to Henry Laurens, John Adams, and John Jay, 10 Sept. 1783.
24. BF to Charles Thomson, 13 May 1784, and BF to Richard Price, 16 Aug. 1784.
25. BF to Thomson, 13 May 1784.
26. BF to Jonathan Shipley, 22 Aug. 1784, and Richard Bache to William Temple Franklin, 14 Dec. 1784. See also Lopez, *My Life with Franklin*, 179–80.
27. Elbridge Gerry to Adams, 16 June 1784, in Paul H. Smith et al., eds., *Letters of Delegates to the Congress, 1774–1789* (Washington, D.C.: Library of Congress, 1976–), 21:686.
28. F.H. to William Temple Franklin, 1 Nov. 1784.

29. Thomas Jefferson to Ferdinand Grand, 23 Apr. 1790, in Julian P. Boyd et al., eds., *The Papers of Thomas Jefferson* (Princeton, N.J.: Princeton University Press, 1953), 16:369.
30. François Steinsky to BF, 17 June 1789; J. Thiriot to BF, 1 July 1784; Erasmus Darwin to BF, 29 May 1787; Marquis de Condorcet to BF, 20 Aug. 1784; —— Thomas to BF, 20 Sept. 1787; —— Taillefert to BF, 18 Feb. 1788; Pierre Ox to BF, 6 Sept. 1784; J.-P. Brissot de Warville, *New Travels in the United States of America, 1788,* trans. Mara Soceanu Vamos and Durand Echeverria (Cambridge, Mass.: Harvard University Press, 1964), 184.
31. Jefferson to James Monroe, 5 July, 28 Aug. 1785, in Boyd et al., eds., *Papers of Jefferson,* 8:262, 446.
32. BF to John and Sarah Jay, 21 Sept. 1785.
33. BF to Thomas Paine, 27 Sept. 1785.
34. BF to Paine, 27 Sept. 1785.
35. On the Philadelphia aristocrats' reaction to Franklin, see Keith Arbour, "Benjamin Franklin as Weird Sister: William Cobbett and Philadelphia's Fears of Democracy," in Doren Ben-Atar and Barbara Oberg, eds., *Federalists Reconsidered* (Charlottesville: University of Virginia Press, 1998), 179–80.
36. BF to Jane Mecom, 4 Nov. 1787.
37. BF to Jonathan Williams, 16 Feb. 1786. When he wrote in 1787 to his former colleague John Jay, secretary for foreign affairs in the Confederation, to recommend someone as vice consul in Bordeaux, he first had to wonder whether "my Recommendation might have any weight." Such was his sense of his position in American politics. BF to Jay, 10 Nov. 1787.
38. BF to Thomas Jordan, 18 May 1787.
39. William Parker Cutler and Julia Perkins Cutler, *Life, Journals and Correspondence of Rev. Manasseh Cutler, LLD* (Cincinnati, 1888), 1:267–68; 2:363.
40. Madison, 25 May 1787, in Farrand, *Records of the Convention,* 1:4.
41. Pierce, in Farrand, *Records of the Convention,* 3:91.
42. BF, Speech in the Convention on the Subject of Salaries, 2 June 1787, in *Franklin: Writings,* 1131.
43. BF to William Strahan, 16 Feb., 19 Aug. 1784. See also BF to Joseph Galloway, 12 Oct. 1774, 25 Feb. 1775, in *Papers of Franklin,* 21:333–34, 509; BF to Shipley, 17 Mar. 1783, BF to Laurens, 12 Feb. 1784, BF to George Whately, 23 May 1785, and BF to John Wright, 4 Nov. 1789.
44. BF, Speech on Salaries, in *Franklin: Writings,* 1134; Madison, 2 June 1787, in Farrand, *Records of the Convention,* 1:85.
45. BF, Last Will and Testament, 23 June 1789.
46. BF to Sarah Bache, 26 Jan. 1784. Despite Franklin's opposition to the Society of the Cincinnati, the State Society of Pennsylvania in July 1789 unanimously elected him to an honorary membership in the organization. We have no record of Franklin's response to this election. (I owe this information to Ellen

McCallister Clark, librarian of the Society of the Cincinnati in Washington, D.C.)

47. BF, Queries and Remarks on Hints for the Members of the Philadelphia Convention, 1789.
48. Franklin to Pierre-Samuel du Pont de Nemours, 9 June 1788.
49. Jefferson to Monroe, 5 July 1785, in Boyd, *Papers of Jefferson,* 8:262.
50. William Temple Franklin, Sketch of William Temple Franklin's Services to the United States of America, 23 May 1789.
51. BF to Thomson, 29 Dec. 1788. In earlier notes for this letter to Thomson, Franklin said that he was "sorry and asham'd that I asked any Favour of Congress" for his grandson. "It was the first time I ever ask'd Promotion for myself or any of my Family." And he vowed it "shall be the Last." Notes for BF to Thomson [1788?].
52. BF to Cyrus Griffin, 29 Nov. 1788.
53. BF to Thomson, 29 Dec. 1788.
54. Notes for BF to Thomson [1788?].
55. BF, Sketch of Services of B. Franklin to the United States, 29 Dec. 1788.
56. BF to Thomson, 29 Dec. 1788.
57. As early as 1785 Franklin had complained to Jefferson of being "extremely wounded" by Congress's treatment of his requests. "He expected," said Jefferson, "something to be done as a reward for his own service." Jefferson, however, thought that Franklin's pride would make him "preserve a determined silence in the future." Jefferson to Monroe, 5 July 1785, in Boyd, *Papers of Jefferson,* 8:262.
58. BF to Thomson, 29 Dec. 1788.
59. *Journals of the Continental Congress, 1774–1789* (Washington, D.C.: Library of Congress, 1937), 34:603n.
60. BF, *Autobiography,* 161–62.
61. BF, *Observations Concerning the Increase of Mankind* (1751), in *Papers of Franklin,* 4:231.
62. BF to John Waring, 17 Dec. 1763, in *Papers of Franklin,* 10:396.
63. BF to Benjamin Rush, 14 July 1773, in *Papers of Franklin,* 20:314.
64. Lopez, *My Life with Franklin,* 196–205.
65. BF, An Address to the Public (1789) in *Franklin: Writings,* 1154–55.
66. Claude-Anne Lopez and Eugenia W. Herbert, *The Private Franklin: The Man and His Family* (New York: Norton, 1975), 301. President Washington was sure that the petition against slavery would go nowhere in Congress. It was "not only an illjudged piece of business," he told an in-law back in Virginia, "but occasioned a great waste of time. . . . The memorial of the Quakers (and a very mal-apropos one it was) has at length been put to sleep, and will scarcely awake before the year 1808," the year Congress gained the constitutional authority to deal with the slave trade. Henry Wiencek, *An Imperfect God: George Washington, His Slaves, and the Creation of America* (New York: Farrar, Straus and Giroux, 2003), 276.

67. 1st Cong., 2nd Session, *Annals of Congress,* ed. Joseph Gales (Washington, D.C., 1834), 2:1197–1205, 1414–15, 1474.
68. BF, Sidi Mehemet Ibrahim on the Slave Trade (1790) in *Franklin: Writings,* 1157–60.
69. Arbour, "Franklin as Weird Sister," 179–98.
70. Franklin had been thinking about this bequest for a number of years. See BF to Charles-Joseph Mathon de la Cour, 18 Nov. 1785. Even into the second decade of the nineteenth century, said Benjamin Rush, it was "scarcely safe to mention Dr. Franklin's name with respect in some companies in our city." Rush to Adams, 6 Aug. 1811, in John A. Schutz and Douglass Adair, eds., *The Spur of Fame: Dialogues of John Adams and Benjamin Rush, 1805–1818* (San Marino, Calif.: Huntington Library, 1980), 184.
71. Alfred Owen Aldridge, *Franklin and His French Contemporaries* (New York: New York University Press, 1957), 212–38; Gilbert Chinard, "The Apotheosis of Benjamin Franklin, Paris, 1790–1791," American Philosophical Society, *Proceedings* 99 (1955): 457, 461. See also Kenneth N. McKee, "The Popularity of the 'American' on the French Stage During the Revolution," American Philosophical Society, *Proceedings* 83 (1940): 479–91.
72. Julian P. Boyd, "The Death of Franklin: The Politics of Mourning in France and the United States," in Boyd et al., *Papers of Jefferson,* 19:81.
73. Adams to Rush, 4 April 1790, in L. H. Butterfield, ed., *Letters of Benjamin Rush* (Princeton, N.J.: Princeton University Press), 2:1207.
74. *The Diary of William Maclay and Other Notes on Senate Debates,* ed. Kenneth R. Bowling and Helen E. Veit, vol. 9 of *Documentary History of the First Federal Congress of the United States of America* (Baltimore: Johns Hopkins University Press, 1988), 341, 369–70; Boyd, "Death of Franklin," 19:81–90.
75. Robert Middlekauff, *Benjamin Franklin and His Enemies* (Berkeley: University of California Press, 1996), 103.
76. Aldridge, *Franklin and His French Contemporaries,* 234.
77. William Smith, "Eulogium on Benjamin Franklin, L.L.D., Delivered on March 1, 1791," in *The Works of William Smith, D.D., Late Provost of the College and Academy of Philadelphia* (Philadelphia, 1803), 1:43–92; Nian-Sheng Huang, *Benjamin Franklin in American Thought and Culture, 1790–1990* (Philadelphia: American Philosophical Society, 1994), 28–29. In 1802 when Smith came to publish his collected works he added to his eulogy a poem written by the loyalist Jonathan Odell. After celebrating Franklin's scientific achievements, the poem ends with several devastating stanzas:

    Oh! Had he been wise to pursue,
    The path which his talents design'd
    What a tribute of praise had been due
    To the teacher and friend of mankind!

But to covet political fame,
Was, in Him, a degrading ambition;
A spark which from Lucifer came,
Enkindled the blaze of sedition.

Let candor, then, write on his urn—
Here lies the renowned inventor,
Whose flame to the skies ought to burn,
But, inverted, descends to the center!

Smith, like Franklin's other enemies, thought that this poem was "beautifully . . . descriptive of the character of Dr. Franklin": Franklin may have been a great scientist, but he had been a terrible politician. Smith, "Eulogium on Franklin," 1:92.

78. Otto, quoted in Aldridge, *Franklin and His French Contemporaries,* 234.
79. Cobbett, quoted in David A. Wilson, ed., *William Cobbett, Peter Porcupine in America: Pamphlets on Republicanism and Revolution* (Ithaca, N.Y.: Cornell University Press, 1994), 40. On Cobbett's campaign against Franklin in the 1790s, see Arbour, "Franklin as Weird Sister," 179–98.
80. Joseph Dennie, *The Port Folio* 1 (14 Feb. 1801): 53–54, conveniently reprinted in Lemay and Zall, eds., *Franklin's Autobiography,* 249–53. See also Lewis Leary, "Joseph Dennie on Benjamin Franklin: A Note on Early American Literary Criticism," *PMHB* 72 (1948): 240–46.
81. Rufus King, quoted by an English correspondent, in Richard D. Miles, "The American Image of Benjamin Franklin," *American Quarterly* 9 (1957): 120.
82. For a survey of some of the different images of Franklin in the generation following his death, see William C. Kashatus III, "Hero and Hypocrite: The American Images of Benjamin Franklin, 1785–1828," *Valley Forge Journal* 5 (1990): 69–87.
83. BF, *Autobiography,* 27.
84. See Paul Leicester Ford, *Franklin Bibliography: A List of Books Written by, or Relating to Benjamin Franklin* (Brooklyn, 1889).
85. Dennie, *The Port Folio,* in Lemay and Zall, eds., *Franklin's Autobiography,* 252.
86. Thomas Earle and Charles Congdon, eds., *Annals of the General Society of Mechanics and Tradesmen of the City of New York, from 1785–1800* (New York, 1882), 32. (I owe this citation to Nathaniel Frank.) Even the older Masonic organizations that had been dominated by gentry were now completely taken over by middling sorts who celebrated distinctions based on merit alone. Steven C. Bullock, *Revolutionary Brotherhood: Freemasonry and the Transformation of the American Social Order, 1730–1840* (Chapel Hill: University of North Carolina Press, 1996), 86, 109–33.
87. Stephen Botein, "Printers and the American Revolution," in Bernard Bailyn and John Hench, eds., *The Press and the American Revolution* (Worcester, Mass.: American Antiquarian Society, 1980), 53, 57.

88. George Warner, *Means for the Preservation of Political Liberty: An Oration Delivered in the New Dutch Church, on the Fourth of July, 1797* . . . (New York, 1797), 13–14.
89. Gordon S. Wood, *The Radicalism of the American Revolution* (New York: Knopf, 1992), 279–83; Howard B. Rock, *Artisans of the New Republic: The Tradesmen of New York City in the Age of Jefferson* (New York: New York University Press, 1979), 264–322.
90. Mason L. Weems, *The Life of Washington,* ed. Marcus Cunliffe (Cambridge, Mass.: Harvard University Press, 1962), 203–21.
91. Weems, *Washington,* 203–14.
92. Dennie, *The Port Folio,* in Lemay and Zall, eds., *Franklin's Autobiography,* 250. Dennie promised to write more on Franklin as the symbol of the getting and saving of money, but he came to realize "that every penurious parent, who prescribes, as horn-book lesson, to his son, that scoundrel maxim a penny saved is a penny got, would cry—shame!" He thus thought better of confronting too directly Franklin's emerging image as the hardworking entrepreneur in an increasingly democratic and capitalistic society. "The world, quoth Prudence, will not bear it; 'tis a penny-getting pound hoarding world—I yielded; and shelter myself in my garret against that mob of misers and worldlings I see gathering to hoot me." Dennie, quoted in Leary, "Dennie on Franklin," 244.
93. David Jaffee, "The Village Enlightenment in New England," *WMQ* 47 (1990): 345; Rena L. Vassar, ed., "The Life or Biography of Silas Felton, Written by Himself," American Antiquarian Society, *Proceedings* 69 (1959): 129.
94. Jaffee, "Village Enlightenment," 328, 345, 329.
95. Huang, *Franklin in American Thought,* 47.
96. Henry P. Rosemont, "Benjamin Franklin and the Philadelphia Typographical Strikers of 1786," *Labor History* 22 (1981): 427–28; Huang, *Franklin in American Thought,* 81–88. On the Franklin Institute established in 1824, see Bruce Sinclair, *Philadelphia's Philosopher Mechanics: A History of the Franklin Institute, 1824–1865* (Baltimore: Johns Hopkins University Press, 1974).
97. Thomas Mercein, "On the Opening of the Apprentices' Library in 1820," in Paul A. Gilje and Howard B. Rock, eds., *Keepers of the Revolution: New Yorkers at Work in the Early Republic* (Ithaca, N.Y.: Cornell University Press, 1992), 53.
98. M. L. Weems, *The Life of Benjamin Franklin; with Many Choice Anecdotes and Admirable Sayings of This Great Man, Never Before Published by Any of His Biographers* (Philadelphia, 1829), 23.
99. Weems, *Life of Franklin,* 49, 65–66, 220–31, 236–38; Carla Mulford, "Franklin and Myths of Nationhood," in A. Robert Lee and W. M. Verhoeven, eds., *Making America/Making American Literature* (Atlanta: Rodopi, 1996), 50–55.
100. Mellon, quoted in Huang, *Franklin in American Thought,* 46; Irvin G. Wyllie, *The Self-Made Man in America: The Myth of Rags to Riches* (New Brunswick, N.J.: Rutgers University Press, 1954), 15–16. See also Louis Wright, "Franklin's Legacy to the Gilded Age," *Virginia Quarterly Review* 22 (1946): 268–79.

101. Wood, *Radicalism of the American Revolution,* 342.
102. J. A. Leo Lemay and P. M. Zall, eds., *The Autobiography of Benjamin Franklin: A Genetic Text* (Knoxville: University of Tennessee Press, 1981), lvi.
103. *The Narrative of Patrick Lyon, Who Suffered Three Months Severe Imprisonment in Philadelphia Gaol . . .* (Philadelphia, 1799); William Dunlap, *History of the Rise and Progress of the Arts of Design in the United States* (1834; reprint, New York: Dover, 1969), 2:375; "Liberty on the Anvil, 1701–2001," The Historical Society of Pennsylvania, www.HSP.org; Ron Avery, "America's First Bank Robbery," www.USHistory.org; Laura Rigal, *The American Manufactory: Art, Labor, and the World of Things in the Early Republic* (Princeton, N.J.: Princeton University Press, 1998), 179–203, 241; and Melissa Dabakis, *Visualizing Labor in American Sculpture: Monuments, Manliness, and the Work Ethic, 1880–1935* (Cambridge: Cambridge University Press, 1999), 10–12, 15–16.
104. For an elaboration of this theme of the changing attitude toward labor, see Wood, *Radicalism of the American Revolution,* 36–38, 277, 284–86, 337, 355.
105. In less than a half century following the Declaration of Independence, writes Joyce Appleby, Americans moved "from the end of traditional society—'the world we have lost'—to the social framework we are still living with." Appleby, *Inheriting the Revolution: The First Generation of Americans* (Cambridge, Mass.: Harvard University Press, 2000), 8.
106. Joyce Appleby, ed., *Recollections of the Early Republic: Selected Autobiographies* (Boston: Northeastern University Press, 1997), 10, 183, 167; Mulford, "Franklin and Myths," 44.
107. Carla Mulford, "Figuring Benjamin Franklin in American Cultural Memory," *New England Quarterly* 72 (1999): 415–43.
108. Alexis de Tocqueville, *Democracy in America,* ed. J. P. Mayer (New York: Doubleday, 1969), 550–51.
109. Tocqueville, *Democracy in America,* 620n.
110. BF to Richard Bache, 11 Nov. 1784. This, of course, is the same advice Franklin had given Benny's father, Richard Bache, a decade earlier when he himself had failed to gain an office in the British government. See p. 138.
111. Ronald W. Clark, *Benjamin Franklin: A Biography* (New York: Random House, 1983), 46; BF to Mathon de la Cour, 18 Nov. 1785.
112. Rosemont, "Franklin and the Philadelphia Typographical Strikers," 398–429.
113. BF to Catherine Ray Greene, 2 Mar. 1789; BF to Duc de La Rochefoucauld, 24 Oct. 1788. For two superb studies of printers and publishers in the early republic, see Rosalind Remer, *Printers and Men of Capital: Philadelphia Book Publishers in the New Republic* (Philadelphia: University of Pennsylvania Press, 1996); and Jeffrey L. Pasley, *"The Tyranny of Printers": Newspaper Politics in the Early American Republic* (Charlottesville: University of Virginia Press, 2001).

Illustration Credits

Page	
18	Courtesy of The Bostonian Society/Old State House.
58	Courtesy of the Harvard University Portrait Collection, bequest of Dr. John Collins Warren, 1856. Photographed by Katya Kallsen. © 2004 President and Fellows of Harvard College.
86	Courtesy of the American Philosophical Society.
87, left	White House Historical Association (White House Collection [981]).
87, right	National Portrait Gallery, Smithsonian Institution/Art Resource, NY.
88, left	Philadelphia Museum of Art: gift of Mr. and Mrs. Wharton Sinkler.
88, right	Philadelphia Museum of Art: purchased.
89	Courtesy of the American Philosophical Society.
126	Courtesy of the Pennsylvania Academy of the Fine Arts, Philadelphia. Gift of Maria McKean Allen and Phebe Warren Downes through the bequest of their mother, Elizabeth Wharton McKean.
141	Courtesy of the Fogg Art Museum, Harvard University Art Museums, bequest of Grenville L. Winthrop. Photographed by

	Photographic Services. © 2004 President and Fellows of Harvard College.
161	Private Collection. Photograph courtesy of the Frick Art Reference Library.
173	Franklin Collection, Yale University Library.
175	The Louvre. Photograph courtesy Erich Lessing/Art Resource, NY.
176, upper left	Philadelphia Museum of Art: gift of Mrs. John D. Rockefeller, Jr., 1946.
176, upper right	Philadelphia Museum of Art: gift of Mrs. John D. Rockefeller, Jr., 1946.
176, lower left	Courtesy of the Huntington Library, Art Collections, and Botanical Gardens, San Marino, California.
176, lower right	The Walters Art Museum, Baltimore.
178, upper left	RSA, London.
178, upper right	The Metropolitan Museum of Art, gift of John Bard, 1872 (72.6). Photograph all rights reserved, The Metropolitan Museum of Art.
178, lower left	The Metropolitan Museum of Art, The Friedsam Collection, bequest of Michael Friedsam, 1931 (32.100.132). Photograph all rights reserved, The Metropolitan Museum of Art.
178, lower right	Courtesy of the American Philosophical Society.
179	Courtesy of the University of Pennsylvania Art Collection, Philadelphia, Pennsylvania.
199	Courtesy Winterthur Museum.
214	Courtesy of the Pennsylvania Academy of the Fine Arts, Philadephia. Bequest of Mrs. Sarah Harrison (The Joseph Harrison, Jr., Collection).
242	John Neagle, American, 1796–1865; *Pat Lyon at the Forge,* 1826–27; oil on canvas, 238.12 x 172.72 cm (93¾ x 68 in.); Museum of Fine Arts, Boston; Henry H. and Zoe Oliver Sherman Fund, 1975.806. Photograph © 2004 Museum of Fine Arts, Boston.

Index

Page numbers in *italics* refer to illustrations.

About the Author

Gordon S. Wood is the Alva O. Way University Professor and professor of history at Brown University. His 1969 book, *The Creation of the American Republic, 1776–1787*, received the Bancroft and John H. Dunning prizes and was nominated for the National Book Award. His 1992 book, *The Radicalism of the American Revolution,* won the Pulitzer Prize and Emerson Prize. Wood contributes regularly to *The New Republic* and *The New York Review of Books.*